UNDERMINED ESTABLISHMENT

STUDIES IN CHURCH AND STATE

JOHN F. WILSON, EDITOR

The Restructuring of American Religion:
Society and Faith Since World War II
by Robert Wuthnow

Shintō and the State, 1868–1988
by Helen Hardacre

Redeeming Politics
by Peter Iver Kaufman

Undermined Establishment: Church-State
Relations in America, 1880–1920
by Robert T. Handy

UNDERMINED ESTABLISHMENT

CHURCH-STATE RELATIONS IN AMERICA,
1880–1920

Robert T. Handy

PRINCETON UNIVERSITY PRESS PRINCETON, NEW JERSEY

Library of Congress Cataloging-in-Publication Data

Handy, Robert T.
Undermined establishment : church-state relations in America,
1880–1920 / Robert T. Handy.
p.   cm. — (Studies in church and state)
Includes bibliographical references and index.
ISBN 0-691-07385-6
1. Church and state—United States—History.   2. United States—
Religion.   I. Title.   II. Series.
BR516.H22   1991
322'.1'097309034—dc20   91-10200   CIP

This book has been composed in Linotron Sabon

Princeton University Press books are printed on acid-free paper,
and meet the guidelines for permanence and durability of the
Committee on Production Guidelines for Book Longevity of the
Council on Library Resources

Printed in the United States of America by Princeton University Press,
Princeton, New Jersey

10   9   8   7   6   5   4   3   2   1

To Winthrop S. Hudson ————————————————

SCHOLAR · TEACHER · FRIEND

Contents

Foreword

Undermined Establishment: Church-State Relations in America, 1880–1920 is the fourth volume in the series "Studies in Church and State" sponsored by the Project on Church and State at Princeton University and funded by the Lilly Endowment. The project has two goals. The first is to sponsor scholarly publications on the interaction of religion and its political environment, primarily but not exclusively in the United States. The second is to draw on disciplines beyond those traditionally concerned with church-state issues to investigate the interaction of religious and political culture.

The Studies in Church and State are designed to fulfil these goals. The first volume examined how religion has changed in the United States since World War II. The second analyzed the Japanese state's relationship with Shinto. The third delineated various patterns of interaction between religious and political authority created in the medieval and early modern West following the Emperor Constantine's adoption of Christianity. Later volumes will explore aspects of the interrelationship of religion and politics, of church and state, in India, Latin America, and Europe as well as U.S. experience with the issue in the revolutionary and Jacksonian eras. A community study of a multiethnic, midsized industrial city in the northeastern United States will also be part of the series, and a summary volume will consider the issue as it has developed throughout U.S. history.

Apart from this series, the project has sponsored a two-volume bibliographical guide to literature on the church-state question in the United States and a casebook on church-state law compiled by John T. Noonan, Jr.[1]

Although the project cannot sponsor studies on all the church-state topics that deserve scholarly treatment, we hope that by demonstrating the potential for new work on the issue we can broaden current discussion and stimulate further scholarship.

Robert Handy's volume examines four decades during which American society changed very rapidly. The population doubled, largely because of immigration. Industrialization and urbanization altered the landscape and brought citizens and government into new relationships. Religious

---

[1] John F. Wilson, ed., *Church and State in America: A Bibliographical Guide*, Vol. 1, *The Colonial and Early National Periods*; Vol. 2, *The Civil War to the Present Day* (Westport, Conn.: Greenwood Press, 1986, 1987). John T. Noonan, Jr., *The Believer and the Powers that Are* (New York: Macmillan, 1987).

bodies proliferated as existing denominations divided and new faiths arrived with the immigrants. Together these developments challenged Protestantism, which until this point had felt itself the dominant religious and moral force in the government and law and in the society at large. Critics both inside and outside the centrist denominations began to question these long-held assumptions and to define new issues that would play a major role in the religious life of the country in subsequent decades. Handy makes extensive use of contemporary sources to examine this period of ferment and to show how these issues took shape.

The development of the Project on Church and State has benefited enormously from the support and guidance of Robert Wood Lynn of the Lilly Endowment and his successor, Craig Dykstra. Yoma Ullman, as project coordinator, brought us her many skills, high standards, and great dedication. We are, further, grateful to the Princeton University Press and particularly to Walter H. Lippincott, its director, and Gail M. Ullman, history editor, for their interest, encouragement, and support.

John F. Wilson
Stanley N. Katz
Albert J. Raboteau

Acknowledgments ———————————————————

MANY PERSONS have been helpful in the preparation of this book. Conversations with colleagues in the Project of Church and State at Princeton University have been illuminating. The patient work of library staffs of Columbia, Drew, and Princeton universities and of Union and Jewish Theological seminaries in New York are much appreciated. Especially helpful has been the careful reading of the first draft by three persons: project director John F. Wilson, project coordinator Yoma Ullman, and Robert Wood Lynn, formerly senior vice president for religion of the Lilly Endowment. I thank James D. Hudnut-Beumler, Mark S. Massa, and Richard Hughes Seager for their wide-ranging essays that focus on the period of this volume in *Church and State in America: A Bibliographical Guide*, Vol. 2, *The Civil War to the Present Day*, ed. John F. Wilson (New York: Greenwood Press, 1987).

I am also grateful to Shlomith Yahalom, author of a Ph.D. dissertation at the Hebrew University of Jerusalem of which the English title is "American Judaism and the Question of Separation Between Church and State" (1981). With her cooperation, the bulk of the thesis, translated into English, is in the possession of the author and the project office. Because the sections of the dissertation were separately translated and paginated, I refer here to the titles of those separate sections; they are cited: "Church-State Separation and Education," "Sunday Laws," and "The Demands of War and the Principle of Freedom of Religion."

The editors of two symposia to which I have contributed essays have given permission to adapt parts of them for this book: "Changing Contexts of Church-State Relations in America, 1880–1920," in *Caring for the Commonweal: Education for Religious and Public Life*, ed. Parker J. Palmer, Barbara G. Wheeler, and James Fowler, 23–43 (Macon, Ga.: Mercer University Press, 1990), and "Protestant Theological Tensions and Political Styles in the Progressive Period," in *Religion and American Politics: From the Colonial Period to the 1980s*, ed. Mark A. Noll, 281–301 (New York: Oxford University Press, 1990).

Lines from "The Second Coming" are reprinted with permission of Macmillan Publishing Company from *The Poems of W. B. Yeats: A New Edition*, edited by Richard J. Finneran. Copyright 1924 by Macmillan Publishing Company, renewed 1952 by Bertha Georgie Yeats.

UNDERMINED ESTABLISHMENT

Introduction

IF ONE understands by the familiar phrase "church and state" two rela-tively well-defined and quite separate entities that are often in tension with one another, then the period from 1880 to 1920 does not seem to be particularly important in the long story of the relations between religion and government in American history. Much of the literature, past and present, on church-state themes tends to focus on earlier or later periods. Much has been written on how the religion clauses of the Constitution and the First Amendment were composed and what that meant for the development of religion and society in the new nation in the first half of the nineteenth century. There is also a vast and growing body of writing on the years since the early 1920s. This material has focused with increas-ing intensity on the rapidly multiplying Supreme Court cases that bear on church-state issues, which surged to new numerical highs in and after the 1940s. In *Cantwell* v. *Connecticut* (1940) and especially *Everson* v. *Board of Education* (1947), the Fourteenth Amendment was interpreted to ap-ply the First to not only the nation at large but also the individual states and by implication to all arms of government. Those and the many sub-sequent cases have tended to perpetuate the familiar definitions of the church-state terminology.

If, however, we understand that the traditional terms "church" and "state" have been stretched in remarkable ways during the course of American history, then our attention can shift from a narrow focus on historic constitutional documents and their interpretation—important as those remain—to the actual varieties and complexities of religious life and the bewildering network of governmental agencies of various types at many levels, and to the interactions between them. The familiar usage derived historically from the European experience of relatively homoge-neous states, most of which had a dominant and legally established church. In American experience, those terms have in fact long been ap-plied to an increasingly diversifed religious situation in a country with a growing population rooted in many histories and cultures. When the fa-miliar words are used simplistically, as they often are, they obscure rather than illumine.

From the wider perspective, the last two decades of the nineteenth cen-tury and the first two of the twentieth can be seen as a time when the earlier religious settlement was tested and challenged. Although many did not want to face the fact, long-accepted assumptions about the relation of religious movements and institutions to governmental structures and agencies were no longer adequate to express the dramatic societal and cultural changes in progress. The familiar church-state terminology, deeply rooted in American consciousness and preserved by popular and scholarly reference systems, continued to be used freely. But the realities to which the old terms pointed were significantly different and still changing as the nation moved into the post-World War I years. Ahead loomed continuing struggles to redefine the situation. The nature of twentieth-century dilemmas of religion and government comes into fuller view against the background of these four decades of expansion and tension: long-familiar views and practices, accepted by many, became increasingly problematical for others.

There were many sources of this expansion and tension. Conspicuous among them was the growth in population. Estimated at fifty million people in 1880, the population had more than doubled to over one hundred million in 1920. In considerable part this growth occurred because of a remarkable surge of European immigration from 1880 to 1915—a movement of Western peoples that dwarfed previous records. Technological improvements in transportation, manufacturing, and construction speeded the migrations and made possible the rapid, though often insufficiently planned, growth of vast urban areas. The far-reaching changes brought on by population growth, industrialization, and urbanization necessitated governmental expansion at both local and national levels to provide for basic services and to face, however imperfectly, mounting societal problems in a period of increasing tension. In consequence, the enlarging maze of legislative, administrative, and judicial agencies that we call "the state" came ever closer to the lives of most Americans. At the same time, the number (and in most cases, the size) of identifiable religious bodies increased because of schisms from older institutions, the transplantation of previously unrepresented groups from Europe and Asia, and the founding of new indigenous organizations. The great bulk of members of religious institutions were in Catholic or Protestant churches, but immigrants included adherents of various Eastern Orthodox churches; the number of Jewish synagogues notably increased, and by 1920 most gathered in a complex network of Reform, Conservative, and Orthodox organizations. Adherents of yet other historic faiths were also becoming visible in certain localities. Even so, many Americans were not formally related to any religious body, while others let their ties become nominal.

In this situation of widening governmental and religious complexity the terms "church" and "state" were less and less descriptive of realities. Their continued usage both obscured the depth of the underlying changes and perpetuated the customary view that the United States was a Christian, indeed primarily a Protestant, nation. The old terms were not self-explanatory, and persons from various backgrounds understood them in differing ways and used them for various agendas. This was the fate of such views as those of Thomas Jefferson; in 1802 he wrote that the First Amendment's clauses on religion had the effect of "building a wall of separation between church and state"—words cited affirmatively in a major Supreme Court decision just prior to the opening of the 1880s. Thus written into the law of the land, the phrase became a precedent for later court cases. Although some were convinced that the relationship between religion and government had been decisively settled and that religious freedom was thereby guaranteed for all, others found such claims qualified, if not denied, by widely held attitudes and actions that limited their exercise of religious freedom. Alternative visions of American life and destiny had often come into conflict before, but in the widening religious pluriformity as one century closed and another opened, the long-dominant Protestant perspectives on religion and the state, closely though not monolithically related to what had long been the nation's leading religious denominations, came increasingly under fire.

The most visible resistance came primarily from Catholics, but to some extent also from those of other philosophical as well as religious traditions. Minorities long opposed to various aspects of the broad but somewhat uneven consensus that had characterized Protestant approaches to issues of religion and government were gaining in strength, even as the dynamic changes of the times were shaking some foundations of that consensus and undermining its promises. Some criticism and questioning came from within Protestant ranks. Confident assertions that the church-state problem had been solved were still being made on familiar grounds, but the old answers were not fully meeting the contemporary challenges. Many participants in the debate were seeking new ways of dealing with the issues. Questions and problems that emerged in the twentieth century's middle decades were shaped in considerable measure by what had transpired from 1880 to 1920.

In that period, the general consensus on matters of religon and government that Protestants had worked out even as they debated some of its details was challenged by those who disagreed with certain features of their position. The stakes were getting higher as the power of government was mounting, especially but not only at the national level. Cultural patterns that had been defined largely in Protestant terms were slowly being diversified by the pressures of industrialization, immigration, secularization, and pluralism, and the voices of outsiders and newcomers were becoming bolder. Yet the Protestant forces, though divided denominationally, confidently expected to prevail despite increasing pressures and to maintain and extend their informal "establishment" indefinitely. Soon after the 1920s new ways of redefining relationships between the institutions of religion and the agencies of government were needed, but there was much resistance to such an effort in the new, highly controversial period in church-state history that was then emerging.

To review the deeper forces at work in the four critical decades of expansion and transition in American religious and social life that led to the later displacement of older, long-dominant church-state views and the groping toward new ones is the principal purpose of this book. Such an effort can provide a fuller understanding of that subsequent struggle to define and deal with a situation that had been significantly changing in ways that only later became more discernible.

1

The Protestant "Establishment" in Late Nineteenth-century America

BY THE closing decades of the nineteenth century the separation of church and state was widely acclaimed in the United States as the best framework for relationships between religious institutions and the arms of government. Legal establishments of religion, prohibited at the national level in 1791, had then been renounced by the few states in which they had survived. But an establishment of another informal and voluntary type, without legal or financial support by government, persisted. Though independently organized, the leading Protestant denominations worked together selectively through various voluntary associations in an effort to bring their nation more fully into accord with their understanding of what a Christian state and society should be. In this quest, the Protestant forces often cooperated informally with government officials.

A dramatic illustration of contacts between prominent political figures and the Protestant establishment occurred at Carnegie Hall in New York City on April 21, 1900, the first day of an Ecumenical Missionary Conference sponsored by the agencies of many denominations and societies. A great gathering was addressed by conspicuous Protestant leaders on that Saturday afternoon. In the evening the famous hall could hold only half those who wanted to enter. The record reflected the excitement: "Punctually at eight o'clock an outburst of cheering at the rear of the stage betokened the approach of President McKinley, and as he was . . . making his way to the front of the platform, the whole audience rose, cheering him vociferously, and saluted him with the waving of handkerchiefs and hats."[1] Speaking effusively of the struggles and sacrifices of missionaries, the president concluded on a high religious note: "May this great meeting rekindle the spirit of missionary ardor and enthusiasm 'to go teach all nations,' and may the field never lack a succession of heralds who shall carry on the task—the continuous proclamation of His gospel to the end of time!" (40). After the singing of the national anthem, another political figure spoke: Theodore Roosevelt, then governor of the state where the meeting was held, but soon to be vice-president and, when

[1] *Ecumenical Missionary Conference in New York, 1900* (New York: American Tract Society, 1900), 38.

William McKinley fell at the hand of an assassin, president. Roosevelt spoke primarily of the importance of mission work in the American West, assuring the delegates that "you are doing the greatest work that can be done" (43). The response to the two high-ranking speakers was given by the honorary president of the conference, himself a former president of the nation, Benjamin Harrison.

That episode and others like it gave a certain visibility to the informal but often effective Protestant establishment at the turn of the century, midway in the period (1880–1920) within which this book is cast. That such informal relationships between Protestant leaders and executive, legislative, and judicial figures in government influenced certain actions and decisions in ways favorable to the churches will be illustrated in the pages that follow. But so will certain counterforces then at work in undermining the Protestant establishment, forces that were increasing in intensity and paving the way for new and quite different definitions and practices concerning the relationship of church and state. Such pressures decisively emerged as the twentieth century unfolded, especially after 1940.

Protestant Churches in the Context of American Life, 1880–1900

By 1880, the leading Protestant denominations—Baptist, Congregational, Disciples of Christ, Episcopal, Lutheran, Methodist, Presbyterian, Quaker, and Reformed—had an estimated total of close to nine million members, or about 18 percent of the population.[2] The bulk of them were descendants of the settlers who had arrived from the early seventeenth century onward. They had come primarily from western and northern Europe, but among them were also slaves imported from Africa. Denominational memberships had steadily increased throughout the nineteenth century as a percentage of the total population, through not only immigration but also the assimilative power of the various traditions as they drew into themselves individuals and groups from quite different backgrounds by conversion, marriage, social aspirations, and cultural success. The English-speaking Protestants, who especially regarded themselves as the custodians of that culture, had become accustomed to their formative role in American life.

Indeed, although their still-growing formal memberships never came close to enrolling half the population in this period, they often spoke as if

[2] Estimates based on the work of Edwin Scott Gaustad, *Historical Atlas of Religion in America*, rev. ed. (New York: Harper & Row, 1976), pt. 2, esp. 111. On the difficulties of gathering and interpreting statistics on religion, esp. for the period of this study, see Kevin J. Christiano, *Religious Diversity and Social Change: American Cities, 1890–1906* (Cambridge: Cambridge University Press, 1987).

they were prescribing the moral direction of the nation as a whole. They claimed that the Protestant faith had been predominant in the colonial and national periods and assumed that many who were not actually members of churches were part of their larger constituencies or at least in general sympathy with them. That view contained a considerable measure of truth, and it encouraged them to speak with a certain assurance when they discussed the American way of relating church and state. As Joseph P. Thompson, retired pastor of New York's Broadway Tabernacle, put it: "In reading the statistics of the American churches, it should be borne in mind that the term *members* by no means represents the total of worshippers in the several congregations, or of nominal adherents to a confession, but only those who by their own act have united with the church proper, the spiritual body, and who partake of its sacraments."[3] Participants in the outer circle who were not full church members usually understood themselves to be part of the denomination of the congregation they attended.

The denominations had many differences, reflecting their varying histories, points of origin, polities, and theologies. They are more accurately described as complex "denominational families," for most of them were also internally divided along sectional, ethnic, racial, or theological lines. In many ways the Lutherans, originating from German and Scandinavian countries primarily, showed some distinctive differences from the others, which shared similar backgrounds in either the British Protestant traditions or Calvinism—and often both. Furthermore, some churches became entrenched largely in certain sections of the country, worked out close affinities with particular racial and ethnic groups, or became associated more directly with a given class in society than another; then social factors provided often hidden or immediately less obvious but nonetheless significant reasons for continued separation.[4] Yet they all claimed to be a part of the continuing heritage of the Protestant Reformation of the sixteenth century, and despite many tensions and quarrels they shared certain common emphases and values that were direct or (more often)

[3] *Church and State in the United States* (Boston: James R. Osgood, 1873), 93. A German edition was published in Berlin by Leonhard Simion.

[4] For a classic analysis, see H. Richard Niebuhr, *The Social Sources of Denominationalism* (New York: Henry Holt, 1929). His own correction of an overemphasis in that work can be found in his *The Kingdom of God in America* (New York: Harper & Bros., 1937). Informative histories that deal primarily with the Protestant churches in America include: Jerald C. Brauer, *Protestantism in America: A Narrative History*, rev. ed. (Philadelphia: Westminster Press, 1965); Winthrop S. Hudson, *American Protestantism* (Chicago: University of Chicago Press, 1961); Martin E. Marty, *Righteous Empire: The Protestant Experience in America* (New York: Dial Press, 1970); Sidney E. Mead, *The Lively Experiment: The Shaping of Christianity in America* (New York: Harper & Row, 1963).

indirect consequences of that major turning point in Christian history as they interpreted it.

With variations in details, the leading denominational families were trinitarian, Bible-centered, broadly evangelical, and missionary-minded. Prominent among their shared values was an insistence on the centrality of the Bible and the importance of personal and group freedom, and the literature that dealt with such matters was widely read across denominational lines. They believed strongly in religious freedom; it not only protected them against interference by government, but it also opened the door for them to win whomever they could to their version of Christian faith by the means of persuasion. The efficacy of persuasion in building vital congregations and denominations conscious of their mission had been amply demonstrated in the religious awakenings of the colonial and early national periods. By 1880, with some exceptions and in varying degrees of intensity, most leading denominational families had been strongly influenced by the theologies and practices of revivalism. Through the means of persuasion and the organizational vitality that voluntaryism had brought, they hoped to win increasing numbers to the Christian faith, at home and abroad.

With somewhat different emphases on such particular issues as Sabbath observance and temperance, the denominational families tended to be reformist in style, some more cautiously than others. Various reform causes, such as antislavery and abolition, had been conspicuously championed by important segments of the Protestant world earlier in the century.[5] Enthusiasm for reform cooled somewhat in the decades following the Civil War, but as social and economic problems mounted toward the end of the century, various reformist measures were again advocated in the wider culture and slowly gathered support among church constituencies in the face of considerable opposition.

The rise of various social Christian movements in the period of this study significantly influenced attitudes toward church-state issues. Hence attention to such movements emerges at appropriate points in chapters that follow, with particular attention to those progressive Protestant aspects that became known as the social gospel. The development of social Christianity heightened the interest of growing numbers of church people in public issues in ways that have given a distinctive cast to twentieth-century religious history. The controversial social Christian movements—some relatively small and short-lived but others having a lasting impact on many denominations—injected new dimensions into the way the institutions and religion and government related to one another.[6]

[5] See, e.g., C. C. Goen, *Broken Churches, Broken Nation: Denominational Schisms and the Coming of the American Civil War* (Macon, Ga.: Mercer University Press, 1985).

[6] For fuller discussion of social Christianity in general and the social gospel in particular, primarily as it bears on church-state matters, see chaps. 3, 5.

Protestant Views of a Christian America

Although the growing Protestant bodies actually enrolled far less than half the country's population in their formal memberships by 1900, they confidently believed that they formed the majority religious voice in the culture. As Edwin Scott Gaustad has stated, the large denominations "participated fully in the larger society, believing that they bore the heaviest responsibility for guiding the nation, sustaining its moral vision and its watchful walk along the paths of righteousness."[7] Claiming that their nation's civilization was rooted in the premises of Protestant Christianity, its leaders aimed to make that civilization more fully Christian. For example, as Robert E. Thompson, a Presbyterian who taught sociology at the University of Pennsylvania, said to students at Princeton Theological Seminary in 1891: "There is no peace for us but in becoming a more Christian nation, and discovering anew the pertinence of the Ten Words of Sinai and the Sermon of the Foundations to our social condition."[8]

The conviction that America was indeed a Christian nation was expressed by many contemporary writers. But they had to deal with the dilemma posed by an allegedly Christian nation whose constitutional provisions explicitly forbade its government to institute religious tests for public office, establish religion, or prohibit its free exercise. One of the most ambitious attempts to resolve this tension was offered in a lengthy book by Presbyterian minister Isaac A. Cornelison, who stated in some detail the Protestant establishment's position on the relationship of religion to civil government in America. On the one hand, he rejoiced "in the fact that we have, in this country, a grand system of political institutions, entirely separate from all ecclesiastical institutions."[9] On the other hand, he believed, along with so many other nineteenth-century Protestants, that "the government of these United States was necessarily, rightfully, and lawfully Christian" (341). His way to resolve the tension was to stress the rights of the majority: "Christianity in a proper sense is the established religion of this nation; established, not by statute law, it is true, but by a law equally valid, the law in the nature of things, the law of necessity, which law will remain in force so long as the great mass of the people are Christian" (362).

Perhaps the best observation on the nature of the voluntary establish-

[7] "The Pulpit and the Pews," in *Between the Times: The Travail of the Protestant Establishment in America, 1900–1960*, ed. William R. Hutchison (Cambridge: Cambridge University Press, 1989), 23.

[8] *De Civitate Dei: The Divine Order of Human Society* (Philadelphia: John D. Wattles, 1891), 4.

[9] *The Relation of Religion to Civil Government in The United States of America: A State without a Church, but not without a Religion* (1895; reprint, New York: Da Capo Press, 1970), vi.

ment came from an outsider. The distinguished British observer Lord Bryce, speaking of the relationship of religion and government in America, said:

> The whole matter may, I think, be summed up by saying that Christianity is in fact understood to be, though not the legally established religion, yet the national religion. So far from thinking their commonwealth godless, the Americans conceive that the religious character of a government consists in nothing but the religious belief of the individual citizens, and the conformity of their conduct to that belief. They deem the general acceptance of Christianity to be one of the main sources of their national prosperity, and their nation a special object of Divine favour.[10]

These perceptions pointed to a dilemma for the leaders of the Protestant establishment: every vehicle that they adopted to further their plan for a more Christian nation (as they defined it) logically contradicted the separation of church and state in a culture infused by religion. Protestant positions at that time on religious ceremonies at public events, education, Catholicism, immigrants, and the nature of missionary work illustrate this difficulty, and Protestant pronouncements on the relation between church and state often exemplified tortuous argument.

Religious Interpretations of Secular Life

Defenders claiming that America was indeed a Christian nation frequently referred to the continuing presence and power of religion in secular life. In stating a unanimous decision of the Supreme Court in 1892, Associate Justice David J. Brewer summed up with considerable precision the conventional Protestant position in this regard. After referring to many events, state constitutions, and court decisions to the effect that Americans were a religious people and that the morality of the country was deeply rooted in Christianity, Brewer concluded:

> If we pass beyond these matters to a view of American life as expressed by its laws, its business, its customs and its society, we find everywhere a clear recognition of the same truth. Among other matters note the following: The form of oath universally prevailing, concluding with an appeal to the Almighty; the custom of opening sessions of all deliberative bodies and most conventions with prayer; the prefatory words of all wills, "In the name of God, Amen;" the laws respecting the observance of the Sabbath, with the general cessation of all secular business, and the closing of courts, legislatures, and other similar public assemblies on that day; the churches and church organizations which abound in every city, town and hamlet; the multitude of charitable organizations exist-

[10] *The American Commonwealth*, 2d ed. (London: Macmillan, 1891), 2: 576–77.

ing everywhere under Christian aupisces; the gigantic missionary associations, with general support, and aiming to establish Christian missions in every quarter of the globe. These, and many other matters which might be noticed, add a volume of unofficial declarations to the mass of organic utterances [a reference to the state constitutions] that this is a Christian nation.[11]

Cornelison, too, subscribed to this view, but a tinge of doubt began to appear in the argument. His clear commitment to the patterns of the voluntary Christendom so dear to Protestants at the time was evident when he reasserted a familiar position:

> The government ought not to discontinue any Christian practice or exercise which has become established by custom; such as the opening of the daily sessions of the Congress of the United States and of the legislatures of the States, with prayer; the employment of Christian ministers as chaplains in the army and navy, in the prisons, hospitals, and homes under its charge; and the opening of the daily exercises of the public schools with religious exercises [363–64].

Cornelison knew that time brought changes, but should such exercises as listed be discontinued, he declared that it ought not be for any reason derogatory to Christianity. Affirming that the formal meeting of large numbers for a common object is impressive and "excites an emotion which naturally tends upward," he tried to draw the line between public events at which prayer was or was not suitable:

> It is perfectly natural that the great National and State political conventions should be opened with prayer; not so natural that the meetings of the National executive committees should be opened with prayer; perfectly natural that the National and State Teachers' Associations should be opened with prayer; not so natural that the meetings of sections and committees should be so opened; perfectly natural that the daily sessions of Congress and the legislature should be opened with prayer; not so natural that the meetings of their committees should be so opened; perfectly natural that the daily sessions of the public school should be opened with prayer; not so natural that the meetings of the Board of Directors should be opened with prayer [364–65].

Actually he was describing practices then current, but to make the point that as it was "natural" for prayer to be omitted in some situations and not in others, an unbeliever's claim that the omission should be made

[11] *Church of the Holy Trinity v. United States*, 143 U.S. 457 (1892) at 471. Extensive selections from the case are reprinted by John T. Noonan, Jr., *The Believer and the Powers that Are: Cases, History, and Other Data Bearing on the Relation of Religion and Government* (New York: Macmillan, 1987), 208–11. Brewer continued to popularize the points he made in the decision of 1892 in writings and addresses; see his *The United States a Christian Nation* (Philadelphia: John C. Winston, 1905).

general would be hardly just, for in the cases of omission the public authorities have neither come over the unbeliever's ground nor made the
omissions for his reasons at all. He thus attempted to make a tortuous
line of argument credible, but to many at home in the Protestant establishment of that time his approach seemed "perfectly natural."

Education

In the colonial period the many close ties between religion and the schooling of the young often involved considerable cooperation between private
and public educational institutions. But in the nineteenth century, with
the major exception of the conservative Lutheran Missouri Synod and
some others' experimentation with church day schools, the Protestant denominations lacked the resources and the will to develop systems of parochial education; instead, they became ardent supporters of the common
school systems as developed throughout the nineteenth century.[12]

On these foundations, Protestants generally believed a Christian America could be further cultivated. They rallied around the public school as
an agency that could operate as a unitive force by providing some fundamental understanding of the American spirit and traditions to the children of an increasingly diversified population. Such understanding included belief in God and devotion to civil and religious liberty. In general,
Protestants committed their basic educational task to the common
schools. Many of those responsible for common schools basically agreed.
For example, leaders of public education in Oregon said in 1884 that
"there *must* be a *religious* basis to our educational system; and acknowl-
edgment of our religious obligations, and the natural and common presentation of incentives to piety, must have their place in the common
school, or it utterly fails of its mission, and will soon go the way of all
effete institutions." They insisted that "this does *not* involve either cant
or sectarianism."[13]

What was called a "common presentation," however, often appeared
to be something of a fusion of Enlightenment and Protestant views and
usually favored Bible reading in the schools. There was growing opposition to such a position from various elements in the population, but few
of these voices came from the world of the major Protestant denominations. By the turn of the century, according to Robert Wood Lynn, the

---

[12] For an excellent, broadly based history of education in America that includes considerable treatment of its religious aspects, see Lawrence A. Cremin, *American Education*, 3
vols. (New York: Harper & Row, 1970–88).

[13] From *Proceedings of the State Teachers Association, 1884*, as cited by David Tyack,
"The Kingdom of God and the Common School," *Harvard Educational Review* 36 (1966):
465.

school had become for Protestants "symbolic of both our national unity and God's handiwork in history. As such it was a sacred cause, worthy of religious devotion."[14] In Christian America, they confidently assumed, the public schools could and should reflect a religious perspective and perform a job that the divided denominations could not. The schools were understood to be nondenominational but certainly not nonreligious.

Cornelison provided a good example of the complex arguments that could arise when Protestant leaders tried to reconcile the role of religion in the state and in the nation with regard to the common schools. Although he had declared that the government ought to provide Christian teaching and nurture for all citizens to whom it stood in loco parentis, he opined that it ought not directly "foster" Christianity in the public schools other than in daily opening exercises. Yet he finally made an important exception in the interests of what he regarded as the rights of the majority. Distinguishing between elementary and more advanced education, he insisted "that the State is under obligation to require that all the teaching in the high schools, universities, military and naval academies, be in accordance with the fundamental truths of Christianity. Here is ground upon which there can be no neutrality" (375). His argument was that in many subjects as taught at secondary educational levels, including those in both the sciences and the humanities, the teaching must be either for or against Christianity, and in a Christian land it must conform with the fundamental truths of that faith.

Anti-Catholicism

Among the forces that gave a generic movement such as "American Protestantism" a measure of identifiability and direction was not only what it supported but also what it opposed. The depth of anti-Catholicism throughout the Protestant world may be hard to understand for many whose perceptions reflect our own era in which religious pluralism is taken as a fact of life. The mutual dislike and hatred between Catholics and Protestants were rooted deep in the religious wars of the sixteenth and seventeenth centuries. The wounds left by those bloody struggles were kept open by a widening stream of historical and polemical literature that flowed down the decades. The bitterness of both religious and political conflict spilled over in sermons, tracts, histories, and theologies; some were intended to be fair as they interpreted past struggles from a particular perspective, but many were shameless in excessive partisanship and scurrility. In England centuries of bitter contention set a strong anti-Catholic bias on the national consciousness. Colonial penal legislation

---

[14] *Protestant Strategies in Education* (New York: Association Press, 1964), 22.

against the Catholics showed that the derivative colonies across the Atlantic followed suit. That period largely ended with the Revolution, but deep-seated fears and persistent prejudices flared up periodically throughout the nineteenth century. One such occasion occurred in the 1880s.

A new anti-Catholic hate group, the American Protective Association (APA), founded in 1887, was virulent enough but did not stir up the violence of some similar movements of the 1840s and 1850s.[15] Yet Protestant leaders who resisted such extremes often perpetuated the rhetoric of anti-Catholicism. For example, in the same year that the APA was founded, Samuel Lane Loomis published a book based on the religious problems of cities. Trying to be evenhanded, he observed that "the religion of Rome is far better than none, and we may believe that many humble souls under the leadings of the Spirit have found their way through tangled meshes of falsehood with which she has covered it, down to the eternal truths on which her venerable faith is based. . . . The Romanism of America is likely to be better than that of Europe." But he explained that "Romanism is not the religion we wish for our fellow-citizens," and he provided a list of particulars:

> It conceals the fatherhood of God behind the motherhood of the Church, and the brotherhood of Christ behind the motherhood of the Virgin. It degrades the atonement by making its benefits a matter of barter; it leads to idolatry and image-worship; it snatches from the believer the great gift bought with the blood of Christ, by thrusting in a priest between him and his heavenly Father. It has kept the people from the Word of God and compelled them to accept forced and unscholarly interpretations of it. It has lowered the tone of morality. It has quenched free thought, stifled free speech, and threatens to throttle free government.[16]

Centuries of conflict lay behind such statements, which voiced prevailing opinions in the Protestant world of their time. Denominations that divided bitterly over the interpretation of common Protestant legacies found in their characteristic opposition to Catholicism a cause that brought them closer to each other.

Immigration

To a considerable measure, of course, the resurgence of anti-Catholic animus was a response to the unprecedented increase in Catholic popula-

---

[15] The full story has been told by Donald L. Kinzer, *An Episode in Anti-Catholicism: The American Protective Association* (Seattle: University of Washington Press, 1964). For more on the APA, see Chap. 2.

[16] *Modern Cities and Their Religious Problems* (New York: Baker & Taylor, 1887), 87–88.

tion. The estimated Roman Catholic membership of six million in 1880 had doubled by 1900. Negative reactions to this remarkable development often combined religious with ethnic hostilities. The overriding consideration for church-state study is not so much the sheer increase as it is the immigrants' sources. In the 1880s the flow from predominantly Catholic central, southern, and eastern Europe greatly increased, and Irish immigration continued. That decade also registered the high point of arrivals from Germany, but of the latter probably only about 30 percent were Catholics. Among the wave of immigrants from Italy the vast majority were Catholics. The same can be said of the new influx of Poles, Czechs, and Slovaks, while many Catholics were present among the Lithuanians and the Ruthenians (Ukrainians). Two other major groups of immigrants also contributed vast numbers to the rapidly growing Catholic church in the United States: French Canadians and Mexicans. "These ten groups of immigrants," as Jay P. Dolan summed up a complex situation, "made up the bulk of Catholics living in the United States in the early twentieth century."[17] Their languages, cultures, and habits often seemed strange and threatening in the culture that had long been developing in America.

After 1880, therefore, many Protestants found themselves increasingly alarmed by the waves of so many newcomers from conspicuously different backgrounds, outsiders who seemed to jeopardize their social and religious hegemony in the culture. One of the most conspicuous persons—in both his own time and the historical literature since—to respond to this unprecedented migration across the Atlantic was a Congregational clergyman, Josiah Strong. Born in Illinois, he served in pastoral and home missionary positions after graduation from Lane Seminary in 1871. His best-seller of the mid-1880s, Our Country, highlighted in alarmist fashion seven perils confronting the nation. Significantly the first two were immigration and Romanism, and the seventh—the city—was pictured as the point at which all the dangers converged. "Because our cities are so largely foreign," he insisted, "Romanism finds in them its chief strength."[18]

Strong was, however, convinced that the future of America as a Protestant nation was safe; he was confident that the Anglo-Saxon race—representative of the two great ideas of civil liberty and pure *spiritual* Christianity—would finally dominate all others. Because he used the term

---

[17] *The American Catholic Experience: A History from Colonial Times to the Present* (Garden City, N.Y.: Doubleday, 1985), 135. There is an extensive literature on the history of immigration; good basic works are by Oscar Handlin, *The Uprooted: The Epic Story of the Great Immigrations that Made the American People*, 2d ed. (Boston: Little, Brown, 1973); and John Higham, *Strangers in the Land: Patterns of American Nativism, 1860–1925*, rev. ed. (New York: Atheneum, 1973).

[18] *Our Country: Its Possible Future and its Present Crisis* (New York: Baker & Taylor, 1885), 129.

"Anglo-Saxon" broadly to include all English-speaking persons, Strong was able to report that in 1880 they numbered nearly one hundred million, half of them in the United States. He explained, citing ethnologists of his time, that Anglo-Saxons have highly mixed origins, that mixed races are superior to "pure" ones, and that in time the incoming races "may be expected to add value to the amalgam which will constitute the new Anglo-Saxon race of the New World" (172). He predicted that "this race of unequaled energy, with all the majesty of numbers and the might of wealth behind it—the representative, let us hope, of the largest liberty, the purest Christianity, the highest civilization—having developed peculiarly aggressive traits calculated to impress its institutions upon mankind, will spread itself over the earth." With that faith in the power of assimilation despite the immediate perils, he concluded: "I cannot think our civilization will perish; but I believe it is fully in the hands of Christians in the United States, during the next fifteen or twenty years, to hasten or retard the coming of Christ's kingdom in the world by hundreds, and perhaps thousands, of years. We of this generation and nation occupy the Gibraltar of the ages which commands the world's future" (180). Typical of many religious leaders of his generation, when he said Christians he often meant Protestants—in his view the representatives of "pure *spiritual* Christianity." Such Christianity was the type that he and many others felt would command the religious future, in not only America but also the world.

The Missionary Advance

The home missionary movement had long been dedicated to the work of winning America to Christ, but in the 1880s the foreign missionary movement, dedicated to winning the world to the Christian cause, rapidly expanded. As evidenced by Strong and others, the confidence in the growing spiritual importance of America on the world scene was significantly bolstered by the remarkable surge of enthusiasm for missions abroad. "Prior to 1880 missions had been maintained by relatively small and specially dedicated groups of believers, but now they blossomed into a major interest of the churches and a significant interest of the nation," according to Charles W. Forman, a prominent historian of missions. His statistics dramatize the missionary resurgence of the century's closing decade: "The number of American foreign missionaries, which stood at 934 in 1890, reached nearly 5,000 a decade later and over 9,000 in 1915."[19]

[19] "The Americans," *International Bulletin of Missionary Research* 6 (April 1982): 54.

That fivefold increase in the 1890s was a remarkable indication of missionary vitality.

Many reasons have been given for the great increase of missionary enthusiasm, in not only the churches but also the environing culture. The enthusiasm for that cause of the famous urban lay evangelist, Dwight L. Moody, was among the most important. In 1886 he called together a conference of college men at Mount Hermon, near Northfield, his birthplace in Massachusetts. With others, he challenged the students to commit themselves to overseas Christian service, and a hundred did so. Two years later the Student Volunteer Movement for Foreign Missions (SVM) was organized; its motto, "the evangelization of the world in this generation," brought excitement and challenge to college campuses and to the churches. Thousands of young persons were drawn into overseas missions through its activities. For thirty years its first chairman, John R. Mott, a Methodist layman who was the dominant leader of the intercollegiate and international Young Men's Christian Association (YMCA), was a central figure in organizing and spreading the missionary crusade. He enlisted and encouraged a large circle of devoted leaders and followers, many of whom served their denominations as missionaries. The whole movement was well publicized and became widely known in both the churches and the culture at large.[20] The excitement of an expanding world perspective in which the United States and its churches were playing an increasing role heartened many youthful persons to commit themselves to the missionary enterprise. The promising scenario was pictured in many ways; for example, a rising theologian, Lewis French Stearns, could exult that "the future of the world seems to be in the hands of the three great Protestant powers—England, Germany, and the United States. The old promise is being fulfilled; the followers of the true God are inheriting the world."[21] Inspired by such hope and confidence, missionaries fanned out across the world; in time their mounting presence and growing influence abroad further complicated American understandings of church and state.

Relations between Church and State

In 1936, theologian William Adams Brown declared that "it has often been assumed by American Protestants that, through the wisdom of the founders who framed the Constitution, the question as to the proper re-

---

[20] See James F. Findlay, Jr., *Dwight L. Moody: American Evangelist, 1837–1899* (Chicago: University of Chicago Press, 1969), and C. Howard Hopkins, *John R. Mott, 1865–1955: A Biography* (Grand Rapids, Mich.: Eerdmans, 1979).

[21] *The Evidence of Christian Experience* (New York: Scribner, 1890), 366.

lation of church and state, which under other forms of political organization has proved to be so baffling, has been finally and forever settled."[22] This assumption had become a widely unifying conviction during the course of the nineteenth century among the restless, growing, self-confident but denominationally divided Protestant traditions. A religious settlement, framed in the 1780s, featured several constitutional statements: "no religious Test shall ever be required as a qualification to any Office or public Trust under the United States"; "Congress shall make no law respecting an establishment of religion, or prohibiting the free exercise thereof."[23] These sentiments provided an atmosphere of freedom in which religious bodies that put forth vigorous efforts found they could attract new followers. The percentage of their members in a rapidly expanding population correspondingly began steadily to rise when they discovered that the voluntary way in religion worked better for them than the older patterns of legal establishment. By the end of the century Protestant authors who wrote on the issues of religion and government routinely emphasized the importance of the principle of voluntary association and the value of the distinction between the religious and the political spheres, yet without minimizing the usefulness of cooperation between them.

Outstanding among such writers was Philip Schaff. Born in Switzerland and educated in Germany, he came to Pennsylvania in 1844, joined the German Reformed Church, and taught first at its seminary in Mercersburg. By 1870 he had become a Presbyterian and joined the faculty of New York's Union Seminary, where he served almost to his death in 1893. Enthusiastically embracing the patterns of religious freedom, voluntaryism, and the separation of church and state that he found in his adopted land, Schaff contributed to the centennial celebration of the Constitution an important work on *Church and State in the United States*, observing that the subject had not yet received the attention it deserved. He discussed the First Amendment as "the Magna Charta of religious freedom in the United States," for it marked a significant turning point in Western history and practice and provided "the first example in history of a government deliberately depriving itself of all legislative control over religion, which was justly regarded by all older governments as the chief support of public morality, order, peace, and prosperity."[24]

[22] *Church and State in Contemporary America* (New York: Scribner, 1938), v.

[23] These are the closing words of Article VI of the Constitution and the opening words of the First Amendment.

[24] *Church and State in the United States: or The American Idea of Religious Liberty and Its Practical Effects* (New York: Putnam, 1888), 22–23. On this book, see John F. Wilson, "Civil Authority and Religious Freedom in the United States: Philip Schaff on the United States as a Christian Nation," in *A Century of Church History: The Legacy of Philip Schaff*,

Although Schaff was a firm believer in religious freedom as safeguarded by Article Six of the Constitution and the establishment and free exercise clauses of the First Amendment, he was also committed to the voluntarily supported Christendom that had been worked out on the American scene. He did not believe in a complete separation of religion and government; because Christianity, "the pillar of our institutions," promotes and serves the public welfare, "an absolute separation is an impossibility" (16, 44). He was deeply sincere in his view that "the separation of church and state as it exists in this country is not a separation of the nation from Christianity" (53). As one who continued to travel widely in Europe and in lands surrounding the western Mediterranean, Schaff believed firmly that "the American nation is as religious and as Christian as any nation on earth, and in some respects even more so, for the very reason that the profession and support of religion are left entirely free" (55). He cited cases to show that in a limited way Christianity was part of the law of the land "as far as the principles and precepts of Christianity have been incorporated in our laws, and as far as is consistent with religious and denominational equality" (58). The learned scholar supported this contention with reference to many particulars concerning religious activities, legislative acts and court decisions, presidential acts and proclamations, exemptions from taxations, appointments of chaplains, marriage legislation, Sunday laws, and the use of the Bible and prayer in the public schools—a line soon to be followed by such writers as Brewer and Cornelison.

The content of his short but informative treatise supported a boldly framed answer to his introductory rhetorical question about the distinctive character of American Christianity as compared to European: "It is a FREE CHURCH IN A FREE STATE, or a SELF-GOVERNING CHRISTIANITY IN INDEPENDENT BUT FRIENDLY RELATION TO THE CIVIL GOVERNMENT" (9). He thus defended what can be called a very benevolent view of separation and regarded it as a guarantee of religious freedom for all, despite its distinct preference toward Christianity. Many offered opinions on the meaning of the separation of church and state: some defined it more rigorously than Schaff, and others suggested that "separation" was too strong a word. Augustus Hopkins Strong, for example, Baptist theologian and president of Rochester Theological Seminary, celebrated the 400th anniversary of Columbus's famous voyage with a pamphlet comparing

---

ed. Henry W. Bowden (Carbondale: Southern Illinois University Press, 1988), 148–67. A good, compact biography is by George H. Shriver, *Philip Schaff: Christian Scholar and Ecumenical Prophet* (Macon, Ga.: Mercer University Press, 1987). For Schaff's earlier reflections on the American cultural and religious situation, see his *America: A Sketch of the Political, Social, and Religious Character of the United States of North America* (New York: Scribner, 1855).

state and church in 1492 and 1892 and discussing broadly the role of
American Christianity as a factor in the progress of civil and religious
liberty. His point of departure was to press the distinction between the
two spheres. On the one hand, he explained that "the foundation of the
church is the spiritual connection of the individual believer with the living
Christ, his Saviour and his King," and as "his reign is a spiritual one, his
laws are enforced solely by spiritual sanctions." On the other hand, he
said, "Side by side with the Church, but in entire independence of it,
stands the State. It, too, is a divine institution and is clothed with a divine
authority. But it has to do only with men's outward and earthly and temporal affairs."[25] Neither church nor state, he insisted, was to intrude into
the other's sphere. The state is to help the church only by protecting it
from external violence and securing the right of all citizens to exercise
their faith so long as others' rights are not violated. The church is to help
the state by declaring that the powers that be are ordained by God and
that in civil matters the citizen owes obedience to constituted authority.
He spoke for an "entire separation, yet friendly cooperation" of the two
(6). As Schaff had done, Augustus Strong praised the voluntary way in
religion, concluding that "the separation of Church and State has harmed
neither of the two; but, where State aid has wholly ceased, religion has
prospered as never before" (44). Although he advocated a stricter separationist position than Schaff, he did not separate himself from the prevailing view that in a Christian nation "friendly cooperation" would continue to the mutual advantage of both church and state.

As the spell of the ideal of Christendom had held its sway over centuries
of Christianity, so the continuing vision of a voluntary establishment long
retained its appeal across decades of American Protestantism. Difficult
problems, however, were emerging as the nineteenth century drew to a
close. Some Protestant leaders who addressed church-state issues indeed
wondered about the usefulness of the concept of separation. When Robert E. Thompson delivered the Stone Lectures at Princeton Seminary, he
dealt with the range of social issues that were emerging in the early 1890s
with a new urgency. When he got to the "many nice problems" that the
relation of the church to the nation presents, he declared that they "are
not solved by assuming that the two forms of society constitute entirely
separate spheres of life and activity":

> They are best kept distinct; they never can be made separate. A church made
> up of disembodied spirits might be separate from the state. But a church made
> of living men and women, who owe duties to the state, and who require a def-
> inite locality within its area for their assemblies and a home for their protection,

[25] *State and Church in 1492 and in 1892* (Philadelphia: American Baptist Publication
Society, 1892), 6.

is obliged to stand in another relation than that of separation. From the membership of the state the church obtains its membership. Under the laws of the state it owns its property. Through the legislation of the state it secures the weekly day of rest for its worship. Through the police of the state its solemn assemblies are strictly guarded from interference and interruption. By the prohibition of the state it is protected against the offense of public blasphemy [251].

But neither can the state ignore the church, which is a mainstay of the social order and a chief pillar of the state. So well is this recognized, Thompson explained, that persons who have no distinct Christian faith nevertheless contribute to the building and support of churches on social grounds alone. Among proper church functions is its role "as a moral tonic and mediator between opposite parties" (252). The church, however, must not get involved in "the direct discussion and attack of social evils" but "imbue society with the great principles of right action, and to leave these to work themselves into better social methods" (253). The negative example of the medieval papacy, Thompson concluded, stands "as a warning to all churches that they should recognize their proper sphere and its limits, and leave the state to do its proper work" (254). The church does, however, have a mediatorial duty, often neglected, which should be carried out in a nonpartisan way. Although he did not like to emphasize the separation of church and state, Thompson's ideas of relating the two differed little from those of his Christian colleagues who did—evidence of a broad consensus despite minor differences.

Isaac Cornelison was more outspoken in his support of separation in his *The Relation of Religion to Civil Government*. He explained that in his study of the early history of the United States his sympathies had been "wholly with the distinctive political views of Washington and Hamilton; and not with those of Jefferson and Madison" (iii). By identifying himself with a negative and restrictive rather than a positive role for government, he was stating a view widely shared among Protestants. He declared that except in certain special cases it was not part of the proper function of government "to inculcate, propagate, or even foster, Christianity": that is the role of the churches, which were fulfilling their roles well so that "Christianity does not need the fostering of the State" (342, 345). Nevertheless, he argued dialectically, "when Christianity is brought to its notice in such a way as to require positive action, it ought to give preference and favor to Christianity," for that "is the religion of the people" (349, 350). Other religions are entitled to toleration and protection, but not to favor by the state. Just as English, the language of the people, alone is entitled to favor while other languages are tolerated, so too Christianity should receive preference and approval from the state. Yet the state ought to extend "equal protection to Christians, Non-Christians, and Anti-Christians," as long as worship is orderly and not connected with immoral practices (351). All properly conducted meetings of unbelievers were also impartially to be protected, even when assembled on the Lord's Day. But the religious feelings of the Christian are also worthy of protection from offense, so, Cornelison argued, "the State ought . . . to prohibit such acts, displays, and demonstrations on the Lord's day as offend those [Protestant] feelings" (353). On the excluded list were businesses, parades, baseball games, and other shows—a summary of general practice at the time, although Catholics were much more accepting of such events.

The Presbyterian author expressed the common Protestant conviction of the time that the religious aspects of the government should be fully nonsectarian. He affirmed that "the State ought not to take any action which involves the adoption or establishment of any sectarian Christian doctrine" (355). It should neither decide on the truth or falseness of doctrine nor be responsible for protecting bequests for what were technically called *pious uses* because that would involve judging sectarian doctrines. Cornelison confronted a knotty problem in dealing with the issue of the exemption of places of worship from taxation by the state. To be sure he wanted continued exemption for churches, but not on the forbidden ground that the government had a supposed duty to foster Christianity, for then it would logically follow "that the places of worship used by all non-Christians,—Confucians, Buddhists, Mohammedans, and even the synagogues of the Jews" would have to be denied like exemption (365). The principle, Cornelison insisted, was that all property used for public purpose and not for pecuniary profit was to be exempt. When all were exempt, the state was giving them freedom without fostering them, for it would be inconsistent to foster contradictory religious systems. He admitted the logical difficulties: in exempting educational and charitable institutions of many types through the "public purpose" principle a fostering purpose is at work, but discontinuing exemption of Christian institutions discriminates against them.

On state action on a moral question, Cornelison fell back on the majoritarian principle in advising that such action ought to conform to the precepts of Christianity. The courts are incompetent to enforce such precepts that have not been incorporated into law, but legislatures should regard it as an obligation to frame statutes on moral questions in accordance with Christian precepts, which in Cornelison's view were nonsectarian. An abstract code of morals for the state is a fiction. "The code of the people; and in this country, . . . the code of Christianity," is to govern legislation (368). This is especially true, declared this Presbyterian minister, in matters of marriage and divorce: "All Christian people, Roman Catholics and Protestants alike, believe that on this subject the Bible is a divinely given rule of practice, and that there can be therefore no departure from that rule but to the injury of the public welfare" (368). On such a conflict of biblical interpretation as to which is the proper day of the week to observe the Sabbath, Cornelison, falling back on his majoritarian principle, found that Sunday should be the day of rest in the nation. He argued that this did not reject the view that the seventh day is the Sabbath but simply followed the wishes of the largest number (371–72).

In conclusion, Cornelison recapitulated his views: his nation was "a State without a Church, but not without a Religion," as his subtitle put it; and the religion was predominantly Christian. Such authors as Isaac Cornelison, Philip Schaff, Josiah Strong, Augustus Strong, Joseph P. Thompson, and Robert E. Thompson, well-known in their time, were not only describing the views widely accepted within the Protestant establishment of the time, but they were also putting them forth as normative for the country as a whole. They did not take serious account of those whose vision of a Christian or a religious nation differed from their own. But challenges to accepted views and practices were being raised, by not only those outside the circle of the Protestant denominational families but also a few within those households of faith.

Dissonant Voices

Majority sentiment among the Protestant denominations in the later nineteenth century largely accepted and applauded the existing framework of the Constitution and the First Amendment on government and religion as generally interpreted. Yet some believed that in the long run that arrangement would not work to the full advantage of the churches. In typical American fashion a voluntary society, the National Reform Association (NRA), had been formed in 1863 to act on the basis of such views. At its first convention the following January it launched an active program that attracted a number of prominent clergy and lay leaders. The purpose of the association was clearly stated in the second article of its constitution, which in its mature form said:

> The object of this Society shall be to maintain existing Christian features in the American Government; to promote needed reforms in the action of government touching the Sabbath, the institution of the Family, the religious element in Education, the Oath, and Public morality as affected by the liquor-traffic and other kindred evils; and to secure such an amendment to the Constitution of the United States as will declare the nation's allegiance to Jesus Christ and its acceptance of the moral laws of the Christian religion, and so indicate that this is a Christian nation, and place all the Christian laws, institutions and usages

of our government on an undeniable legal basis in the fundamental law of the land.[26]

The NRA found its followers largely among denominations of Calvinist orientation, although some well-known Episcopalians and Methodists were involved. The small Reformed Presbyterian Church, especially active in providing day-to-day support and leadership for the NRA, undertook in 1867 to edit its periodical *The Christian Statesman*, which continued to appear throughout and beyond the period covered by this book. The most conspicuous aim of the NRA, which attracted considerable public attention, was to secure the desired constitutional amendment. The association's first petition in 1874 to amend the preamble to the Constitution, however, was rejected by the House Judiciary Committee. Nonetheless, the petitioners persisted on into the twentieth century, despite a second rejection in 1896.

In the atmosphere of the late nineteenth century, NRA members felt that their main goal was realizable; as late as 1890 of the forty-two states thirty-seven constitutions acknowledged the authority of God in preambles or main articles. Nevertheless, many members of the leading evangelical denominations who were in sympathy with some of the NRA's goals did not support its central concern. For some, only conversion could make people religious, so that recourse to law was futile. This supported the widely popular view that Christians should infuse their values into the culture as individuals by following their biblical principles in all areas of life; those expressing such opinions often echoed the familiar statements discussed in the previous section about keeping the institutions of religion separate from those of civil life. It was enough for Christians to work with others for laws consistent with their own moral standards without confusing the two spheres. They believed that America was a Christian nation, as evidenced, for example, by certain nineteenth-century Supreme Court decisions and found it sufficient to concentrate on aligning it more fully with their principles by the tested and proven means of voluntary persuasion.

In response to criticism, NRA representatives often insisted that their proposed amendment would not unite church and state. Christian moral principles would have explicitly and formally become the basis of American legislation and administration, however, and the great majority re-

---

[26] As printed in the report, "Annual Meeting and National Conference, Philadelphia, April 24–26, 1888," *National Reform Documents* (Philadelphia: Aldine Press), 2, no. 1 (1888), back cover. Brief treatments of the NRA are by Gary Scott Smith, *The Seeds of Secularism: Calvinism, Culture, and Pluralism in America, 1870–1915* (Grand Rapids, Mich.: Christian University Press, 1985), 59–68, and by Anson Phelps Stokes, *Church and State in the United States* (New York: Harper & Bros., 1950), 2: 259–60; 3: 583–87.

mained unconvinced. Hence much opposition to the association's major goal came from within the conservative camp as well as from Christians of other orientations, persons of other faiths, and from the secularly oriented. As Gary Scott Smith concluded in his informative discussion of the movement, "The amendment was defeated primarily because many Americans did not believe it was necessary, fair, or biblically justified to recognize officially the lordship of Jesus Christ over the nation" (65). Yet the NRA articulated a distinctive position on religion and government that attracted considerable attention in the contemporary Protestant as he or she searched for a more fully Christian nation.

Dissonant voices of quite another type were sounded by a few who fully accepted "normative" Protestant efforts to combine commitment to the separation of church and state with the goal that their establishment would continue to dominate America's religious future but who did not share the confidence that things would work out that way. The most conspicuous example was an Episcopal clergyman, William Reed Huntington. In a book that originally appeared in 1870 and ran through a number of editions, he had called attention to what he perceived (and deplored) as a major trend of the time that was running against the continuation of America as a Christian nation by voluntary means. He boldly claimed, at a time when experimentalism of many kinds was in vogue,

> that the experiment of greatest moment now in progress here is not popular government at all, but this, *The mutual independence of Church and State.*
>
> We have dissolved a partnership which for fifteen hundred years the world held sacred.[27]

As a major illustration of the trend, Huntington pointed to the First Amendment's establishment clause, in which "lies wrapped the secret of our national destiny; and on the wisdom or unwisdom of this decision of the fathers hinges the well-being of their children's children." For it means, declared the man who became the rector of New York's influential Grace Church in 1883, "that our Government rests in theory, and must eventually rest in practice, upon a purely secular basis" (100).

Huntington observed that some traces of the old concordat between church and state survived: such matters as the opening of legislatures and courts with prayer, Bible reading in the schools, presidential proclamations, military chaplains, pious mottoes on coins. But in a curiously prophetic passage that flew in the face of prevailing Protestant opinion, he dismissed their significance:

> These vestiges of Christianity, as we may call them, are printed on the sand.

[27] *The Church-Idea: An Essay Towards Unity,* 4th ed. (New York: Scribner, 1899), 94. A fifth edition of the book was published in 1928.

The tide has only to crawl up a few inches further to wash them clean away. There is nothing in the theory of the Republic that makes such usages an essential part of the national life. They rest for the most part upon the precarious tradition of colonial days: or if on statute law, what is statute law but the creature of temporary majorities? The moment popular opinion sets against them, all these relics of an established religion must go by the board. They are not the natural fruit of our system; they are but reminders of an old order of things that has passed away; fossils embedded in the rock on which the existing structure stands. One by one they will probably be chipped out and set aside as curiosities [102].

Huntington knew about the endeavors of "certain very sanguine persons" who launched the movement to incorporate in the Constitution an article recognizing the truth of Christianity, but he declared that "it is too late. The stars in their courses fight against so forlorn a hope" (103). Meanwhile, as America has deliberately chosen the utilitarian scheme, it must continue in that way, unless the people were prepared to agitate for revolution and tear up the social order by the roots. He saw the whole civilized world moving in the same secular direction, quite opposite to Lewis French Stearn's claim that the Christian nations were in the ascendant.

Huntington, however, was in his own way an optimistic American, too. He rejoiced that the ground was decisively cleared so that the church at last had full freedom to do her best—"and for it she has to thank those who in the interest of secular government cut the knot of Church and State" (106). Were the process to continue to its utmost possible limit and the gap between church and state become wider, the Church need not flinch. As human government renounces diviner functions, he argued, then people "will look about them to see whether there be not some social organism capable of supplementing the deficiencies of the secular machine." That will be the church's opportunity: "The food and drink that are withheld at the Capitol must be sought for in the Temple. The more thoroughly the State secularizes human life, the more earnestly ought the Church to labor to spiritualize and ennoble it" (107). A secular state is perfectly competent to deal with morality and crime, he explained, but it does not know or care to know about sin and holiness. The church must therefore furnish a high and pure standard of morality and leave with the state the responsibility of conforming its action more or less closely to it.

The Episcopal rector questioned whether the Christian church was properly organized to do this. He advocated closer cooperation among the various denominations and is now remembered primarily as a pioneer of the ecumenical movement. As churches moved toward a larger unity, he believed that they would be better prepared to make the most of their opportunities in an increasingly secular American state.

Few people in either churches or government at that time were prepared to accept Huntington's logic, though some shared his doubts. For example, George Harris, a Congregationalist theologian, prized the separation of church and state but welcomed the "mutual friendliness and recognition" between them, especially as it permitted Bible reading and prayer in the public schools.[28] As he surveyed the increasing religious pluriformity in the nation of the 1890s, he reluctantly concluded that "we must be prepared to relinquish what remains of religious observance" in public education. He wanted to let things remain as they were for the time being but saw that "when an issue is made, it should be acknowledged that the State cannot assume the function of religious teaching" (388).

Few people in the Protestant churches were prepared to accept the logic of a Huntington or the doubts of a Harris; the majority continued to hope and work for a more fully Christian America as they defined it. At the same time, however, various other religious bodies, some expanding explosively, were growing restive with the limits that they perceived the Protestant establishment, cooperating with public authority, to be placing on their freedom.

[28] *Moral Evolution* (1896; reprint, New York: Arno Press, 1977), 385.

2

Protestantism Challenged: Latter-day Saints and Roman Catholics

IN THE 1880s, the prevailing views on religion and government as generally held within the major evangelical Protestant denominational families were being resisted at crucial points by two other Christian traditions, the Catholic and the Mormon. They were, of course, vastly different in their origins, history, size, teachings, and emphases—different both from one another and from the Protestant churches. From the point of view of the latter, they both posed serious threats to the continuation of hard-won, prized patterns of religious, moral, and political life.

In his famous book *Our Country*, Josiah Strong named Mormonism and "Romanism" among the "seven perils" confronting America—the only two religious traditions on his list. In 1886, both religions worried leaders of the American branch of the Evangelical Alliance, a voluntary agency that drew its members from across the Protestant spectrum as it worked to advance religious liberty, resist superstition and infidelity, and deepen fellowship among evangelicals. As Philip D. Jordan summarized one of their major fears, "The geometric growth of Roman Catholics and the expansion of Mormonism into states neighboring Utah threatened the fabric of the Republic."[1] In the turmoil of American life in the late nineteenth century, one of these traditions was forced to make a crucial adjustment to survive in a land where the Protestant moral code was so deeply embedded in the culture, while the older and much larger body dramatically resisted the transmission of that culture through the public schools. In the ensuing struggles, issues of the role of religion and religious institutions in public life were hotly debated. As new perceptions and realities emerged, some positions relating to church and state hardened, while others were modified.

Latter-day Saints: A Change of Direction

Although there were certain similarities between Mormonism and evangelical Protestantism, the new movement took a distinctive direction from

[1] *The Evangelical Alliance for the United States of America, 1847–1900: Ecumenism, Identity and the Religion of the Republic* (New York: E. Mellen, 1982), 154.

the start. "It began as a movement that understood itself as Christian," Jan Shipps has written, "but as 'the new dispensation of the fulness of times' commenced with the publication of the Book of Mormon, the 'restoration' of the Aaronic priesthood, and the recognition of Joseph Smith as prophet, these nineteenth-century Latter-day Saints (as they came to be called) embarked on a path that led to developments that now distinguish their tradition from the Christian tradition as surely as early Christianity was distinguished from its Hebraic context."[2] The three formative events mentioned occurred in 1829 and 1830, when Smith claimed—and was accepted by his family and a growing circle of believers—that the Book of Mormon was his translation, under divine guidance, of golden plates that had been hidden for fourteen hundred years until revealed to him. The book tells the story of a small band of Hebrews who fled the Holy Land just before the Babylonian invasion, then journeyed by sea to the western coast of what came to be known as the Americas. Conflict divided the group, until the resurrected Christ appeared, brought them together, and organized his church. For some two hundred years all went well, but conflict broke out again; one group destroyed the other and then, apparently mixed with other peoples, became ancestors of the Indians. The last prophet of the destroyed group, Moroni, son of Mormon, buried the plates where they remained until, as Smith claimed, he was led to them, guided in their translation, and instructed by revelation in the organizing of the new church.

Founded in Fayette, New York, in April 1830, the church began to grow and spread as it sent out missionaries who drew converts into the new fold. It established its center in the vicinity of Kirtland, Ohio, but also dispatched groups to Missouri as the new Land of Zion. Soon other writings based on what the new church recognized as revelations added to the core of sacred writings. As news of the growing movement spread, however, many rejected its claims, and some became its bitter enemies; it was finally forced out of Kirtland in 1838 and, after some battles and a massacre, out of Missouri by the following year. A new refuge was found back across the Mississippi in Nauvoo, Illinois. As Mormon missions succeeded at home and abroad, especially in England, the church soon reached an estimated overall membership of thirty thousand. Persecution followed the new, rapidly growing tradition; Smith himself was murdered in 1844, and Mormon continuation in Nauvoo became untenable. Two years later temporary settlements were set up in Iowa, and in 1847 the historic trek to find a permanent home in the western territories located the new headquarters at Salt Lake City, with Brigham Young as the new

[2] *Mormonism: The Story of A New Religious Tradition* (Urbana: University of Illinois Press, 1985), ix–x.

leader. During that stormy decade the reported membership had doubled. In its inner growth, the new tradition drew on both Old and New Testaments and on its own sacred texts, which were accepted as arising out of divine revelations to the prophet and his successors. So, as Shipps said at the conclusion of her work, "While it perceives of itself as Christian, Mormonism differs from traditional Christianity in much the same fashion that traditional Christianity, in its ultimate emphasis on the individual, came to differ from Judaism."[3]

Very early in the new tradition's development, and partly because it followed ancient patriarchal examples with considerable literalness, the practice of "plural marriage"—polygamy, or bigamy as it was often called at the time—entered Mormon history. It was sanctioned by what was believed to be a revelation to the founder and prophet, which was not written down until 1843 and not made public for nine years after that. This departure from the Western moral code stirred up tensions within Mormonism, where it was practiced only by a minority, and much increased the already great antipathy to the movement among most other Americans. It ran directly contrary to the teachings and practices of the existing Christian denominations, in which the monogamous family was viewed as divinely established. Many protested against what they regarded as scandalous behavior. As there was no law in Utah Territory against it, rising pressure spurred Congress to pass the Morrill Anti-Bigamy Act in 1862; the legislation not only made bigamy a felony but also dissolved the charitable incorporation of the Church of Jesus Christ of Latter-day Saints and limited church property holdings to $50,000.[4] While national attention was riveted on the Civil War and its aftermath, the enforcement of that law in Utah became ineffective, and it was largely ignored.

Not until the 1870s, when increasing numbers of non-Mormons came into Utah following completion of the transcontinental railroad, were serious anti-Mormon measures taken by the government. At that point Mormon authorities, believing the 1862 act to be unconstitutional,

[3] Ibid., 148. See also John F. Wilson, "Some Comparative Perspectives on the Early Mormon Movement and the Church-State Question," *Journal of Mormon History* 8 (1981): 63–77. For a useful survey history, see Leonard J. Arrington and Davis Bitton, *The Mormon Experience: A History of the Latter-day Saints* (New York: Knopf, 1979).

[4] Kenneth David Driggs, "The Mormon Church-State Confrontation in Nineteenth-Century America," *Journal of Church and State* 30 (1988): 277. Various Mormon sects arose through the years, many of them gathered in the Reorganized Church of Latter Day Saints (RLDS, 1860), but it is the larger body centered in Salt Lake City that I discuss briefly in this book. For full-length treatments, see Edward Leo Lyman, *Political Deliverance: The Mormon Quest for Statehood* (Urbana: University of Illinois Press, 1986), and Edwin B. Firmage and Richard C. Mangrum, *Zion in the Courts: A Legal History of the Church of Jesus Christ of Latter-day Saints, 1830–1900* (Urbana: University of Illinois Press, 1988).

sought to test it by means of the case of George Reynolds, who was convicted of polygamy in 1875. The complexities of the appeal process meant that the case was not reviewed by the Supreme Court until late 1878, with the unanimous decision handed down the following January by Chief Justice Morrison R. Waite. In the course of marshaling the evidence, Waite quoted favorably Jefferson's interpretation of the First Amendment given in 1802 as "thus building a wall of separation between church and State," a precedent for many later church-state cases. Waite also made a much-quoted distinction in explaining that "Congress was deprived of all legislative power over mere opinion, but was left free to reach actions which were in violation of social duties or subversive of good order."[5] Noting with considerable documentation that polygamy had always been odious in Western civilization, he drew the line:

> We think it may safely be said there never has been a time in any State of the Union when polygamy has not been an offence against society, cognizable by the civil courts and punishable with more or less severity. In the face of all this evidence, it is impossible to believe that the constitutional guaranty of religious freedom was intended to prohibit legislation in respect to this most important feature of social life [165].

So Reynolds went to jail, justly from the viewpoint of Gentiles, but a hero to Mormons.

Latter-day Saints (LDS) publicly defied the antipolygamy laws. A high official in the church and the Utah delegate to Congress, George Q. Cannon, even published a sharp critique of the Supreme Court's decision. Congress responded in 1882 with the Edmunds Act, which set higher prison terms and fines for persons convicted of the felony crime of polygamy and disqualified practicing polygamists from holding public office, voting, and sitting as jurors on polygamy cases. This provided the basis for what Mormons called the "raid" when federal marshals were dispatched to Utah Territory to arrest men involved in plural marriage. Voter registration officials often interpreted the law to exclude Mormons generally; in neighboring Idaho Territory they were completely disenfranchised. The latter action was challenged by a Mormon monogamist, but he was convicted of having voted and conspiring with others to vote in 1888. The Supreme Court unanimously upheld the jurisdiction of the district court, emphasizing that bigamy and polygamy were crimes by the laws of all civilized and Christian countries. "To extend exemption from punishment for such crimes would be to shock the moral judgment of the

---

[5] *Reynolds* v. *United States*, 98 U.S. 145 (1879) at 164. Significant parts of this and several related cases have been reprinted, along with brief commentary, by Noonan, *The Believer and the Powers that Are*, 197–98.

community," wrote Justice Stephen J. Field in stating the judgment of the court. "To call their advocacy a tenet of religion is to offend the common sense of mankind."[6] With the pressure on, some prominent Latter-day Saints fled the country; others aided by a Mormon underground, went into hiding. Hundreds of convictions were obtained by 1890.

In 1887 the federal government used another weapon. The Morrill Act of 1862 had limited Mormon holdings; now amendments to the Edmunds Act directed the attorney general to take steps to seize all the church's assets, as well as those of its agency that financed the immigration of thousands of European LDS converts. A number of actions were undertaken; consolidated into one case, the Supreme Court upheld the seizures, this time in a seven-to-two vote. In declaring the decision of the Court, Justice Joseph Bradley said: "The organization of a community for the spread and practice of polygamy is, in a measure, a return to barbarism. It is contrary to the spirit of Christianity and of the civilization which Christianity has produced in the Western world."[7] Although LDS leaders had been searching for a compromise, that decision, wrote Kenneth Driggs, "forced Mormon leaders to realize that no compromise was possible. They had to elect between loyalty to their unique social, political, and economic customs and their very survival."[8] A moral practice that conflicted with a position deep-rooted in American culture was a highly emotional issue for evangelical Protestants; it stood squarely in the way of the Mormon future.

The decisive action to avert destruction was taken by the head of the church, First President Wilford Woodruff. In 1888 he had affirmed that "the Lord never will give a revelation to abandon plural marriage" for "we cannot deny principle."[9] But after the decisions of 1890, he wrote in his diary, "I have arrived at a point in the history of the Church of Jesus Christ of Latter-day Saints when I am under the necessity of acting for the temporal salvation of the church" (135). From the outside, the observer sees the Mormons yielding to the superior strength of the government and giving up a practice that offended the moral commitments of Western Christian civilization. But as the Mormon historian Lyman phrases it, "Even if the church was figuratively backed to the wall and practical considerations demanded concessions, that does not necessarily deny the possibility of the divine inspiration Woodruff and his associates claimed as his ultimate motivation" (136). On September 24, 1890,

---

[6] *Davis* v. *Beason*, 133 U.S. 333 (1890) at 341; Noonan, *The Believer and the Powers that Are*, 202–3.

[7] *The Late Corporation of the Church of Jesus Christ of Latter-day Saints* v. *United States*, 136 U.S. 1 (1890) at 49; Noonan, *The Believer and the Powers that Are*, 205.

[8] "Mormon Church-State Confrontation," 287.

[9] As quoted by Lyman, *Political Deliverance*, 106.

Woodruff believed that he had received spiritual direction. He discussed it with other leaders of the church and issued the "Woodruff Manifesto" in the form of a press release the next day. Responding to reports that plural marriages had continued to be contracted and encouraged by the church, he declared:

> I, therefore, as President of the Church of Jesus Christ of Latter-day Saints, do hereby, in the most solemn manner, declare that these charges are false. We are not teaching polygamy or plural marriage, nor permitting any person to enter into its practice, and I deny that either forty or any other number of plural marriages have during that period been solemnized in our Temples or in any other place in the Territory. . . .
>
> Inasmuch as laws have been enacted by Congress forbidding plural marriages, which laws have been pronounced constitutional by the court of last resort, I hereby declare my intention to submit to those laws, and to use my influence with the members of the Church over which I preside to have them do likewise [296].

On October 6 a General Conference assembled by the church unanimously accepted the manifesto as authoritative and binding.

The change made it difficult for those already involved in plural marriages, but in general the matter was left for the families to handle as best they could. They were urged not to violate covenants made and yet to honor the law of the land, to live so that the world would recognize the sincerity of the change. Many apparently handled the matter by being very quiet about their continuing relationships. As it became clear that no new plural marriages were officially being allowed, the government made concessions gradually. Amnesty for those who had been indicted was promised; confiscated church property was restored when it became clear that it would not be used to advance the banned practice. Although it took more than five years to complete the process, the path was now open for Utah to become a state. Some perhaps thought the practice of plural marriage could or would be quietly resumed, but after 1890 it was increasingly evident that the distinctive boundary that had decisively separated more than two hundred thousand Latter-day Saints from the main patterns of American culture had been removed. The statements made and steps taken led progressively to a point where no return was practically possible. An old order was passing away, but the LDS church survived—and after a difficult transition period it thrived in a different way. Plural marriage was not officially reintroduced in the main body of Mormon life, but as enforcement relaxed it did continue quietly for a few years and was perpetuated in some splinter groups.[10]

---

[10] Shipps, *Mormonism*, 114–15, 125–26; Arrington and Bitton, *Mormon Experience*,

The struggle between a church and a determined government, pressed by an evangelical Protestantism aroused on a moral issue, had led to the religious body's capitulation. On the way it met tests before the Supreme Court that became precedents often cited in church-state litigation and discussion. "Mormons of the period believed their sincere religious beliefs were protected by the First Amendment," concluded Kenneth Driggs, "and they were bitterly disappointed to find the Constitution would not protect them in the face of widespread public hostility."[11] Protestants saw the outcome as a sign that a peril to their dream for a Christian America had been overcome. Although retaining their distinctiveness as a new religious tradition, Mormons had entered the mainstream of American culture.

Catholic Educational Strategy: A Firm Stand

From the time of the American Revolution, Roman Catholics had welcomed the nation's tradition of religious freedom and accepted the patterns of church-state separation as they evolved. The outstanding Catholic leader throughout the period of this study was James Gibbons, who was American-born though he had spent much of his boyhood in Ireland. Elevated to the episcopacy in 1868, he rose quickly to prominence while he demonstrated efficiency in administration and a talent for reconciliation. Only nine years later, he became archbishop of Baltimore, the oldest archdiocese in the nation; its incumbent at that time served as unofficial but virtual primate in the American church. Just ten years after that, in 1887, Gibbons was named a cardinal.

In view of the long centuries in Catholic historical experience in which church and state often were (and remained) closely related in theory and practice, Gibbons was exhibiting a deep conviction when, in a sermon as he took possession of his titular church in Rome as a new cardinal, he said forthrightly: "For myself, as a citizen of the United States, without closing my eyes to our defects as a nation, I proclaim, with a deep sense of pride and gratitude, and in this great capitol of Christendom, that I belong to a country where the civil government holds over us the aegis of its protection without interfering in the legitimate exercise of our sublime mission as ministers of the Gospel of Jesus Christ."[12] Although American

esp. chap. 13, "Church and Kingdom: Creative Adjustment and Reinvigoration." See also Driggs, "After the Manifesto: Modern Polygamy and Fundamentalist Mormons," *Journal of Church and State* 32 (1990): 367–89.

[11] "Mormon Church-State Confrontation," 289.

[12] As reprinted by John Tracy Ellis, ed., *Documents of American Catholic History*, 4th ed. (Wilmington, Del.: Michael Glazier, 1987), 2: 462.

Catholics expressed such sentiments in various ways, he was stating a widely held view of Catholic acceptance of American church-state patterns. At the very time he spoke, however, a new surge of anti-Catholicism was rising. Alarmed by the rapid increase in Catholic numbers as a result of the shift in patterns of immigration in the 1880s, many Americans could not believe that such sentiments as Gibbons voiced were sincere. They feared that their own freedoms would be jeopardized if the power of Catholicism in their country increased.

While many traditional antipathies between Catholics and Protestants persisted into the tensions of the 1880s and 1890s, they were increasingly focused and intensified by the mounting controversies that swirled around issues of education—disputes that had important implications for the ways in which the relationship of religion and government was understood. The growing political strength of Catholics gave a new seriousness to the struggles. Immigration from Ireland had begun in the colonial period, but the large influx of the 1840s and 1850s from the Emerald Isle predated the arrival of vast numbers of foreign-speaking Catholics from southern and eastern European lands; accordingly, Irish Catholics felt more at home in American political life. Significantly, when a Catholic was nominated for mayor of New York in 1880 some people feared that the public schools would be "romanized," but Irish-American William R. Grace was elected anyway. During that decade Catholic mayors were also elected in Boston and other New England cities. In some other northeastern and midwestern states Catholics gained strong, if not dominant positions in the Democratic party.[13] Hence fights over issues in education increasingly entered the political arena.

The heart of the controversy, however, remained in conflicting approaches to religious and moral issues. Public school systems were growing rapidly in this period. Their defenders argued that, pervaded by a broadly religious but nonsectarian spirit, they communicated sound moral and spiritual values to the pupils. The schools were seen as important sources of unity in a nation that was receiving millions of persons from diverse cultures. Thomas Jefferson Morgan, a Baptist, summarized the point in 1889: "If the heterogeneous masses that are coming to us from all parts of the world are to be melted and molded into a homogeneous mass, if the children that come here with all their inherited prejudices from Germany, and France, Italy, and all over the world, are to be blended into a great nationality, it will be because of the work done by the public schools." Illustrating the piety that many Protestants invested

[13] Lloyd P. Jorgenson, *The State and the Non-Public School, 1825–1925* (Columbia: University of Missouri Press, 1987), 121–22.

in the common school, he added, "They seem to be God's machinery of assimilation."[14]

Although many Protestants wanted to have Bible reading at the opening of the school day, they often concurred with the view that religion need not be taught as part of the curriculum. But some who disagreed with that particular point nevertheless did not quarrel with the wider agreement: religious and moral emphases could be advanced without sectarian overtones. Addressing his Baptist brethren in 1889, Leighton Williams declared that "I feel it right to push every bit of moral view into the public school system that I can; and if I feel that the Bible is a good moral textbook I am content to use every means in my power to push Bible instruction into the schools; I never want to push any sectarianism; I do want to push all the moral, all the religious force that I can into every department of the Government."[15] On the basis of his study of the Calvinistic tradition in this period, Gary Scott Smith concluded that "until at least 1915 the theistic but nonsectarian view continued largely to control American public education, especially in small towns and rural areas."[16] With few exceptions Protestant churches believed in the common schools and found their support to be a point of unity across denominational lines, but the great majority of nominal Protestants not formally on church rolls evidently endorsed them, too.

Roman Catholics, despite their inner differences on many matters that often grew out of their various ethnic heritages, in general shared a distinctive ethos setting them apart on educational issues. As part of a worldwide church with centuries of tradition informing it, the Catholics saw education based primarily in the family and the church. For them, true religion was not only sectarian but also rooted in Catholic truth, formally and authoritatively defined by the teachings of the sixteenth-century Council of Trent and reinforced by the declaration of papal infallibility on matters of faith and morals in 1870. Growing numbers of Catholics wanted that element included in the education of their children. As developments in educational theory and trends in economic life meant that schools were replacing families as the basic institution of education, the nation at large increased its attention to educational institutions and carefully scrutinized what the schools did. Although Catholics differed in attitudes toward the public school, they strongly tended, encouraged by their priests and bishops, to prefer education in the context of church life. Much as churches of various traditions had established schools in the co-

---

[14] As quoted by Francis Paul Prucha, *American Indian Policy in Crisis: Christian Reformers and the Indian, 1865–1900* (Norman: University of Oklahoma Press, 1976), 305.

[15] Informal remarks recorded in *Proceedings of the Baptist Congress* (New York: Baptist Congress Publishing Co., 1889), 138.

[16] *Seeds of Secularism*, 85.

lonial and early American periods, Catholic parishes started schools, often locating them in church buildings.

As the drive for universal, tax-supported, nonsectarian common schools matured during the nineteenth century, many Catholics found that such schools did not meet their needs. They increased the number of their own educational institutions, at their own expense, during a time when they were struggling to build churches to deal with the waves of Catholic immigrants. Early efforts to gain a share of public funds were generally unsuccessful, and some bitter clashes took place. As a result, efforts to teach religion in the public schools declined, though brief devotional exercises were often retained. Thus as Catholics grew in numbers, so did their network of schools, parallel to the maturing systems of public education. Jay Dolan wrote that the parochial school "became the principal educational institution in the Catholic community, and Catholic educators promoted it with the same type of zeal found among public school crusaders. By the 1880s, the parochial school, rather than the men's college, was the most important school in the Catholic community."[17]

At its Third Plenary Council of Baltimore in 1884 the American Catholic hierarchy, with the strong urging and support of the Vatican, threw its growing weight into the extension and improvement of the parish schools. The month-long council was an impressive affair: its membership roll of top church leaders was headed by fourteen archbishops and fifty-eight bishops.[18] Among the most important matters decided by the council was that of education, at both elementary and advanced levels. Of special significance was the ruling on the former, for the prelates directed that within two years a parochial school should be attached to all existing parishes; responsibility for so doing was placed upon the pastors. Parents were required to send their children to the parish schools, unless they could provide for their Catholic education at home or in other suitable educational institutions. Steps to improve the quality of education in those schools were taken. A measure to deny the sacraments to parents who did send their children to public schools was narrowly defeated; always controversial and sometimes practiced, that measure had previously become "a popular tactic to force parents to send their children to the Catholic school."[19] But it was recognized that some parishes, both in crowded cities and in thinly populated areas, simply lacked the resources

[17] American Catholic Experience, 262.

[18] For a brief, informative account of this important gathering and its outcome, see Thomas T. McAvoy, A History of the Catholic Church in the United States (Notre Dame: University of Notre Dame Press, 1969), 255–62.

[19] Dolan, American Catholic Experience, 270.

to start a school. Hence considerable internal tension arose over the practicality of launching schools in such situations.

That such a measure had been so thoroughly discussed, however, indicated the church's seriousness about its schools. The strong swing to parochial education was clear; whereas in 1880 there had been 2,246 schools, by 1900 there were 3,811.[20] Parish schools were popular among immigrants, who generally were anxious to impart their own religious, cultural, and linguistic traditions to their children. A very important factor in the growth of the system was the availability of teachers, largely from women's religious communities. By 1900 there were forty thousand Catholic sisters in the country, the great majority involved in staffing the schools, at a sufficiently low cost to make the vast and growing enterprise possible. If the public school system was a "sacred cause" for many of its supporters, the Catholic network was an even more visibly and institutionally unified movement that combined basic education with a particular Christian stance.

As they were both maturing, the two educational approaches had frequently clashed, especially at state level. In 1869, for example, a Cincinnati school board proposal to bring the systems together at public expense prompted feuding between Catholics and Protestants. The Catholic archbishop John P. Purcell was not willing to go quite as far as the measure suggested; but in the furore over the episode the religious pluralism of the city was emphasized, and the board decided to exclude the Bible from the city's public schools. A superior court injunction thwarted the board, but in 1873, after the controversy had calmed down somewhat, Ohio's Supreme Court unanimously reversed the superior court's decision. Thus, the "Cincinnati Bible War" resulted in a stalemate, later apparent in other places, that has characterized the struggle between two major educational approaches ever since. A Catholic bid for public support of parish schools had been rejected, but Protestants had lost Bible reading in the public schools in a major city—a precedent that figured in subsequent disputes.[21]

At the national level, another example of stalemate soon emerged. In 1876 James G. Blaine introduced into the House of Representatives a resolution proposing an amendment mandating that no money raised by any state by taxation or derived from any public funds or lands for the support of public schools "shall ever be under the control of any religious

---

[20] James Hennesey, *American Catholics: A History of the Roman Catholic Community in the United States* (New York: Oxford University Press, 1981), 187.

[21] There is a brief account of the "Cincinnati Bible War" in Jorgenson, *The State and the Non-Public School*, 119–20; for a more detailed treatment, see Robert Michaelsen, *Piety in the Public School: Trends and Issues in the Relationship between Religion and the Public School in the United States* (New York: Macmillan, 1970), 89–98.

sect" or "be divided between religious sects or denominations." The House passed the amendment, but it was hotly debated in the Senate, where some felt that existing constitutional guarantees were adequate, others preferred that such issues be left to the states, and many voiced strong Catholic opposition. Various attempts to revise the measure failed, and it was narrowly defeated. The controversy, quiet after that, was revived again in the 1880s when serious efforts were made in Congress to secure direct appropriations of money from the national treasury to the states to aid the development of the public schools. Especially conspicuous in this effort was a senator from New Hampshire, Henry W. Blair, who tried no less than five times in the decade to get such a measure passed in one form or another, without success. It became clear that such aid would not be forthcoming unless private schools could be included. The enveloping stalemate was thus further fixed into America's educational history.[22]

As the school controversy flared up again in the 1880s, past debates were recalled, old charges were renewed, often with great intensity, and the anti-Catholic spirit was once again embodied in various writings and actions. For example, Daniel Dorchester, a Methodist pastor who had served several terms in political office, published in 1888 a massive history of *Christianity in the United States* and devoted five chapters to Catholicism. Drawing extensively on Catholic sources, he dealt with the past in a fairer way than most non-Catholics by paying tribute to Catholic participation in the American Revolution, commending the zealous and self-sacrificing spirit of missionaries on the frontier, and providing informative passages on the lives of prominent church leaders. When he approached his own time, however, the tone sharply changed as he expressed alarm at the way "European Romanism" seemed well on its way to becoming a state religion, especially in New York. He reflected a fear of immigrants, three-fifths of whom he believed were of Catholic stock, by exclaiming: "How grievously have morals been debauched, pauperism, insanity, and crime augmented, and moral progress retarded by these exotic masses!"[23]

In that same year Dorchester focused more directly on educational issues in *Romanism* versus *the Public School System*, where he rehearsed past fights and quoted contemporary newspaper reports indicating that

---

[22] Stokes, *Church and State in the United States*, 2: 722–28; Jorgenson, *The State and the Non-Public School*, 141–44. A detailed treatment in a broad context is by Gordon C. Lee, *The Struggle for Federal Aid: First Phase: A History of the Attempts to Obtain Federal Aid for the Common Schools, 1870–1890* (New York: Bureau of Publications, Teachers College, Columbia University, 1949), 88–168.

[23] *Christianity in the United States: From the First Settlement down to the Present Time* (New York: Phillips and Hunt, 1888), 764.

in some places parents were excommunicated for not sending children to parish schools. Dorchester repeated the familiar plea that the Christianity of Christ and not of the sects be taught in public education and expressed his view that the best way would be to forbid private schools of any kind, Catholic, Jewish, or Protestant, until children had reached their fourteenth year—a law that he claimed would be entirely "unsectarian"![24]

His strictures were mild compared to those of another entry into the field, Justin D. Fulton, who had been ordained a Baptist but later built and served a large People's Church in Brooklyn. He resigned in 1887 to head the Pauline Propaganda, a society of dues-paying members that published his books. These bore such titles as *Washington in the Lap of Rome* and *Woman in the Toils of Rome*. In 1889 Fulton wrote *The Fight with Rome*, setting the tone for his polemic in his opening pages with these words:

> Rome tramples on decency and virtue. Her priests can drink to drunkenness, in conversation they can be foul-mouthed, in private they can be abusers of themselves, they can outrage virtue and bring scandal on homes, separate husbands from wives, and use language with young and inexperienced girls which would not be tolerated in the professedly good and which could only characterize the infamously abandoned and the utterly vile; and yet society tolerates all this, and when the priests are berated and denounced for it they simply laugh at the indignation of the community, and push on as if they were masters of the situation. They pass from the brothel to the altar and celebrate the mass, and from a state of utter inebrity to perform the most solemn sacraments; and all this is borne with because they are Romanists. . . .
>
> Seven millions of people are compelled to vote as the cardinal, archbishops, bishops and priests may command. Parents are compelled to take their children out of the public schools or have the sacraments withheld.[25]

He criticized the Evangelical Alliance because it treated "the Roman Catholic Church as one of the religious denominations and as a part of the Christian world" at a time when he believed no neutral ground was possible, for Romanism was a "terrible and implacable foe" of Christianity (352).

Not only did a torrent of words erupt in many other such books, but various organizations devoted to anti-Catholicism also emerged. Some were local, but others were national in scope; most were short-lived. A number of them, such as the Pauline Propaganda, appear to have gathered around an articulate leader. The central figure in the National

---

[24] *Romanism versus the Public School System* (New York: Phillips and Hunt, 1888), see esp. 97, 114–15, 163, 178.

[25] *The Fight with Rome* (1889; reprint, New York: Arno Press, 1977), 1–2.

League for the Protection of American Institutions (NLPAI), organized in 1889, was its general secretary, a Methodist minister named James M. King, who persuaded a number of well-known persons to let their names appear in connection with its activities; historian John Jay, for example, was its first president. Despite its name, this largely paper organization, centered in New York, was especially concerned with protecting the common school system. By far the most conspicuous organization to appear was the American Protective Association (APA), a much broader based society and one prone to exploit the more disreputable aspects of anti-Catholicism—Justin Fulton, for example, was one who appeared on its platforms. Founded in Clinton, Iowa, in 1887, the APA was centered in the Midwest, although it did become a national organization that remained active in the 1890s.

The principal founder and leader of the APA was a self-educated lawyer, Henry F. Bowers, who was deeply interested in politics as a committed Republican active in various county and state party offices. He remains a somewhat enigmatic figure; as Donald L. Kinzer delicately put it, "the evidence of his speeches and the very few examples of his writings that exist suggest that he did not submit to the discipline of facts" but approached truth by accepting or rejecting evidence according to his own intuitive conception.[26] Bowers justified founding the association by affirming that the condition of affairs in the country "was such that the institutions of our Government were controlled and the patronage was doled out by an ecclesiastical element under the direction and heavy hand of a foreign ecclesiastical potentate" (37). For him, "political Romanism" stood in the way of true Americanism, but he apparently retained personal friendships with Catholics and helped families of that persuasion without fee in hard times. When a revised list of principles was adopted by the APA, at its peak of influence in 1894, it emphasized its commitment to "non-sectarian free public schools, the bulwark of American institutions, the best place for the education of American children" (45).

The strong anti-Catholicism of the movement showed up especially in its lodgelike secret ritual, during which an initiate took oaths to denounce the pope, his priests and emissaries, and "the diabolical work of the Roman Catholic church" (49). Largely through the work of its local councils, which were formed in most states, the APA influenced elections in 1892 and 1894, in part through the circulation of forged documents purporting to be Catholic, and it became briefly the dominating influence in the anti-Catholic movement. By the middle of the decade, however, as inner tensions combined with attacks by both Roman Catholics and Protestants (conspicuously by social gospel leader Washington Gladden) and

[26] *An Episode in Anti-Catholicism*, 38.

by independent journalists, the movement had fallen into decline. But during its days of influence, it played a major role in highlighting the Catholic-Protestant stalemate on schools in the public mind.

The various organizations of which the APA became for a time the most conspicuous were often labeled the "patriotic" societies, for their members insisted that they were true Americans in a way Catholics could not be. This affront to the Catholics, who understood themselves to be loyal and patriotic Americans, was deeply resented. Although they criticized the public schools, often sharply, as they expanded their own system of education, they disagreed that they were thereby attacking God, the Bible (though they did prefer their own Douai translation), or their nation or supporting schools in any way un-American. In the pastoral letter of 1884 that reported the results of the Third Plenary Council to their congregations, the bishops declared:

> We repudiate with equal earnestness the assertion that we need to lay aside any of our devotedness to our Church to be true Americans, and the insinuation that we need to abate any of our love for our country's principles and institutions, to be faithful Catholics. . . .
>
> No less illogical would be the notion, that there is aught in the free spirit of our American institutions, incompatible with perfect docility to the Church of Christ.[27]

Charges of un-Americanism kept coming, however, both in the blatant language of the anti-Catholic groups and in the milder verbiage of various denominational presses. Without the violence that had erupted in the 1830s and 1840s or the excesses of the "Know-Nothing" period at mid-century, this upsurge of anti-Catholicism was bitter enough and reinforced the negative attitudes of many toward the other in both traditions of Christianity. The hostility between the two was mutual, but in his researches Jay Dolan has not been able to trace among Catholics extreme anti-Protestant behavior that ran into violence: "The reason why Catholics did not engage in violent anti-Protestant behavior was that they were outnumbered. They were a minority group and perceived themselves as such; thus they avoided any extreme public actions that would weaken their already tenuous position in the United States. Catholics wanted desperately to be accepted as 100 percent American, and overt anti-Protestant behavior clearly was not conducive to such acceptance."[28] The per-

---

[27] As quoted in Hugh J. Nolan, ed., *Pastoral Letters of the United States Catholic Bishops* (Washington, D.C.: National Conference of Catholic Bishops, United States Catholic Conference, 1983–1984), 1: 215–16.

[28] "Catholic Attitudes toward Protestants," in *Uncivil Religion: Interreligious Hostility in America*, ed. Robert N. Bellah and Frederick E. Greenspahn (New York: Crossroads,

sisting hostility between the two positions often became especially evident in the stalemate over schooling.

One particular, and unusual, aspect of the clash in educational approach that also heightened the Catholic-Protestant tension was related to the nation's long, terrible, and tragic struggle with the Indians, the real native Americans. Through the 1880s, that story was just becoming better known through the publication of such works as Helen Hunt Jackson's *A Century of Dishonor: A Sketch of the United States Government's Dealings with Some of the Indian Tribes* (1881). One chapter in the painful history that was intended to be better than those marked by the savagery of the past was initiated by President Grant in what became known as the "peace policy" (1869–1882). This arrangement gave power to churches that cooperated with the government actually to control its Indian agents. It greatly expanded and intensified the program of federal aid to Indian missions and education, which had been going on for many decades. It exacerbated religious tensions, for of the seventy-three agencies allotted to the denominations only seven went to the Catholics, even though they were by far the largest single church with long and distinguished record in Indian missions. Some Catholics accused the program of harking back to the colonial past with its Protestant establishments of religion.

In a well-documented study, Robert H. Keller, Jr., quoted a contemporary Catholic complaint that the program was a reversion to "the old Colonial *State Church* . . . a feeler and experiment in *State*-Churchism."[29] Keller declared that the peace policy "provided federal support for sectarian missions and worship, violated the constitutional ban against religious tests for public office and, perhaps most serious of its legal transgressions, denied religious liberty as guaranteed by the First Amendment" (176). That the Indians had any rights to their own religious traditions was rarely considered by missionaries, so sure were they of the vast superiority of their faith against the paganism of the "savages." In the final section of his study, Keller concluded: "As for the relationship between Church and State, the Peace Policy can be viewed equally as the culmination of the idea of a Christian Commonwealth and as a flagrant violation of the First Amendment, but the second possibility simply did not occur to many people in the 1870s" (213). As the century wore on, however, many people became more sensitive about violations of the Constitution—not so much out of their concern for the Indians, to whom most white Americans seemed to think the First Amendment did not apply, but

---

1987), 73. In the same work, see also an important chapter by Barbara Welter, "From Maria Monk to Paul Blanshard: A Century of Protestant Anti-Catholicism," 43–71.

[29] *American Protestantism and United States Indian Policy, 1869–1882* (Lincoln: University of Nebraska Press, 1983), 171.

often because of their mounting anxieties that one denomination might gain an advantage over others.

Although Grant's peace policy was terminated in 1882, the support from public funds for what were called "contract schools" operated by denominations for Indians was not only continued but also increased. One somewhat ironic but significant outcome of the policy was that Catholics, believing Protestants were more highly organized for Indian missions than they were, created a Bureau of Catholic Indian Missions (founded 1874) that was far more effective than any Protestant agency. By the end of the 1880s, Catholics were in control of almost two-thirds of the funds for contract schools. A struggle over those Indian schools intensified the continued conflict over parochial and public education. A focus of controversy was the appointment in 1889 by the Harrison administration of Thomas J. Morgan as commissioner of Indian affairs. An ordained Baptist minister, Morgan was principal of Rhode Island's state normal school, a prominent vice-president of the National Education Association (NEA), and a strong enthusiast for the public schools and compulsory education in the English language for all children. Some of his remarks at NEA meetings had given some clues to his anti-Catholic stance, but he tried to keep that under tight rein as commissioner. His appointment of Daniel Dorchester as commissioner of Indian education brought increased criticism, for his new associate's anti-Catholic views had been clearly and publicly stated, especially in his book *Romanism* versus *the Public School System*.

The brunt of Catholic criticism of the way the Indian bureau was being run in the early 1890s thus continued to be borne by Morgan as its head. He and others wanted the contract school system ended because it was weakening the stance taken by so many Protestants that no sectarian schools should receive public funds. In 1892 Methodists, Congregationalists, Presbyterians, and Episcopalians, "preferring to lose their own meager benefits than to see the Catholics profit,"[30] withdrew from Indian school contracts. The Catholic case for continuing them at the time was carried by the able, outspoken director of the Bureau of Catholic Indian Missions, Joseph A. Stephan. A priest who had opposed in vain the appointments of Morgan and Davenport, Stephan continued to charge them with bigotry during their terms. Consequently Morgan cut all links between the two bureaus, though the contracts with Catholic Indian schools, which he bitterly opposed in principle, were continued. The forceful attacks on Morgan by Stephan and others were at least one factor in the defeat of Harrison's Republican party at the polls in 1892 when Cleveland won his second term. From a new post in his own denomina-

---

[30] Prucha, *American Indian Policy in Crisis*, 318.

tion, Morgan's deep anti-Catholic feelings were given full expression as he appeared on APA platforms, where he was celebrated as something of a martyr.

The clash over the contract schools finally closed them down and hardened the lines of the growing stalemate over education. Funds for the contract schools were soon reduced and disappeared altogether by 1900 as, in Prucha's words, "the close ties between the churches and government in Indian matters were finally cut by the sharp knife of intolerance."[31] An observation by Keller highlights the impact of all these events on church-state relations: "not until American Catholicism began to grow in size did 'strict separation' become a Protestant constitutional doctrine."[32] It was a response to the mounting challenge to Protestant power. Attitudes of many Catholic and Protestants, hardened in this period of intense school controversy, persisted well into the next century. The conceptual wall of separation between church and state had been raised higher in many minds. Various efforts toward effecting some kind of compromise between public and parochial education did not last as tension heightened. One of the most successful and long-lasting of these experiments had gone on for some years in Poughkeepsie, New York, since 1873: parochial school buildings had been rented to public school boards for a nominal fee during school hours, and teachers nominated by the local priest were approved and paid by the boards to teach the public school curriculum. Religious instruction and observances were permitted only before and after regular school hours. Similar programs were undertaken in other communities—thirty-two were listed in one effort to count them.[33]

The colorful archbishop of St. Paul, John Ireland, dramatically proclaimed himself friend of the public school and regretted only its neglect of religion. He backed compromise plans for Faribault and Stillwater, Minnesota, but in the climate of the early 1890s they lasted only a year or two. By 1898 even the Poughkeepsie plan had been ruled out by the state; in Dolan's apt summary, "the wall separating church and state was now high enough that such a compromise was no longer a viable solution to the Catholic-school issue."[34] But the issue had grown beyond the historic conflict between Catholics and Protestants; some governmental agencies at various levels now tended to act as "disinterested" third parties to keep sectarianism in any form out of the public schools. One outcome of this trend toward the secularization of the schools had long been

[31] Ibid., 56.

[32] *American Protestantism and United States Indian Policy*, 214.

[33] E.g., see Robert D. Cross, *The Emergence of Liberal Catholicism* (Cambridge: Harvard University Press, 1958), 139.

[34] *American Catholic Experience*, 275.

a cause for Catholic criticism, but the process accelerated in the twentieth century, especially after World War II. It moved more quickly in some sections of the country than in others; in general, criticism grew faster in the northeastern than in the southern states. The intense educational stalemate in the 1890s was a contributing factor toward minimizing religion in public school curriculums.

3

Signs of Change: Religion and Public Affairs in the 1890s

IN THE 1890s church-state patterns that had been hammered out in the course of the nineteenth century seemed to change little. The Supreme Court had made its strict judgments in the Mormon cases of 1890 and then two years later had unanimously agreed that the United States was indeed a Christian nation. Although debates about the meaning of "a wall of separation between church and state" did not cease, that metaphorical barrier continued to define the situation, a fence raised a little higher primarily as a consequence of resurgent anti-Catholicism. Yet the decade itself was troubled and exciting: massive immigration continued, cities burgeoned, corporations grew, financial panic and economic depression hit, and a short war awoke imperialistic dreams. A closer look from a vantage point of nearly a hundred years later discloses that the church-state situation was not static. Just as the observer near the surface of a body of water cannot see into the depths as a person at a higher elevation can, so the interpreter who looks back from a distance can discern things going on beneath the surface that in time contributed to significant changes in the perception and conduct of relationships between religious institutions and governmental agencies. Seeds of developments that later surprised, baffled, and often annoyed various groups of people sprouted; some were choked off, and others flourished. In matters broadly relating to the public aspects of religious life, some emerging patterns disclosed their deeper significance only later in twentieth-century life.

Religion and Changing Political Realities

Important clues as to relationships between religion and politics can be traced in the way members of religious bodies vote. To assess what influence American religious movements may have on politics when ballots are cast is not easy, though sophisticated techniques that have been developed yield informative results. But difficulties remain, whether one approaches the question from either religion or politics. Denominations have long been reluctant to be too specific about political parties and their candidates: not only has the tradition of the separation of church and

state usually meant that churches should not get involved in partisan politics, but also churches have expressed a primary desire to reach out to all
persons with their religious messages. Even when hopes and efforts to
make the nation more fully Christian were running high, the prevailing
idea was that individuals acting out their faith in social and political
spheres would do it. Yet at given times and places certain political parties
demonstrably attracted more followers from some religious traditions
than from others. "Considerable evidence shows that there is high unanimity within religious groups on political matters," sociologist John L.
Hammond has written, "frequently far more than can be explained by
the similarity in social status of the members."[1]

When one turns to the parties, however, to assess with some precision
the impact of religion, problems arise. "No political party has ever wholly
conformed to retrospective descriptions of it," said Paul Kleppner, author
of many books about voting behavior. "Party activities and behaviors
have always been sufficiently varied to elude simple descriptive generalizations."[2] He has emphasized that analyses of voting must deal with the
spectrum of ethnocentric values relating to family, religion, education,
and community; this helps explain why it is difficult to be precise about
any one factor, such as religion, in the mix.

Nevertheless, more precise generalizations about religion and political
behavior can be made for some periods than for others. The years preceding the 1890s were such a time; the relation of religious allegiance to
voting was then in the main still quite predictable. In his probing book
The Winning of the Midwest, Richard J. Jensen went so far as to declare
that "religion shaped the issues and the rhetoric of politics, and played
the critical role in determining the party alignments of the voters." Focus-
ing on the midwestern states and using rather broad categories, he identified two polar theological positions, the pietistic and the liturgical,
which "expressed themselves through the Republican and Democratic
parties, respectively."[3] He found that religion was then politically more
important than culture, for partisanship followed religious lines more
closely than cultural divisions. The significance of this is made clearer
when one realizes that estimates show more than 70 percent of the midwestern population was church-affiliated (a much wider category than
church membership) by 1890. Jensen's research showed that the two
broad theological positions were in conflict in every denomination. This

---

[1] *The Politics of Benevolence: Revival Religion and American Voting Behavior* (Norwood, N.J.: Ablex Publishing Corp., 1979), 21–22.

[2] *Who Voted? The Dynamics of Electoral Turnout, 1870–1980* (New York: Praeger,
1982), 76.

[3] *The Winning of the Midwest: Social and Political Conflict, 1888–1896* (Chicago: University of Chicago Press, 1971), 58; see esp. chaps. 6 and 7.

meant that politics led to some unlikely combinations. For example, the liturgically minded German Lutherans largely identified themselves with the Democrats, thereby associating with their traditional religious opponents, the Catholics; however, the pietistically inclined followers of Luther more often gravitated to the Republicans. Such political tensions within denominations suggest further clues about why churches usually avoided taking partisan political stands: they sought to preserve their own unity and improve effectiveness in pursuing their primary religious goals.

Although there were various exceptions, the evidence points to a fairly clear religio-political picture as the last decade of the century opened, and not only in the Midwest. In his more recent study of the national scene, in which he focused on the more populous areas and used categories somewhat different from Jensen's, Paul Kleppner came to quite similar conclusions for the late nineteenth century. He found that "as party behaviors began to evoke common meanings for activists, officeholders, and voters, *Democrat* came to represent the outlooks of antipietists, and *Republican* came to resonate emotionally with the dispositions of evangelical pietists." He cited revealing comments by people of that period: " 'Catholics . . . think one is not a Catholic if he is a Republican'; or alternatively, when they pointed to the inconsistency involved in going 'to the Lord's table on Sunday and vot[ing] for Cleveland on Tuesday.' "[4] The latter remark highlights the tension within Protestant ranks between those who found it incongruous to attend communion and then vote for the Democratic candidate, even though he was also a Protestant.

The 1890s, however, saw some significant alterations in that general pattern of political alignments. Certain decisive shifts in voting among groups that appear to have been largely motivated by religious issues occurred at the state level early in the decade. Several well-known episodes were related to the conflicts between public and parochial school systems. Wisconsin, for example, at that point had received more German immigrants than any state; they formed a sizable minority of the state's total population, considerably larger than the Scandinavian group. Over the issue of slavery, both groups had become "an important and dependable bloc in the new Republican party."[5] In 1889, early in the administration of newly elected Republican governor William B. Hoard, the Bennett bill (so named after the committee chairman who had introduced it) was passed unanimously by the assembly. The bill provided for the compulsory education of children between the ages of seven and fourteen and

[4] *Who Voted?* 45–46.

[5] Jorgenson, *The State and the Non-Public School*, 189. See also Thomas C. Hunt, "The Bennett Law of 1890: Focus of Conflict Beween Church and State in Education," *Journal of Church and State* 23 (1981): 69–93.

required that basic education in every school, public or private, be in the English language.

The Lutherans, many of them of German background, reacted strongly against it. The official Catholic response, which appeared in March 1890, stated that the measure was an effort to bring all schools under state control and "gradually to destroy the parochial school system altogether" (194). Hoard defended the Bennett law, but the municipal elections that followed were disastrous for Republicans. A major controversy erupted as the press focused on the issue. Most denominations, other than Lutheran and Catholic, tended to favor the measure. Hoard staked his continuance in office on it in the fall elections, and as the furore increased, "proponents of the law were drawn increasingly into an anti-ecclesiastical posture" (200). On November 4, 1890, the Republicans lost the governorship and both houses of the legislature, an event signaled by papers across the land as a major political upset. Of all the issues in the campaign, the role of religion appeared to many as decisive. This expensive lesson for the Republicans showed that what had long appeared as a settled alliance could quickly change.

A similar measure was passed in Illinois, also then a predominantly Republican state. Known as the Edwards law, after its chief proponent, the superintendent of public instruction, it was passed in 1889. Again the Lutherans, who had nearly three hundred schools in the state, were the first to mount a strong protest; Catholics also sought to modify it. The election of 1890 was less decisive than in Wisconsin, but the Democrats did take over the lower house and unseat Edwards. The decisive change, however, came two years later: The archbishop and bishops of the Catholic province of Illinois then came down firmly against the measure, and the Republicans lost the governorship and both houses of the legislature; the Edwards law was soon repealed. The controversy over the schools then subsided, with the stalemate tacitly accepted on both sides.[6]

At the national level in 1892 the Democrats also did well; they won back the presidency and a majority of both houses of Congress. The main issue was the tariff, with the victors promising to reduce it whereas their opponents had upheld protection. But Grover Cleveland had the unhappy experience of beginning his second term as president (after an interval of four years since his first term) just as a financial panic, followed by mounting unemployment and hard times, hit the nation. Hence the economic factor was primary in the major political realignment that took place in 1896, when William McKinley defeated Williams Jennings Bryan for the presidency. A change in the mutual relationship of political parties and religious denominations can be discerned in that realignment, a

[6] Jorgenson, *The State and the Non-Public School*, 201–4.

change that contributed to not only the Republican victory of 1896 but also to the continuing strength of that party for the first three decades of the twentieth century (except for the period when it split in 1912 and allowed the Democrats to place Woodrow Wilson in the White House for two terms). Several aspects of the changes that took place in the 1890s are relevant to a full understanding of twentieth-century religio-political patterns. First, significant shifting produced new political affinities for a number of Catholics. Second, and not unrelated, politics was becoming increasingly a pragmatic realm as party programs and actions became less directly related to religious affiliation than it had been, without necessarily reducing the larger significance of religion for politics when sensitive issues surfaced.

The Catholic church in the United States has never been as monolithic or unified as it has often appeared to those who felt threatened by it. By the 1890s segments of its rapidly growing numbers were attracted to the Republicans, who at that time were promoting greater national centralization. It was estimated, for example, that by 1894 there were seventy thousand Republican Catholics in New York State. A national figure, the eloquent archbishop John Ireland, was an ardent member of that party who developed considerable influence in its affairs. He deplored the identification of Catholics with the Democrats and played down the anti-Catholic elements in his chosen party.[7]

Republicans had been more favorable to the rising cause of temperance than its major opponent, but that suited Ireland, who was a central figure in the Catholic Total Abstinence Union, which had a half-million members at its peak. Ireland even helped in founding the Anti-Saloon League.[8] His party meanwhile had been broadening its scope by resisting the more extreme, ultraist interpretation of temperance as advanced by outspoken prohibitionists in favor of more moderate, gradualist stands. Illustrating this important shift with reference to developments in Iowa, Jensen pointed to the way that the Republicans there had to draw the line between "responsible temperance and control of the saloon on the one hand, and irresponsible, millenarian prohibition, with its secret dives and bootleggers on the other."[9] After the move to the softer position, the party regained control of the state in 1893, thereby laying the groundwork for McKinley's critical plurality in 1896.

Similar trends were occurring elsewhere, especially in the Midwest and the Northeast. The middle road was proving politically viable. The Republican move toward a measure of moderation came in part because

[7] Samuel T. McSeveney, *The Politics of Depression: Political Behavior in the Northeast, 1893–1896* (New York: Oxford University Press, 1972), 76, 105–6.

[8] Cross, *Emergence of Liberal Catholicism*, 110, 128–29.

[9] *Winning of the Midwest*, 202, see also 195–208.

pragmatic professional politicians were taking a larger role in party affairs. In these same years, the Anti-Saloon League, founded in Ohio in 1893 and organized as a national movement two years later, was laying the groundwork for its later successes. The league eventually attained its goal of prohibition in part because it also relied on the professional experts. Realizing the churches would not be a political annex of any party, the league adopted a nonpartisan, single-issue approach as it sought to serve as the political arm of the church on the temperance question.[10] Although religious issues would continue to surface decisively under certain circumstances (as in the 1928 election), and although older religio-political alliances would long persist, a trend toward more pragmatic, professionally guided politics was discernible. By the middle 1890s, Republicans were finding that they could repudiate connections with anti-Catholic organizations such as the APA without significantly losing the support of traditionally anti-Catholic Protestants, yet at the same time they gained the support of some Catholics. A sign of the new stance was that they chose a rabbi to open their national convention in 1896, not to attract Jewish voters, who had not yet become a significant political force, but to avoid offending either their traditional Protestant following or their growing Catholic constituency.[11]

Influential studies of the returns of the 1896 election have interpreted the results as showing that the Republicans under McKinley won decisively in what came to be called the urban-industrial heartland of the Northeast and Midwest; there they gained support among Catholics and confessional German Lutherans, groups that with few exceptions had been traditionally oriented to the other major party. The Democrats under Bryan not only largely retained their following in the South and West, but they also gathered votes from some former Populist and Prohibition party supporters and citizens concerned about the moral integration of society. But many old-line party regulars, who did not want strong central government, rejected Bryan. In Kleppner's words, "Bryan's advocacy of an active and interventionist government, a posture articulated in evangelically toned rhetoric, repelled many of the party's normal ethnic and religious support groups." Thus, Bryan was supported by many urban native-stock Protestant voters, but there was little enthusiasm for him among many Catholics and German Lutherans. "As a consequence," Kleppner concluded, "at its social base, Bryan's Democratic party was more agrarian and evangelical than that party had been at any earlier

[10] Ibid.; on the Anti-Saloon League, see K. Austin Kerr, *Organized for Prohibition: A New History of the Anti-Saloon League* (New Haven: Yale University Press, 1985), esp. 106–26.

[11] McSeveney, *Politics of Depression*, 37–38, 85.

point in the second half of the nineteenth century."[12] But it was not enough for the party to win in either 1896 or the next three presidential elections: direct affinities between religious and political affiliations were lessening.

For many, support of one party or the other long continued to follow traditional patterns as shaped by their religious orientations; their ties, however, were no longer as fixed as they had been, and such other factors as economic or class considerations could lead to dramatic shifts. The affinities between certain religious groups and political parties, still very strong in certain sections, had on the whole become discernibly weaker. It was one sign of trends toward secularization in the culture and its politics, trends that later influenced the way many Americans thought about the appropriate relation between religious institutions and the arms of government.

Another important change in the political alignments of religious groups in the 1890s occurred among Latter-day Saints. To get coveted statehood for Utah, under which they could have more influence in their region than territorial status permitted, they "adopted a 'line' consistent with the dominant policies of the nation," yet also "sought to preserve as many of their traditional goals as national sentiment would permit."[13] Accordingly the church gave up its previous promotion of cooperative economic enterprises, sold most of its business properties, and—of especial importance for this chapter—disbanded its Utah political party. Until 1891, Utah politics had been dominated by two major territorial parties, the Mormon-controlled People's party and the Liberal party; the latter was largely an anti-LDS coalition that had ties with both major parties nationally. In June of that year church leaders dissolved the People's party and urged Mormons to affiliate with one or the other of the major national parties. Within several years the Liberals faded as a political force. The normal patterns of American politics were taking over. Because the Democratic party had traditionally shown a greater sympathy to the Mormons than the Republicans, the church encouraged some members to affiliate with the latter party in the interests of maintaining a two-party system. Although a Republican administration had decisively pressed measures against polygamy in 1890, many Mormons, somewhat surprisingly, were attracted to the party because of its connections with big business, its protectionism, and its increasing support for Utah's statehood— pragmatic political reasons. "Ironically," noted Lyman, "the party using the heaviest hand ended up benefiting the most politically from the transition so rapidly taking place in Utah."[14]

The political transition took time, however; Harrison lost to Cleveland in 1892, and only then, in his remaining days in the White House, did he grant a petition for amnesty for Mormons who had complied with the law on polygamy. The fluidity of changing electoral politics became evident, however, when the Republican party elected every state and national candidate in the 1895 territorial election. But the Democratic administration could claim credit for restoration of the church's property beginning in 1893 and for the passage by Congress of the Utah Enabling Act in July of the following year. It took a year and a half for statehood to be consummated, for the constitutional convention had to meet and elections for the first state officers be held. The constitution provided that polygamous or plural marriages were forever prohibited. Finally, on January 4, 1896, Cleveland signed the proclamation admitting Utah as the forty-fifth state. Understandably, Utah went heavily Democratic in the fall elections, supporting Bryan and electing a Democratic legislature. This would not have been possible without solid, significant support among LDS voters.[15] The Mormon influence in Utah life continued to be strong, even as that church accepted the dominant political styles and parties of American life. By the early twentieth century the Mormon church was flourishing again under the new conditions. But the trend toward pragmatic and professional approaches to politics in the 1890s in Utah as elsewhere marked a watershed between two centuries: religion became less and less *the* decisive issue in voting behavior. It emerged periodically to affect certain elections, but it lacked the consistency of earlier party alignments.

Another event of the 1890s with marked political consequences was the militant resurgence of the movement, especially in the southern states, to deprive blacks of the right to vote. The Democratic party was deeply involved because it sought to maintain its political hold on the South, but blacks were traditionally Republican. Many leaders of the "Jim Crow" laws that fixed the patterns of racial segregation were prominent in the life of the white churches, as H. Shelton Smith has carefully documented; their voices drowned out those of the few dissenters.[16] Drawing on the currents of Anglo-Saxonism and white supremacy that were popular at the time, the strategists who planned and carried out the disenfranchisement of blacks found little resistance in the South and less than expected

---

[14] *Political Deliverance*, 143; see also chap. 6, "The Emergence of National Parties in Utah."

[15] Ibid., chaps. 7–9; Arrington and Bitton, *Mormon Experience*, 243–49.

[16] *In His Image, But . . . : Racism in Southern Religion, 1780–1910* (Durham: Duke University Press, 1972), chap. 6, "The Triumph of Racial Orthodoxy."

from northern liberals. Many of the latter found it expedient to seek reconciliation with the South politically and went along with its view of race
in its less extreme forms. C. Vann Woodward has called attention to the
way those liberals, some of them former abolitionists, mouthed in the
1880s and 1890s "the shibboleths of white supremacy regarding the Negro's innate inferiority, shiftlessness, and hopeless unfitness for full participation in the white man's civilization. Such expressions doubtless did
much to add to the reconciliation of North and South, but they did so at
the expense of the Negro."[17]

With opposition muted, the way was clear for the drive to deprive
blacks of the franchise; here there was bipartisan support, even though
the great majority of blacks then favored the Republicans. In its constitutional revision of 1890 Mississippi showed the way by passing an
amendment that included a poll tax and barred those who could not read
any section of the state constitution or understand it when it was read to
them. This effectively squeezed out most blacks but less than one-tenth as
many whites. South Carolina followed a similar strategy five years later,
and Louisiana three years after that. Other southern states fell in line soon
after the new century dawned. The effect of all this was devastating; in
1896, for example, some 130,000 Negroes were registered in Louisiana;
two years later the figure was just over 5,000.[18] The Supreme Court offered no opposition. It had invalidated the Civil Rights Act of 1875 eight
years after it was passed, and in 1896 in *Plessy* v. *Ferguson* the Court
found that legislation was "powerless to eradicate racial instincts or abolish distinctions based upon physical differences," thereby sanctioning the
"separate but equal" myth.[19] In Paul Kleppner's apt summary, as more
and more blacks lost their voting rights, "the demobilization that occurred in the post-1900 South was the largest, most extensive, and most
enduring that this country has ever witnessed."[20] The way was then clear
for the passage of extensive and detailed segregationist legislation, even
to the point of a Jim Crow Bible for use in courts. The whole process was
marked by a shameful increase in the number of lynchings.

The Republicans lost many potential voters, for the overwhelming majority of blacks who had voted were of that party. But it was obviously
not a major concern for the Republicans in view of their victories in presidential elections from 1896 through 1908. They knew that about nine-

[17] *The Strange Career of Jim Crow*, rev. ed. (New York: Oxford University Press, 1957),
53.

[18] John Hope Franklin, *From Slavery to Freedom: A History of Negro Americans*, 3d ed.
(New York: Vintage Books, 1969), 338–43.

[19] *Plessy* v. *Ferguson*, 163 U.S. 537 (1896) at 551.

[20] *Continuity and Change in Electoral Politics, 1893–1928* (New York: Greenwood,
1987), 165; see also his *Who Voted?* 56, 65–66.

tenths of the blacks at the time were still in the largely Democratic South, a situation that persisted into the World War I years. Nor did many northern Protestants speak up for their fellow religionists. On the whole their treatment of the black churches was condescending and patronizing; their most substantial help was given to the education of blacks through a network of schools and colleges.

In their predicament, southern blacks greatly prized their religious freedom and the separation of church and state, for they had realized at the close of the Civil War that with few exceptions they were not wanted as equals in white circles; consequently they had poured into their own churches and greatly escalated in size the black Baptist and Methodist denominations especially. Here they controlled a network of institutions, the principal base of both their religious and their community life, their zone of freedom in a threatening environment. Much evidence shows that black Protestants took their Christian and democratic heritages very seriously. August Meier has concluded that "Negroes never abandoned their emphasis upon the Christian and humanitarian and democratic elements in the American tradition."[21] But the wall of segregation largely deprived them of not only political privileges but also wider religious fellowship, in which exchanges could be more open and sincere and understandings and resources genuinely shared. Behind that wall the churches remained major centers of black religious and communal life, and they played strategic roles in developing leadership patterns and preparing the way for the determined efforts of the later twentieth century to reverse what racism—with its patterns of disenfranchisement and enforced segregation—had done in both politics and religion. Continuing reactions to the injustices, dislocations, and costs of the Jim Crow period, borne so heavily by the blacks, were powerful factors in later civil rights struggles to bring about reforms in governmental and religious institutions.

New Currents in Christian Political Thought: Positive Views of the State

During and following the 1940s, many scholars have studied social Christianity, especially in its liberal, progressive forms, which came to be widely known in the twentieth century as the social gospel. Although the movement came to full flower early in the new century along with and in relation to the progressive period in political life, in the 1890s social Christianity had begun to play a significant role in the life of denomina-

[21] *Negro Thought in America, 1880–1915: Racial Ideologies in the Age of Booker T. Washington* (Ann Arbor: University of Michigan Press, 1963), 23.

tional families, particularly the Congregational, Episcopal, Baptist, Methodist, and Presbyterian (primarily in the northern branches of the latter three). For example, in an annual review of books, an editor of a prominent religious journal exclaimed that "the year 1894 has been most prolific in the production of books, good, bad, and indifferent, on the subjects most dear to the public heart,—socialism, social reform, sociology, political economy, and social aspects of Christianity."[22] With few exceptions, early social gospel leaders were attracted to the liberal currents of religious thought that sought to mediate between traditional patterns of faith and the evolutionary, scientific, and critical trends that were so strong in the intellectual life of the later nineteenth century.[23]

One target of the new social thinkers was the individualistic ethic that had come to dominate much American political and social thought, especially among Protestants. Individualism emphasized that one's situation in life was largely the result of that person's own ability and energy and minimized the right of government to interfere with the individual freedom of either the weak or the strong. The economic effects of such a philosophy of individualism were allowing a few to amass much wealth while great masses lived at or near the poverty level in the rapidly expanding, urbanizing, and industrializing nation. Reformers, including growing numbers who were active within the churches, were calling for a stronger, more centralized state to deal with mounting social problems. Protestant advocates of this emphasis often found support in the work of European Christian social thinkers, especially in the writings of such British authors as Christian socialists Frederick Denison Maurice and Charles Kingsley. Because Americans who espoused such views were challenging the long-accepted, well-entrenched theories of a minimalist state, they were usually highly controversial figures. Their emphasis on a more positive role for the state led naturally to questioning conventional understandings of the separation of church and state.

Often called "the father of the social gospel," the well-known Congregational pastor of Columbus, Washington Gladden, was a friend of religious freedom but thought that the separation of church and state had been pushed too far. At the center of his vision for both religious and political institutions was what he called one of "the ruling ideas of the present age"—the coming kingdom of God on earth, an idea being preached and taught forcefully by a growing number of religious and theological leaders. As one popularizer of this emphasis, he developed the theme in sermons, addresses, and books. Gladden characteristically af-

[22] *Bibliotheca Sacra* 52 (1895): 205.

[23] E.g., see William R. Hutchison, *The Modernist Impulse in American Protestantism* (Cambridge: Harvard University Press, 1976); Ferenc M. Szasz, *The Divided Mind of Protestant America, 1880–1930* (University: University of Alabama Press, 1982).

firmed that "the complete Christianization of all life is what we pray and work for, when we work and pray for the coming of the kingdom of heaven."[24] For him, that meant that every department of human life, including politics, was to be governed by Christian law and controlled by Christian influences. Although a romantic idealist and a confident optimist, he knew well that the realities of economic, social, and political life fell far below his vision, as his biographer, Jacob H. Dorn, has made clear.[25] Gladden called for basic changes in attitude and practice, in the lives of both church and society.

Many of his addresses and writings touched on his views on such matters; the patterns of his thought have been helpfully systematized and summarized by Richard D. Knudten. Recognizing the serious lack of ethics and morality in politics, Gladden traced it to the principle of the separation of church and state. He believed, in Knudten's paraphrase of his work, that the American nation had "traveled much further in separation than the nation's forefathers imagined or intended."[26] The rise of sectarianism and the acceptance of the artificial distinction between secular and sacred had played a role in the divorce between the two. He sought a "cooperative union" among the churches so that when "the Church of God is finally united, it will be possible, Gladden contended, to work closely with the State to reintegrate society" (103). In a prophetic way Gladden anticipated the growing importance of ecumenical agencies and their encouragement of governmental action for justice and human welfare in the first half of the twentieth century. The patterns of democracy, as he saw it, opened the way for believers to work together to reformulate the laws and Christianize the state. Some of his dreams were fulfilled in part, but he also envisioned a time when both church and state "will appear to be equally sacred, while equally secular," when "there will be no distinction between them because they will be united in the work of social construction and reconstruction" (147).

In many aspects of his work, Gladden showed that the social gospel, as proclaimed by himself and others, not only reflected an idealistic optimism but also enlivened the hope for a Christian America, which would be brought nearer by a greater measure of justice in the marketplace. He was clearly moving in a different direction from many Protestants, including some who were concerned with social problems and some who stressed separation to resist Catholicism. He forcefully protested against the anti-Catholicism of the APA, for example, and his efforts were later

[24] *The Church and the Kingdom* (New York: Fleming H. Revell, 1894), 8.

[25] *Washington Gladden: Prophet of the Social Gospel* (Columbus: Ohio State University Press, 1967), see esp. 189–97, 230–31.

[26] *The Systematic Thought of Washington Gladden* (New York: Humanities Press, 1968), 146.

recognized by the bestowal of an honorary degree from the University of Notre Dame. Remembered as a resolute defender of evangelical liberalism and a prophet of the social gospel, in the 1890s Gladden challenged the individualism that saw little if any place for governmental action in welfare and reform and advanced a position that was gaining a considerable following even as it remained controversial.

While the influence of Gladden's long career can be traced in several aspects of twentieth-century religious history, it is harder to assess any lasting effect of the meteoric impact of George D. Herron in the 1890s. Widely heard in church and reform circles for a few years, his steady movement toward the theological and social left led to the churches' rejection of his radical views. His dismissal from the Congregational ministry in 1901, however, was formally based on the fact that he was divorced by his wife and speedily remarried. But in his few years of broad influence as a teacher at Iowa College (later Grinnell), he drew headlines and editorials as a magnetic speaker who made vigorous but controversial pleas for a very positive if rather vaguely stated role for the state in human affairs. In a series of lectures, delivered in various cities and later published, Herron denounced existing political and religious institutions and declared the state to be "the only organ through which the people can act together in the organization and perfection of their common life in justice. . . . Only through industrial democracy can the state obtain and insure political freedom, and Christianity cannot accomplish its world mission, save it effect the political organization of human life."[27] At that point he seemingly lacked specific plans for this accomplishment; he merely offered rhetorical proclamation of his vision. He was baffled by the criticism of Gladden and others who found his message impractical, naive, and much too antagonistic to institutions.[28] At the height of his fame, however, before he embraced political socialism, he was widely heard and quoted, in part because he provided an alternative to conventional views about the role of the state.

The impact made by a lay Episcopal economist, Richard T. Ely, was far different and much longer lasting. His active leadership in the emerging social gospel movement was also limited to the last few years of the nineteenth century, but his social Christian writings continued to be widely read and notably influential long after he had turned his attention to other things. He never repudiated what he had said in those works; indeed, in his autobiography, written late in his long life, he remembered them fondly. After earning his doctorate in Germany, where he was steeped in

[27] *The Christian State: A Political Vision of Christ* (New York: Thomas Y. Crowell, 1895), 53–54, 108.

[28] Gladden, "Shall We Abolish Institutions?" *The Congregationalist* 79 (January-June 1894): 791.

the historical school so critical of classical laissez-faire economics, Ely taught at Johns Hopkins University and the University of Wisconsin. In an early book, which indicated the impact of his German education, he reported that "it may rationally be maintained that, if there is anything divine on this earth, it is the state, the product of the same God-given instincts which led to the establishment of the church and the family."[29] From this perspective he understood state and church to be natural allies.

In 1889 he took his place as a central figure in the nascent social gospel movement in an oft-quoted work, *The Social Aspects of Christianity*. The following year he delivered the Carew lectures on "The Church and the World, the Church and the State" at Hartford Theological Seminary; later he repeated them at the famous conference grounds at Lake Chautauqua and thus reached strategic audiences. Like some other conspicuous social Christian leaders, he looked to the parallel social Christian movement in England for inspiration and information and offered a rather positive assessment of the role of the state church there. In comparison, Ely referred to some problems of American disestablishment, which "has led to the separation of our life into two parts, the one sacred and the other secular and to many these are mutually exclusive in the sense that where one begins the other stops."[30] He admitted that the churches formerly established in America had been too narrow in form and wanting in the true idea of a state church. He mingled elements from both classical and voluntary Christendom in describing that idea:

> A state church in modern times cannot be a mere sect. It cannot be an organization for the propagation of any narrow and exclusive creed. It must within itself contain room for a great multiplicity of dogmas and its emphasis as a church must be laid on righteous life. It must not through the coercive power of the state nor yet through its own churchly punishments like excommunication attempt to fasten the minds of men to certain speculative views in regard to the nature, purposes and methods of the Almighty. It must recognize the inner spiritual life as the domain of sovereign individuality and adopt in its attempt to influence rightly this inner individual life the methods of persuasion and not coercion. . . . A state church must be regarded as occupying essentially the large and generous ground of the public schools. . . . It must represent one side of the life of the people and must supplement the activities of the state. It

[29] *The Labor Movement in America* (New York: Thomas Y. Crowell, 1886), 325–26.

[30] "The Church and the World, the Church and the State" (typescript, Ely papers, State Historical Society of Wisconsin, Madison, 1890), 137. A copy of the typescript has been made available to me through the courtesy of Eugene Y. Lowe, Jr., author of an informative study, "Richard T. Ely, Herald of a Positive State" (Ph.D. diss., Union Theological Seminary, New York, 1987); see also Lowe's summary article, "Richard T. Ely: Herald of a Positive State," *Union Seminary Quarterly Review* 42 (June 1988): 21–29.

must serve the state, regarding the establishment of just and loving relations among men as its peculiar mission and as a holy work [137–39].

Because of the multitude of denominations in the United States Ely recognized that "it is manifestly impossible to reestablish a state church among us," but he suggested that the solution lay "in the conception of the state as the true church of the future" (159).

The impact of the unpublished Carew lectures was limited, but their basic thesis was repeated in some of Ely's other writings, particularly in "The State" chapter in *The Social Law of Service*. Observing that family, church, and state are frequently listed together as the three preeminently divine institutions, he declared "that God works through the State in carrying out His purposes more universally than through any other institution; that it takes the first place among the instrumentalities."[31] Soon after the publication of this book he withdrew from direct participation in the social gospel movement, just as it was becoming increasingly influential, to turn his full professional attention to public matters, especially economic life, perhaps because he understood the state to be the most universal of the "three divine institutions." But the two books I cited continued to be read as their author, while remaining active as a lay participant in parish life, let his writings speak for him in the larger world of Protestant life and thought. The work of these three Protestant voices in the 1890s—Gladden, Herron, and Ely—was to bear its fruit when the social gospel flowered early in the following century.

Political thought among Roman Catholics in America was quite different from that of Protestants, for it was much more directly shaped by medieval traditions mediated by the teachings of the Vatican. Positive views of the role of the state in human affairs, accompanied wherever possible by legal church establishment, had been axiomatic for centuries in the Catholic world. The overwhelming acceptance in the United States of the patterns of religious liberty and the separation of church and state by Catholic clergy and laity was something of an exception.

In the later nineteenth century some prominent members of the Catholic hierarchy, drawing on currents of thought that had been stimulated in the church in part by its social environment, enthusiastically advocated the development of democracy with its commitment to religious freedom. They believed that a broadly tolerant approach to the problems of the church in the American republic, given its Protestant flavor, would better disarm opponents and help in assimilating the flood of foreign-born Catholics. Cardinal Gibbons himself was generally favorable to the Americanists, as they came to be called, though the outspoken Archbishop Ireland remained their most eloquent and enthusiastic advocate.

---

[31] *The Social Law of Service* (New York: Eaton and Mains, 1896), 162–63.

The rector of the new (1887) Catholic University of America in Washington, D.C., Bishop John J. Keane, allied himself with the Americanist movement, as did the independent-minded bishop of Peoria, John Lancaster Spalding. Denis O'Connell, named by Gibbons as rector of the American College in Rome in 1885, used his diplomatic skills at the Vatican on behalf of the movement.[32] Americanists insisted that for their country the constitutional provisions regarding religion were consistent with a vigorous Catholic life.

The movement was opposed under the leadership of more conservative clergy, particularly Archbishop Michael A. Corrigan of New York, Bishop Bernard J. McQuaid of Rochester, and a number with German backgrounds, notably Frederick F. X. Katzer, named archbishop of Milwaukee in 1890. In the 1890s the tension between the two groups increased, and bitterness mounted. In addition to differences in their views of the patterns of American culture, a number of specific issues divided them. Of particular importance for this study were those related to elementary and secondary education, for Ireland, as has been noted, especially declared himself a friend of the public school.

At first the Americanist cause fared well. Archbishop Francesco Satolli, soon to be named by Pope Leo XIII as a permanent apostolic delegate to the American hierarchy, came to the country in 1892 and was a helpful mediator, especially in quieting the storm within Catholicism over the public school. He declared in favor of parochial education but indicated that, if unavailable, Catholic children could attend public schools with the bishop's approval. He reaffirmed the decision of the Third Plenary in 1884 that parents could not be excommunicated for sending their children to such schools. At first, guided by Ireland and Keane, he was friendly to the Americanists, but by 1895, as his English improved and he became more fully acquainted with the details of church life in the country, he had changed sides.[33] He defended the rights of German Catholics to retain their language and customs, resisted the tendency of his former allies to enter into conversation with non-Catholics about religious matters, and reflected the conservative currents then resurgent in the Vatican.

Early in 1895 Leo XIII sent an important encyclical, *Longinqua oceani*, to American Catholics. He had words of praise for the American republic

[32] Gerald P. Fogarty, *The Vatican and the Americanist Crisis: Denis J. O'Connell, American Agent in Rome, 1885–1903* (Rome: Università Gregoriana Editrice, 1974), aptly tells the story from a particular perspective but also provides a good account of the movement as a whole; see esp. chap. 4. See also Thomas T. McAvoy, *The Great Crisis in American Catholic History, 1895–1900* (Chicago: Henry Regnery, 1957).

[33] Robert J. Wister, *The Establishment of the Apostolic Delegation in the United States of America: The Satolli Mission, 1892–1896* (Rome: Dissertatio ad Doctoratum in Facultate Historiae Ecclesiasticae Pontificiae Universitatis Gregorianae, 1981), esp. 111–41.

and expressed pleasure at the progress made by its Catholic church under the freedom of religion. Although he considered that the main factor in the church's flourishing condition had been the ordinances and decrees of the synods, especially those convened and confirmed by the authority of the Apostolic See, he also gave credit to the fact that the church lived "unopposed by the Constitution and government of your nation, fettered by no hostile legislation, protected against violence by the common laws and the impartiality of the tribunals"; it was free to live and act without hindrance. "Yet, though all this is true," he continued, "it would be very erroneous to draw the conclusion that in America is to be sought the type of the most desirable status of the Church, or that it would be universally lawful or expedient for State and Church to be, as in America, dissevered and divorced." That the church was enjoying prosperous growth was to be attributed to "the fecundity with which God has endowed His Church." But "she would bring forth more abundant fruits if, in addition to liberty, she enjoyed the favor of the laws and the patronage of the public authority."[34]

In the context of the traditions of the United States this was a very conservative statement, and it troubled the Americanists especially. This encyclical advocated positive roles for governments in matters relating to Catholicism. Ten years before, in the encyclical *Immortale Dei*, on the Christian constitution of states, Leo had drawn on centuries of Catholic teaching to provide theological foundations for the view that a state should publicly profess its allegiance to true religion, carefully defined as Catholicism. Americanists explained that these documents were written in a European context when the church had fared poorly with the spread of liberal democracies in Europe in revolutionary times and had finally lost the papal states. They were sensitive when such statements were cited by critics of their church as an indication that Catholics, should they ever become strong enough, would move against religious freedom and church-state separation. Their conservative opponents within the church effectively used such authoritative declarations in resisting what they regarded as the excesses and dangers of Americanism.

In the closing years of the century, the tide ran strongly against the Americanists, who had been firm in their commitment to their nation's traditions of religious freedom. O'Connell was forced to resign his post at the American College in 1895, though Gibbons arranged for him to stay in Rome. The next year on the initiative of the Vatican, Keane was dismissed as rector of Catholic University. In 1899, despite a vigorous effort by Ireland to stop or delay its publication, Leo XIII sent to Gibbons the encyclical *Testem benevolentiae*. Again, the primary context was Eu-

[34] Ellis, ed., *Documents of American Catholic History*, 2: 502.

ropean ecclesiastical politics as the alleged dangers of "Americanism" became a primary target of conservative church leaders in France. The letter was carefully worded, for it referred to certain erroneous opinions, called Americanism by some, based on such faulty principles as "the Church ought to adapt herself somewhat to our advanced civilization, and, relaxing her ancient rigor, show some indulgence to modern popular theories and methods. Many think that this is to be understood not only with regard to the rule of life, but also to the doctrines in which the *deposit of faith* is contained."[35] The letter found no problem with the term Americanism as it designated the characteristic qualities that reflected honor on the nation's people; but it concluded that if Americanism was to signify or commend doctrinal consequences dangerous for faith and morals deriving from faulty principles, then "there can be no doubt that our Venerable Brethren the bishops of America would be the first to repudiate and condemn it, as being especially unjust to them and to the entire nation as well" (452). Gibbons promptly replied that the "extravagant and absurd" doctrine known as Americanism "has nothing in common with the views, aspiration, doctrine and conduct" of American Catholics.[36] Thus Gibbons did not lose face, but the warning had been heeded. Efforts to interpret the church in American idioms and thought patterns were checked, and the conservative trend that was to dominate Catholic church-state thought well into the twentieth century was clearly ascendant.

Another aspect of the positive view of the state, articulated in Leo's famous encyclical of 1891, was not to bear much fruit until the twentieth century. *Rerum novarum*, with its focus on the condition of the working classes, was influential in helping the Catholic church in America become known as the friend of labor. The document also revealed something of the complexity of the pontiff's thought, for according to historian Robert Cross, "both liberals and conservatives were delighted with Leo's encyclical on the condition of the working class."[37] Not only did it firmly uphold the right to private property and highly criticize socialism, but it also strongly emphasized the importance of governmental concern for the rights of the poor:

As regards the State, the interests of all, whether high or low, are equal. The poor are members of the national community equally with the rich; they are real component living members which constitute through the family, the living

[35] John J. Wynne, ed., *The Great Encyclical Letters of Pope Leo XIII*, 3d ed. (New York: Benziger Bros., 1903), 442.

[36] As quoted by John Tracy Ellis, *The Life of James Cardinal Gibbons, Archbishop of Baltimore, 1834–1921* (Milwaukee: Bruce Publishing, 1952), 2: 71.

[37] *Emergence of Liberal Catholicism*, 123.

body; and it need hardly be said that they are in every State very largely the majority. It would be irrational to neglect one portion of the citizens and favor another, and therefore, the public administration must duly and solicitously provide for the welfare and the comfort of the working classes; otherwise, that law of justice will be violated which ordains that each man shall have his due.[38]

Nor was this left in high generality, for, turning "to things external and corporeal," Leo insisted that "the first concern of all is to save the poor workers from the cruelty of greedy speculators, who use human beings as mere instruments of moneymaking. It is neither just nor human so to grind men down with excessive labor as to stupefy their minds and wear out their bodies" (234).

After the encyclical's initial enthusiastic reception in the United States, the glow soon faded. Preoccupied by such internal disputes as those over the schools and Americanism, involved in defending their church against anti-Catholic attacks, and engaged with founding parishes and cultivating a network of institutions to cope with its growing numbers, church leaders were busy with many other matters. Jay Dolan has indicated that in the 1890s "the ideology of social conservatism, which emphasized charity, rather than justice, was still the dominant force in shaping Catholic social thought."[39] Most bishops and priests tended to emphasize primarily the encyclical's message commending private property and condemning socialism. But at the more practical level, a number of priests, especially those involved with working-class parishes, became acquainted with the labor movement and were often drawn into active sympathy with the unions. They were encouraged by the call for justice in *Rerum novarum*. The seeds that had been planted flourished when reformist social and progressive political movements became important influences in American life early in the new century. In that context, the positive role for the state to "duly and solicitously provide for the welfare and comfort of the working classes" emerged as a more prominent motif in Catholic social thought and life.

Mounting Awareness of Other World Religions

Since the beginnings of European settlement, American awareness of religions other than Christianity had been cast largely in a negative light. The indigenous religions of the North American continent had been regarded for the most part as pagan superstition. Such historic world faiths as Judaism, Hinduism, Buddhism, and Islam had often been used as a foil

[38] Wynne, ed., *Great Encyclical Letters*, 228.
[39] Dolan, *American Catholic Experience*, 335.

for displaying the virtues of Christendom. Christians generally had been taught to believe that theirs was the only way to salvation.

This conviction was a powerful force behind the Protestant missionary enterprise of the nineteenth century. It continued to energize the remarkable increase in missionary enthusiasm of the Protestant denominations in the 1890s, especially among the more conservatively oriented, while the motives of lifting others out of ignorance, poverty, injustice, and spiritual darkness also contributed to the growth of the number of missionaries sent abroad from the United States in the decade from less than one thousand to nearly five thousand.[40] The increase of trade and travel meant that more American Christians came into contact with representatives of other religions than had previously been the case. In colleges and seminaries, courses in comparative religion were developed; true to the spirit of voluntary Christendom they were often slanted to display the superiority of the Christian to other faiths, even in state universities. On the whole, other religions, not really taken seriously, were often used for apologetic purposes.

The major exception was Judaism, for small numbers of Jews had been present in North America since the seventeenth century. Although the centuries-old practice of regarding them as responsible for the crucifixion continued to be part of Christian preaching and to influence liturgical forms, in the colonial period they had been a tolerated, tiny minority. *From Curiosity to Third Faith* was the apt subtitle Joseph L. Blau provided for his compact survey, *Judaism in America*; he pointed to the fact that Jews were generally regarded as a peaceable group entitled to a refuge in a freedom-loving land. In various colonies they had been deprived of certain political privileges, restrictions carried over in the practice of some states but gradually lessened across the decades as discrimination was protested. Blau wrote,

> In 1783, when the American Revolution was barely finished, the enlightened Jewish literary idol of the Berlin salons, Moses Mendelssohn, wrote a short treatise advocating religious freedom and the separation of church and state. How meaningful the geographically remote American experience was to him is indicated by a footnote added to the last page of the first edition of his *Jerusalem*: "Alas! We hear from America that the [Continental] Congress has revived the old tune and is beginning to talk of a dominant religion." From time to time in American history, talk of this sort has recurred. Amendments to the Constitution of the United States declaring it to be a Christian nation have been pro-

---

[40] Robert Pierce Beaver, "Missionary Motivation through Three Centuries," in *Reinterpretation in American Church History*, ed. Jerald C. Brauer (Chicago: University of Chicago Press, 1968), 113–51; James S. Dennis, *Christian Missions and Social Progress*, 3 vols. (New York: Fleming H. Revell, 1897–1906).

posed, but never adopted. Anti-Jewish sentiment among the American people has waxed and waned, but there has never been an official governmental policy of restricting either the opportunities open to individual Jews or the freedom of Jewish worship.[41]

What Mendelssohn feared in 1783 did not happen, though individual Jews did find their opportunities limited by recurrences of anti-Semitism, especially as the numbers of Jews dramatically increased in the latter part of the nineteenth century, and xenophobia combined in specific instances with the deep-seated distaste for those of Hebrew ancestry. Jews, so often subject to persecution in Europe, were drawn by the magnet of the New World, and by 1880 their estimated numbers had swelled to more than a quarter million. Then, in part because of the increase of pogroms in Eastern Europe, their numbers escalated sharply. In an informative doctoral dissertation on American Judaism and the separation of church and state, Shlomith Yahalom has estimated that "from 1880 to 1900 the number of Jews in the United States swelled from 280 thousand to 1 million."[42] Some counts run higher; in her *Encounter with Emancipation*, for example, Naomi Cohen reported that "close to 1.5 million Jews from eastern Europe had emigrated to the United States during the two decades since 1881."[43]

How many of these were active (and to what degree) in synagogue life is not known. The census of 1890, noting that only heads of families could be recorded, reported that there were more than 57,000 communicants in the stricter Orthodox synagogues, and more than 130,000 in Reform Judaism, which had made a much greater accommodation to American life.[44] As Shlomith Yahalom (among others) explains, because of their long, tragic relationship with Christendom, including the "voluntary" form so conspicuous in nineteenth-century America, Jews were ardent upholders of religious freedom and the separation of church and state. Yet while advocating a secular government, the more observant especially resisted the trend toward cultural secularization. A major thesis of Yahalom's work is that until the end of the nineteenth century, however, Jews appealed to the principle of separation between church and

[41] *Judaism in America: From Curiosity to Third Faith* (Chicago: University of Chicago Press, 1976), 27–28.

[42] "American Judaism and the Question of Separation Between Church and State" (partial English translation of Ph.D. diss., Hebrew University of Jerusalem, 1981), section on "Church-State Separation and Education," 32. (See Acknowledgments for further bibliographical information.)

[43] *Encounter with Emancipation: German Jews in the United States, 1830–1914* (Philadelphia: Jewish Publication Society of America, 1984), 239.

[44] As reported by Henry K. Carroll, *The Religious Forces of the United States* (New York: Christian Literature Society, 1893), 161, 164.

state primarily to solve their own internal problems, and as a minority movement in a predominantly Christian environment did not challenge the status quo. They accepted state or municipal privileges extended to allow them to carry out certain duties, particularly to administer marriages and to sell Kosher food certified to meet the standard that was claimed. When civil authority bestowed a monopoly in such matters to a given group, parties not so favored invoked the principle of the separation of church and state in the civil courts, which tended to confirm older customs and forms of prayer in accordance with English precedents.[45] As a minority group, Jews strongly believed in equality before the law in religious matters.

As most Jews, especially newly arrived immigrants, were striving to make a place for themselves in American society, they favored the public schools as a means to that end for their children. Yet they resisted the Protestant overtones in reading the Bible (often the King James version), singing hymns, and observing pseudo-religious celebrations during the Christian holidays. This led to some mixed alliances. As Arthur Gilbert summarized a complex matter, "For many years, Jews were able to count on Catholic support in their protest against religion—usually of Protestant form and substance—in the public schools; and Jews joined Protestants in opposing Catholic efforts to obtain financial aid for parochial schools."[46]

In the late 1880s and 1890s a new set of Jewish institutions that would become the Conservative movement was emerging out of the "historical school" that was seeking a middle way between Reform and Orthodox Judaism. That school "emphasized that traditional faith and Jewish communal existence must be based on the new conditions of modern society: Jewish emancipation, equality of rights, and practical separation of Church and State." Like Reform, it accepted the advantages of equality of rights, freedom, and cultural advances brought by the Enlightenment. But like Orthodoxy, the Conservative movement "strove vigorously to maintain the religious, ethnic and cultural unity of American Jewry and its indissoluble tie with World Jewry."[47] Like the other two, the emerging movement, lacking the resources to develop a network of Jewish schools

[45] Yahalom, "Sunday Laws," 11–12. See also Jonathan D. Sarna's chapter, "Christian America or Secular America? The Church-State Dilemma of American Jews," in *Jews in Unsecular America*, ed. Richard J. Neuhaus (Grand Rapids, Mich.: Eerdmans, 1987), 8–19.

[46] "Jewish Commitments in Relations of Church and State," in *Church-State Relations in Ecumenical Perspective*, ed. Elwyn A. Smith (Pittsburgh: University of Duquesne Press, 1966), 58.

[47] Moshe Davis, *The Emergence of Conservative Judaism: The Historical School in 19th Century America* (Philadelphia: Jewish Publication Society of America, 1963), 19; see also 242–52.

parallel to parochial schools, saw that the contemporary public schools were pervaded by Protestant influences and not really open to religious instruction by various faiths. Hence the Conservative movement focused its first educational efforts on training rabbis and teachers, as the Reform movement had done. Although some Jewish day schools were founded, by the turn of the century the three main branches of Judaism had accepted public education; they were troubled about its religious content "but not to the extent of inducing them to forfeit the benefits it offered."[48] The immigrants had known far greater threats in their countries of origin.

The waves of immigration during the last several decades of the nineteenth century were bringing not only vast numbers of Catholics and Jews but also some Christians of Eastern Orthodox backgrounds and a few representatives of other historic faiths. That the religious map of the United States was steadily changing—given the influx of newcomers of many varieties from the outside and the emergence of indigenous groups of Protestant backgrounds—became widely noticed only much later. But the increasing religious pluralism of the nation was putting pressure on the Protestant denominations, which hoped to maintain their cultural dominance. Toward the end of the century the pluralistic trend became apparent in various ways, one of which was the problem of Sunday laws.

With varying degrees of strictness, most American Protestant denominations placed considerable emphasis on the observance of Sunday and wanted to maintain certain customs and laws that had been part of the legal inheritance from the colonial period. Such state and municipal laws were amended from time to time, especially in the later nineteenth century, accelerated by the impact of immigrants familiar with the freer Sunday patterns of the continent where the "Puritan Sabbath" had not been known. Yet in a majority of the states there were still laws restricting Sunday labor, manufacturing, selling, and public amusements at which an admission fee was collected. The Supreme Court found that such measures were consistent with the Constitution. In a decision handed down in 1885, Stephen J. Field summarized the court's opinion: "Laws setting aside Sunday as a day of rest are upheld, not from any right of government for the promotion of religious observances, but from its right to protect all persons from the physical and moral debasement which comes from uninterrupted labor."[49]

Although Protestants who sought to maintain those laws used such "secular" arguments too, clearly a deep religious feeling motivated their position. In 1900, for example, the Methodist bishops exclaimed: "Unnecessary travel, unnecessary work, the Sunday newspaper, social visit-

[48] Yahalom, "Church-State Separation and Education," 33.
[49] *Soon Hing* v. *Crowley*, 113 U.S. 703 (1885) at 710.

ing, excursions, and amusements encroach more and more on time which God has consecrated to sacred uses." They were alarmed, for, as they saw it, "without Sabbath sanctity our people will suffer moral loss, our sanctuaries will be deserted, and our ministries will be ineffective."[50] In that same year the report of a Presbyterian committee to its General Assembly included such sentences as this: "When the people who should be in the pews in the sanctuary are absorbed in the pursuit of pleasure or business on the Lord's Day, the Church and the Lord's treasury are the immediate and inevitable sufferers."[51] Voluntary associations of Protestants that attracted members across denominational lines, such as the National Reform Association, entered the fray on behalf of maintaining strict observance. Several other voluntary organizations, the American Sabbath Union (1887) and the Lord's Day Alliance (1888), were formed specifically to maintain and enforce Sunday laws, gathering their primary following among the evangelical churches.

The Sunday laws posed serious problems for Jews, for whom the historic Sabbath was Saturday. Those who were observant and adhered to Jewish law could not work on Saturday, and thus at a time when the six-day work week was standard they were cut short on work time. They had learned to distrust "united front" cooperation among Protestant denominations, which so often fueled the drive to make America a Christian nation and played a role in providing an atmosphere in which the seeds of anti-Semitism could grow. One result of the crusade for maintaining Sunday laws led to abrogating some special ordinances that had been enacted as safeguards for Sabbath-observant Jews. Hence when the National Reform Association promoted a campaign for a National Sabbath Rest constitutional amendment, the Conference of Delegates of Reform Judaism's Union of American Hebrew Congregations launched protests in 1890 and 1891.

They were not wholly alone in their objections. On the one hand, resistance to Sunday laws was offered by such liberal organizations as the philosophically minded Francis Ellingwood Abbot's National Liberal League and the eloquent agnostic Robert G. Ingersoll's American Secular League and Free Thought Federation. On the other hand, several small Protestant denominations, which held to a belief that the seventh day was indeed the biblical Sabbath—Seventh-day Adventists and Seventh Day Baptists—also protested. The former were conspicuous in the formation of the National Religious Association (later the Religious Liberty Asso-

[50] David S. Monroe, ed., *Journal of the General Conference of the Methodist Episcopal Church . . . 1900* (New York: Eaton & Mains, n.d. [1900]), 30.

[51] *Minutes of the General Assembly of the Presbyterian Church in the U.S.A.* (Philadelphia: MacCalla & Co., 1900), 30.

ciation of America) in 1888.[52] But in the larger denominations that were deeply concerned about maintaining Sunday as a day of rest, members' opinions differed as to what degree the old "blue laws" (so called because they had originally been printed on blue paper) should be retained. Although Catholics historically had often differed with Protestants on the rigor of the older Puritan Sunday customs, some saw certain advantages in keeping the day distinctive in the face of threats of secularism and apathy. In their effort to identify with and help mold American culture, some Americanist leaders especially found value in efforts to maintain certain restrictions.[53] There were also differences among Jews about how far they should adjust to the prevailing practices of the American environment. Many Reform synagogues held services on Friday evening (for Jews the Sabbath begins and ends at sundown); they often became popular and well-attended events.

A highly publicized controversy over Sunday observance erupted during the planning for the World's Columbian Exposition to celebrate the 400th anniversary of Columbus's historic voyage of 1492. In 1890 a congressional act nationally recognized the coming exposition, which was to be held in Chicago, and provided for a sizable commission to be named by the president to cooperate with the city. When Chicago had raised the required sum of ten million dollars, it applied for a federal loan, some of which was later made as an outright gift. But advocates of maintaining Sunday as a day of rest, led largely by Protestant groups, denominational and nondenominational, pressured Congress to keep the fair closed on Sunday. This touched off a heated congressional debate in 1892, as petitions pro and con poured into Washington. Opponents of Sunday closing protested that such legislation violated the principle of the separation of church and state; they claimed it was governmental interference on behalf of religion. Sunday closing supporters threatened to boycott members of Congress at election time if they did not vote their way. The Supreme Court decision in *Church of the Holy Trinity* v. *United States*, handed down earlier in the year, maintained that "this is a Christian nation," a phrase frequently mentioned in the petitions and stressed by the president of the American Sabbath Union when he appeared before congressional committees during the debates.[54]

The tension in Jewish circles about how best to deal with such a con-

---

[52] Yahalom, "Sunday Laws," 11–14. On the Adventist groups, see Arthur Carl Piepkorn, *Profiles in Belief: The Religious Bodies of the United States and Canada*, Vol. 4, *Evangelical, Fundamentalist, and Other Christian Bodies* (San Francisco: Harper & Row, 1979), 133–36, 153–57.

[53] Cross, *Emergence of Liberal Catholicism*, 129, 178.

[54] The Supreme Court decision is discussed more fully in Chap. 1; Yahalom, "Sunday Laws," 15.

troversy was reflected in somewhat different resolutions passed by two of Reform Jewry's organizations. The Union of American Hebrew Congregations' statement not only objected to Sunday laws but also specifically opposed the exposition's closings. The Central Conference of American Rabbis' declaration was more general because it protested against all such legislation involving religion as subversive of religious liberty, but in final form it did not mention the exposition. After all the furore, the Sunday closing proposal passed easily; the political clout of an aroused evangelical Protestantism could not be ignored.

That did not settle the issue, however. When the exposition opened in Chicago in May 1893, the rule was observed at the outset, but not on the last Sunday of the month when the fair remained open. Subsequent legal wranglings temporarily closed it again. By early summer it was opened on Sunday and remained so for the fair's duration because the legal situation was still clouded. The champions of Sunday closing, however, were successful in passing such legislation for later expositions at St. Louis (1901) and Jamestown (1906).[55] They saw those victories as a contribution to what they hoped would be a "Christian" century.

Religion and the Chicago Exposition

The World's Columbian Exposition provided a setting for several gatherings concerned with religion, sponsored by the World Congress Auxiliary. A Catholic Congress brought together clergy and laity; it called attention to problems of Indians and blacks, considered social problems in the light of *Rerum novarum*, and protested the arms race in which "Christian nations" were engaged.[56] The World Evangelical Alliance held a general meeting there at the invitation of its American branch; it focused on the social mission of the churches and increasing cooperation among them.[57] But by far the most unusual and colorful gathering was the World's Parliament of Religions, which met in September and lasted for seventeen days. There had been nothing like it before—nor has there been since. Buddhists, Confucians, Hindus, Jains, Muslims, Parsees, Shintoists, Taoists and others from abroad were among those who mingled with representatives of the faiths best known to Americans. Many were glad of the chance to explain and defend the faiths to which they had committed their lives. The parliament was not all addresses and lectures, however; Cardinal Gibbons in his scarlet robes opened the gathering with

[55] Ibid., 14–19; Stokes, *Church and State in the United States*, 3: 158–61, 573.
[56] Hennesey, *American Catholics*, 191, 200.
[57] Jordan, *Evangelical Alliance*, 177–81.

the "universal prayer," the Lord's prayer, in which, it was noted, most joined. Later, Philip Schaff, present against his physicians' advice, later led the assembly in the same prayer. He was too weak, however, to deliver his address on "The Reunion of Christendom," which was read by another as he listened from the platform.

Representatives of the various religions of the world attended for many reasons and with varying degrees on enthusiasm. "The hope that the Parliament would promote the Christian faith was foremost in the minds of a number of its leading American supporters," wrote Egal Feldman in his interpretation of the parliament.[58] Martin Marty's Part I of the first volume of his *Modern American Religion*, "The Modernists," opens with an account of the parliament and calls attention to those who were seeking a universal outlook, the one truth underlying all, "a main modernist tenet."[59] Some liberals of various backgrounds found their sense of the historical conditioning of all institutional religion illustrated by the colorful gathering of religious figures of many nations, languages, and faiths. But such persons as Schaff and other members of the Evangelical Alliance saw in the situation a fresh imperative for a new unity among Christians, and they sought ways to reunite the scattered forces of Christendom into what he called "evangelical Catholicism." For Schaff, believing that the truth of the Christian religion would only be enhanced by comparison with other religions, the parliament was "an epoch-making fact, a new departure in the history of religion."[60] Gibbons was at first hesitant about the gathering because it seemed to put all religions on the same level. But the insistent Ireland and others of the Americanist group urged cooperation when they addressed the delegates; like Schaff, Keane pleaded for the reunion of Christendom and noted that the positive doctrinal divergences that had kept Christians apart were being obliterated. Jews of both Reform and Conservative tendencies were glad of the opportunity to participate. During their preparations, the rabbis agreed that they would seize the opportunity to go beyond their papers on ethical, religious, and historical matters and refute the anti-Semitic charges that were then mounting.[61]

[58] "American Ecumenism: Chicago's World's Parliament of Religions of 1893," *Journal of Church and State* 9 (1967): 182.

[59] *Modern American Religion*, Vol. 1, *The Irony of It All, 1893–1919* (Chicago: University of Chicago Press, 1986), 20; see also 17–24. A good brief bibliography of the Parliament of Religion accompanies his account. See also Joseph M. Kitagawa, "The World's Parliament of Religions and its Legacy," in his *The History of Religions: Understanding Human Experience* (Atlanta: Scholars Press, 1987), 353–58; and Grant Wacker, "A Plural World: The Protestant Awakening to World Religions," in *Between the Times*, ed. Hutchison, 253–55, 259, 261.

[60] As quoted by Shriver, *Philip Schaff*, 103.

[61] Feldman, "American Ecumenism," 186–88, 195–96.

At the time, most who attended the parliament were favorably impressed. There were some tense and embarrassing moments and a few heated exchanges, but on the whole all went well. Nevertheless, some sober second thoughts about what had happened followed the parliament's conclusion. "Designed to show the unity of faiths, it displayed a split within the company of conveners, a set of disparities and disputes among denominations in this world's fair of faiths," Marty concluded. "Instead of dialogue a succession of monologues had occurred."[62] As the reaction against the Americanists mounted, the Catholic presence was viewed by prominent leaders both in Rome and at home as a mistake.

As we look back now from the perspective of a century later, we can wonder if these sober reactions foreshadowed an awareness of the religious pluriformity steadily to increase during the twentieth century—a pluriformity that not only would prevail among and within the Christian and Jewish traditions, but would also include the many faiths of the world. Christian sponsors hoped to promote faith and Jewish participants to correct misunderstandings, but many others had their moment in the spotlight and now wanted a permanent place on the American stage. A Vedanta Society to spread Hindu teachings was founded the year after the parliament by Swami Vivekananda, who made a great impression at the gathering and became convinced that there was a great opportunity for the spread of Oriental religious philosophies in America. Buddhism was soon being taught by a Japanese priest who settled in San Francisco, while even during the parliament an American convert to Islam reported that a Muslim study group was at work in New York. Neither a confident, crusading Protestantism nor a growing, consolidating Catholicism was much troubled at the time, but the fact of the religious spectrum of the world had for a moment been apparent on Chicago's midway. That moment lived on in human memory and set its stamp on the literature of religion.

Not so many decades after 1893, awareness of the realities of religious pluralism strengthened the hands of those who wanted both to keep the institutions of religion and the institutions of government as separate as possible and to weaken the confidence of some who had thought theirs was the only true way but had now encountered others who were sure theirs was the right path. Some deeper significances of the Parliament of Religions appeared only with the passage of time. But before the 1890s ran their course an event of quite another kind had an immediate impact on both religion and government and opened new vistas for the twentieth century.

[62] Marty, *The Irony of It All*, 22.

4

Expansionism in Government and Religion as a New Century Dawns

By 1900 the expansion of the nation and of its religious institutions had long been part of the fabric of American life. The first permanent settlers from Europe in the colonial period soon began pressing inland from their coastline bases. By the time the Constitution was ratified in 1788, the western boundary of the United States stood at the Mississippi, but the movement of the new Americans into Indian country beyond the Allegheny mountains was just beginning. It soon escalated into a flood as increasing numbers caught "western fever" and sought their livelihood in the new lands of opportunity. As the frontier steadily moved westward, hundreds of towns and cities were founded, and new territories and states were added to the Union. Networks of economic, educational, cultural, and religious institutions proliferated as the spirit and reality of expansion indelibly marked nineteenth-century American life. Religious life flourished in the new setting, often by developing novel methods and structures.[1] Newly conceived missionary programs extended visions of peoples under God at home and abroad.

When the census report of 1890 found that settlement had proceeded so far that a frontier line could no longer be drawn, some felt that the age of expansion was over. But as the nation slowly recovered from the depression years of the 1890s, many forces—notably economic interests, political ambition, national pride, journalistic adventurism, and religious zeal—stimulated a revived concern for America's "manifest destiny" as not only a continental but also a world power. The dramatic events of 1898 then served as a catalyst for the powerful emotional current of expansionism that swept over the nation and its churches. Not everyone was carried along; there was considerable resistance to its imperialist overtones, but expansionist fever was running high as one century drew to a close and another opened. Expansionism was a factor in the spread of the power of government and in the increased outreach of the churches abroad. Its high point came in 1898, but its effects long persisted.

[1] Some of the seeds of what Robert Wuthnow was much later to call "the restructuring of religion" were planted in the nineteenth century; see his *The Restructuring of American Religion: Society and Faith Since World War II* (Princeton: Princeton University Press, 1988), esp. 6–8, 22–25, 277–78.

The Splendid Little War

On the night of February 15, 1898, the battleship *Maine* was sunk in Havana harbor with heavy loss of American lives. Those responsible have never been identified, but at the time many jumped to the conclusion that Spain was the guilty party, in part because several New York newspapers competing for circulation had paid much attention to the atrocities committed against Cuban insurgents in the long struggle against their Spanish rulers. War hysteria mounted. Although some prominent church leaders, both Protestant and Catholic, opposed military intervention and worked for peace, increasing numbers discerned in the flow of events convincing evidence that war would be justified. At the end of March the *Evangelist*, a Presbyterian publication, announced that "if it be the will of Almighty God, that by war the last trace of this inhumanity of man to man shall be swept away from this Western hemisphere, let it come!"[2]

After Congress passed joint resolutions authorizing President McKinley to use force to expel the Spanish from Cuba and war was declared on April 25, such preachers as W. H. P. Faunce, for example, provided a typical interpretation of what was transpiring: "Spanish and American civilization could not exist side by side, separated only by a narrow strip of Southern sea, without sooner or later coming into opposition, any more than fire and water could touch without generating steam." The influential Baptist could declare that Spain "stands convicted of incompetence, of oppression, of cruelty, of such incompetence as permits the slow death of one-tenth of Cuba's population and the swift destruction of a ship of a friendly power bound on a peaceful mission."[3] As for Methodists, in whose ranks the president was numbered, Kenneth M. MacKenzie concluded that "war was reluctantly accepted as a necessity, but once having been entered, was to be prosecuted with the vigor of a sacred and humanitarian crusade."[4] Although Catholics discerned not a little anti-Catholicism in much prowar publicity of the time and both Ireland and Gibbons had worked for peace, it was also true that more than half of those who went down with the *Maine* were Catholic. Once war began, the archbishops unanimously declared that "whatever may have been the individual opinions of Americans prior to the declaration of war, there can now be no two opinions as to the duty of every loyal citizen." They affirmed once

[2] As quoted by Stokes, *Church and State in the United States*, 2: 312.

[3] *New York Times*, April 25, 1898, as quoted by John E. Smylie, "Protestant Clergymen and America's World Role, 1865–1900: A Study of Christianity, Nationality and International Relations" (Th.D. diss., Princeton Theological Seminary, 1959), 449.

[4] *The Robe and the Sword: The Methodist Church and the Rise of American Imperialism* (Washington, D.C.: Public Affairs Press, 1961), 57–58.

again that Catholics were true Americans "and as such are loyal to our country and our flag and obedient to the highest decrees and the supreme authority of the nation."⁵ The religious bodies overwhelmingly supported the national cause. The internal debate within the churches had not been long, and it concluded with a high degree of unanimity.

At the moment war was declared, public attention focused on Cuba, but it was almost immediately diverted to the other side of the world. The first major result of the war had been set up several months before by imperially minded Theodore Roosevelt, then assistant secretary of the Navy, who saw to it that the Pacific fleet was ready to deal with Spanish naval forces based in the Philippine Islands. Steaming into Manila Bay on May 1, Commodore George Dewey's squadron sank the anchored Spanish fleet. Suddenly not only was the liberation of Cuba at stake but also the opportunity for the United States to acquire colonies. In the rising tide of expansionism, a long-desired goal of American interests in Hawaii was realized when it was annexed by joint congressional resolution on July 7.

Meanwhile, the Spanish fleet in Cuba was destroyed in an effort to slip out of the harbor at Santiago, and that city fell to the American army on July 16. Puerto Rico was also occupied with little difficulty. Hostilities were terminated on August 12 with an agreement that Cuba was to be free, Puerto Rico and Guam ceded to the United States, and Manila occupied until a final disposition of the Philippines was settled. The war had been won despite gross inefficiencies and many blunders. Because the value of a strong Navy had been demonstrated, those who wanted to increase and centralize the power of the national government were encouraged. Also, as Robert H. Ferrell has aptly put it, "the importance of. the Spanish-American War for the diplomatic history of the United States lies in its appeal to the new sentiment of manifest destiny, its lending of substance and a feeling of achievement to what hitherto had been largely dreams and hopes. . . . The experience was thrilling to the national psyche."⁶ The dream of America as a world power was coming true. This exhilarating prospect led to the excitement with which the nation added colonies at that point. Ernest R. May has argued that "practically every American scholar who has studied the record has come to the same conclusion—that the taking of these new territories was a result of a temporary emotional upswell among the public."⁷ Yet it did not go unresisted at the time.

Even before the short war was over the debate about what to do with

---

⁵ As quoted by Frank T. Reuter, *Catholic Influence on American Colonial Policies, 1898–1904* (Austin: University of Texas Press, 1967), 11–12.

⁶ *American Diplomacy: A History* (New York: W. W. Norton, 1959), 210. On the course of the conflict, see Frank Freidel, *The Splendid Little War* (Boston: Little, Brown, 1958).

⁷ *From Imperialism to Isolationism, 1898–1919* (New York: Macmillan, 1963), 31.

the surprising outcome of what John Hay dubbed "the splendid little war" was in full swing. The prevailing mood supported those willing for the nation to become vigorously imperialistic, but organized resistance emerged in the fall of 1898. The anti-imperialists, among whom were persons of eminence in the literary and intellectual world, based their appeal largely on political principle. They resisted the idea of expanded military forces, involvement in overseas wars, and responsibility for peoples they believed to be racially incapable of governing themselves.[8] Although prominent religious leaders had generally favored entering the war to free Cuba, they were divided on the imperialist issue. As Winthrop S. Hudson has demonstrated, a number of illustrious clerical leaders adhered to an anti-imperialist position, and some widely read denominational periodicals remained unswayed by their anticolonialist stance. Very early in the debate, Unitarian layman David Starr Jordan, then president of Stanford University, saw the drawing power of imperialism with its victories and applause but rejected it nevertheless: "It is un-American; it is contrary to our traditions; it is delicious; it is intoxicating." Late in the year, when the issue was moving quickly toward settlement, from his prestigious Presbyterian pulpit in New York the eloquent Henry Van Dyke asked rhetorically, "are we still loyal to the principles of our forefathers . . . or are we now ready to sell the American birthright for a mess of pottage in the Philippines?"[9]

Many other ministers went the other way and urged annexation of the Philippine islands. Especially influential was Lyman Abbott, pastor of Brooklyn's Plymouth Church and editor of the *Outlook*, who step by step moved from a questioning to a clearly imperialist stance. He advocated protectorates over Cuba, Puerto Rico, and the Philippines so that they might have the blessings of freedom: free schools, a free (i.e., "non-Catholic") church, and equal justice under the law. In an oft-quoted phrase, he called it "the new imperialism—the imperialism of liberty."[10] Washington Gladden preached that the anti-imperialists were wrong in claiming that annexation would violate American principles, for "semi-civilized races" could govern themselves only after extensive preparation. He declared it "simply amazing that grown men, with the pages of history

---

[8] Robert L. Beisner, *Twelve Against Empire: The Anti-Imperialists, 1898–1900* (New York: McGraw-Hill, 1968); Richard Hofstadter, "Cuba, the Philippines, and Manifest Destiny," in his *The Paranoid Style in American Politics and Other Essays* (New York: Vintage Books, 1967), 171–74.

[9] Jordan and Van Dyke quotations from Winthrop S. Hudson, "Protestant Clergy Debate the Nation's Vocation, 1898–1899," *Church History* 42 (1973): 114, 117.

[10] *Outlook* 59 (August 27, 1898): 1004, as quoted by Ira V. Brown, *Lyman Abbott, Christian Evolutionist: A Study in Religious Liberalism* (Cambridge: Harvard University Press, 1953), 170.

open before their eyes, should go on applying the maxims of our Declaration of Independence to populations like those of the Philippines."[11] Such voices as these—and there were many others—allowed those opting for annexation to dismiss the views of the anti-imperialist clergy, for a moral consensus was not expressed. Among Catholic bishops, only John Lancaster Spalding was conspicuous in opposing the acquisition of colonies as he pled for a return to the principles on which America was founded. Many among the Irish laity had supported intervention in Cuba but opposed imperial expansion.[12]

After McKinley had instructed the American peace commissioners who were meeting with the Spanish delegation in October 1898 in Paris to demand the cession of the Philippines, the die had been cast. McKinley is reported to have explained his action to a group of fellow-Methodists in words frequently quoted: "I walked the floor of the White House night after night until midnight, and I am not ashamed to tell you, gentlemen, that I went down on my knees and prayed Almighty God for light and guidance more than one night." In a way he could not explain, it came to him that various options—returning the islands to Spain, or turning them over to commercial rivals like France or Germany, or letting them alone to sink into anarchy—would not work. So, he concluded "there was nothing left for us to do but to take them all, and to educate the Filipinos, and uplift and civilize and Christianize them, and by God's grace do the very best we could by them, as our fellowmen for whom Christ also died."[13] The Spanish diplomats resisted but gave in when $20 million was offered, and the treaty was signed in December. The national debate continued, for it marked a departure from past policy. But the treaty was finally ratified by the Senate early in February.

The currents of thought and feeling that had helped sweep America into acquiring new colonies slowly ebbed. Even the word imperialism was bypassed: expansionism became the more familiar noun. Thus, though the expansionist mentality and activity persisted in matters of economics, culture, and religion, few more territories were added. "Many factors contributed to America's loss of stomach for imperial ventures," Hudson concluded, "but certainly the fact that the views of opinion leaders among the Protestant clergy once again began to coalesce as qualms developed about the 'pious justifications' advanced for the adoption of a colonial system helps to explain in part why American flirtation with a policy of

[11] From sermons of November 25 and December 18, 1898, as quoted by Jacob Dorn, *Washington Gladden*, 412.

[12] Hennesey, *American Catholics*, 205.

[13] As quoted by Ferrell, *American Diplomacy*, 205. The remark was reproduced several years later by one who had heard it, but it appears to be a fair representation of what McKinley actually said.

territorial expansion ended so quickly."[14] The vocabulary of expansionism, however, was increasingly relied upon as that of imperialism faded.
Robert L. Beisner has observed how the leaders of the time "drew imaginatively from a dictionary of denial in finding the language—protectorates, expansionism, Roosevelt Corollary [to the Monroe Doctrine], hemispheric security, containment—that would provide the tongue and mind
a way to evade confessing what still felt like the crime of imperialism."[15]
The "expansionist" spirit, certainly persistent in many forms, unveiled
exciting prospects for American influence in the world as the new century
opened.

Josiah Strong chose as the title of a new book for the times *Expansion:
Under New World-Conditions*. He had resigned his post with the Evangelical Alliance in 1898 to cofound and give major attention to the
League for Social Service. He devoted a large part of his new work to
interpreting the studies of the specialists to a wider public through lecturing, editing, and writing. His 1900 book characteristically combined a
great array of facts gleaned from many sources with sweeping generalizations to dramatize his central points. At that point he clearly favored
imperialism; he cited one of its prominent champions, Navy captain Alfred T. Mahan, who read several of his chapters in advance. Strong
stressed the need for new foreign markets and increased industrial expansion for the good of America and the world. The Pacific became for him
the new Mediterranean, soon to become the center of the world's population and commerce and hence the center of wealth and power. He
voiced none of the alarmism of the "seven perils" of his earlier *Our Country*, but he pictured a struggle between two great, rapidly growing races
for the domination of the Pacific.

Strong's contrast was sharp: "The Anglo-Saxon is the supreme representative of civil and religious liberty; the Slav [he referred primarily to
Russia] is the supreme representative of absolutism, both in state and
church."[16] He pleaded for the retention of the Philippines and claimed
that other action would be "treason to ourselves, to the Anglo-Saxon
race, to humanity, and to Western civilization" (204). Noting that many
lands touching the Pacific flew Anglo-Saxon flags, he saw in it all the
work of an intelligence higher than human knowledge: "Such facts are
God's great alphabet with which he spells for man his providential purposes" (212). He resisted anti-expansionist arguments about the necessity
of gaining the consent of the governed, for the new conditions had so
shrunk the world that savage, backward, disease-ridden races "must be

---

[14] "Protestant Clergy Debate the Nation's Vocation," 118.

[15] "Formative Events from Columbus to World War I," in *American Character and Foreign Policy*, ed. Michael P. Hamilton (Grand Rapids, Mich.: Eerdmans, 1986), 19.

[16] *Expansion: Under New World-Conditions* (New York: Baker & Taylor, 1900), 190.

controlled by enlightened nations both for their own sake and for the sake of the world" (245). A certain amount of military force might be necessary as a last resort, but he closed his book with an appeal "to recognize the place in the world which God has given us, and to accept the responsibilities which it devolves upon us in behalf of Christian civilization" (302). His presentation of "expansionism" contributed to the immense confidence with which many Americans, especially those in positions of leadership, greeted the new century.

"Providence, Piety, Politics, and Patriotism"

The mood of expansion provided a favorable context for the already growing missionary movement as talk of "world conquest" became increasingly familiar. Although Christians had disagreed on the issues of territorial imperialism, they rarely hesitated to stress the importance of missionary expansion for their own denominations, both in the areas where they already had long since ventured and in the new places made available by the events of 1898 and their outcomes. Some tensions between foreign missions and other forms of American expansionism arose, but in general they were mutually reinforcing. In many ways missionary enthusiasm was an early form of the expansionist spirit and helped prepare the way for its spread. The story of the founding of the Student Volunteer Movement for Foreign Missions (SVM) in 1888 and the popularity of the famous watchword, "the evangelization of the world in this generation," has been told many times. It meant various things to different people, but Clifton J. Phillips has concluded that "the much-flaunted watchword, no matter how variously interpreted, served to epitomize the optimistic self-confidence of a rapidly expanding Anglo-Saxon empire which was bringing both the virtues and the vices of Western civilization to bear on 'backward races' and non-Christian societies all over the earth."[17]

The SVM was but one of the many organizations that enlivened and magnified the growing missionary movement; of the others, some were related to denominations while many gathered support wherever they could find it. The way the missionary and expansionist movements swept forward together in the closing years of the old century has been expressed by Gerald H. Anderson in a colorful sentence: "The potent blend

[17] "Changing Attitudes in the Student Volunteer Movement of Great Britain and North America, 1886–1928," in *Missionary Ideologies in the Imperialist Era, 1880–1920*, ed. Torben Christensen and William R. Hutchison (Aarhus: Aros, 1982), 135. On the SVM, see Chap. 1, and also Hutchison, *Errand to the World: American Protestant Thought and Foreign Missions* (Chicago: University of Chicago Press, 1987), esp. 119, 130–33.

of Providence, piety, politics, and patriotism surged in support of foreign missions in 1898–99 with the Spanish-American War, especially with regard to the Philippines."[18] The same yeasty mix could be discerned in other fields: with his eyes primarily on China, Paul A. Varg concluded that "the missionary movement and imperialism were wheels driven by the same explosive energy generated by a sense of superiority, moral duty, and the ego satisfaction to be gained in developing the underdeveloped areas of the world."[19] The number of American Protestant foreign missionaries doubled in first fifteen years of the twentieth century; though estimates vary somewhat, Anderson finds that slightly more than four thousand in 1900 had exceeded nine thousand by 1915.

The work overseas, with its promise of spreading the values of Western civilization and uplifting those who lacked its faith and its advantages, appealed not only to those prominent in church leadership but also to many on its margins. A layman who attended an SVM meeting in 1906 was so moved by the zeal of the students that he participated in founding the Laymen's Missionary Movement. This organization sponsored well-publicized mass meetings across the nation, successfully heightening public interest and raising funds for the cause of the churches's world outreach. Larger in size than both was the interdenominational woman's foreign mission movement. More than three million women were on the membership rolls of the female missionary societies of some forty denominations by 1915. With local societies in most evangelical churches, the movement inspired and informed churchwomen at home and enlisted many for foreign service. By the early years of the twentieth century, more than 60 percent of mission personnel were women.[20] The mission study books, prepared largely for lay audiences under both denominational and interdenominational auspices, further cultivated enthusiasm for America's role in the world among the many who read them.

The informal mutuality between religion, especially in its Protestant forms, and nationalism worked well at home; people assumed that something similar would be a blessing abroad. Schooled for more than a century in the "fair experiment" of religious freedom and alert to any threats to it, evangelical leaders could hardly see any weaknesses in their stance on the way religion and government should be related—legally separated but committed to many ideals in common and open to voluntary coop-

[18] "To the Ends of the Earth: American Protestants in Pursuit of Mission," in *A Century of Church History*, ed. Bowden, 173.

[19] *Missionaries, Chinese, and Diplomats: The American Protestant Missionary Movement in China, 1890–1952* (Princeton: Princeton University Press, 1958), 81–82.

[20] Patricia R. Hill, *The World Their Household: The American Christian Woman's Foreign Mission Movement and Cultural Transformation, 1870–1920* (Ann Arbor: University of Michigan Press, 1985), esp. 3, 14.

eration. "While Protestant leaders were very much aware of the evils resulting from a formal connection between church and state they were, to
say the least, less conscious of the equally grave perils in religious endorsement of a particular way of life," wrote Sidney Mead. "Consequently under the system of official separation of church and state the
denominations eventually found themselves as completely identified with
nationalism and their country's political and economic systems as had
ever been known in Christendom."[21] When American missionaries went
abroad, they often carried some such understanding with them, usually
quite unself-consciously.

Many of the missionaries from other nations had the official support
of their governments, but Americans went as private persons. What they
wanted from their state department was what any citizen abroad
sought—protection of life and property. When J. Bruce Nichols, who has
focused his major attention on religion, refugee work, and American foreign policy since World War II, looked back into the early decades of the
century he noted that "most foreign policy bore the imprimatur of the
dominant Protestant culture" yet found that "the agents of government
and organized, largely Protestant religion carried on their labors in relative independence, secure that they were after all members of the same
family."[22] Missionaries were often unaware of how much they were products of American life in their attitudes toward religion and government,
among other things. In their zeal for the faith and the salvation of those
who had not come under the sway of the Christian gospel and their conviction that theirs was the true and best way, they reflected the concept of
Christian expansion by conquest, often unintentionally creating conflict
in the cultures they encountered.[23] Yet from my own limited researches in
these areas I find myself in agreement with a summary judgment offered
by Arthur Schlesinger, Jr.: "Whatever links the missionary enterprise
might develop along the way with traders or bankers, politicians, gener-
als, or diplomats, however much it might express in its own way the aggressive energies of the West, the desire to save souls remains distinct
from the desire to extend power or to acquire glory or to make money or
to seek adventure or to explore the unknown."[24] Missionaries, part of the

[21] *The Lively Experiment*, 156–57.

[22] *The Uneasy Alliance: Religion, Refugee Work, and U.S. Foreign Policy* (New York:
Oxford University Press, 1988), 9.

[23] E.g., see Joseph L. Grabill, "The 'Invisible' Missionary: A Study in American Foreign
Relations," *Journal of Church and State* 14 (1972): 93–105; and Valentin H. Rabe, "Evangelical Logistics: Mission Support and Resources to 1920," in *The Missionary Enterprise in
China and America*, ed. John K. Fairbank (Cambridge: Harvard University Press, 1974),
89.

[24] "The Missionary Enterprise and Theories of Imperialism," in *Missionary Enterprise*,
ed. Fairbank, 342.

culture in which they had been nurtured, shared many of its values, yet their commitment to faith as they understood it was normally deeply sincere and gave them their priorities and a certain independence of spirit and action as they worked.

In such areas as the former Spanish islands, the Near East, and China the missionary attitude toward matters involving religion and government can be depicted. In his thoughtful study of Catholic influence on American colonial policies, Reuter pointed out how differently the separation of church and state could be interpreted by U.S. government officials and by Catholic leaders in the former Spanish territories, where their church had been legally established. To many officials governing seemed a simple matter of applying constitutional principles: "Colonial administrators would remove all traces of clerical influence from colonial administration and withdraw from the Church all forms of governmental financial support."[25] State-owned property, whatever its use, would go to the state, and church-owned property would be returned. But to many Catholic officials separation meant only that state influence in religious affairs would be removed and the church would be free, for the ancient privileges of patronage that had given the Spanish monarchy a strong hand in church affairs would be revoked. The officials hoped that their church would continue to hold not only strictly ecclesiastical but also income-producing property that had traditionally been used for its support. Between these two extremes was a range of options, settled in somewhat different ways by compromises on both sides. The peace treaty bound the United States to recognize the religion of the inhabitants and to protect all religious property in lands now under their control. But how to meet those obligations while guaranteeing the freedom of religion, and hence opening the way to Protestant missionary activity, raised many problems.

The most serious church-state problem quickly surfaced in the Philippines. The Catholic church, present for nearly four hundred years, had built an impressive archdiocese that claimed six-sevenths of the native population and was staffed by more than sixteen hundred priests, nearly two-thirds of whom were Spanish, the rest native. Even critics of Catholicism were surprised at the depth of devotion found among the Filipinos. Hence it was difficult at first for Americans to understand how such loyal Catholics could so strongly dislike the Spanish friars who served in the priesthood. But for many natives, the friars represented the oppressive bureaucracy of the country under whose rule they had so long lived because, along with their priestly duties, many had also served as government officials and landlords.

The Filipino animosity for the friars became clear when the forceful

---

[25] *Catholic Influence on American Colonial Policies*, 36.

leader Emilio Aguinaldo, with the support of the American forces, proclaimed a provisional government in June 1898. He extended his control among the provinces, and by August he was holding thousands of prisoners, among them well over one hundred Spanish friars, members of four mendicant orders that many Filipinos had found especially obnoxious. Aguinaldo soon clashed with American occupation forces, however, and launched a bitterly fought guerrilla war, in the course of which the clerics were freed by the American forces. That war lasted three years, cost more than four thousand American and far more Filipino lives, and stimulated the critical reaction of the anti-imperialist movement at home. But the question of what to do with the Spanish friars remained unresolved. Some other unfortunate events occurred, such as when American occupation troops looted Catholic institutions. Sensitized by the long struggle against anti-Catholicism, the American Catholic press was quick to pounce on these incidents. There was also much concern over American plans to create a nonsectarian public school system—at a time when the educational stalemate in the United States had hardened.

The situation began to improve with William H. Taft's appointment as head of a commission that replaced the military government in 1901; he then served as the first civilian governor general of the islands. Through long and complicated negotiations that included a trip to Rome, he proved instrumental in helping the Catholic church not only to recover most of its church properties but also to receive compensation for some of its lost income-producing lands. Taft was able to help American Catholics understand and cooperate in the development of the islands' public school system—no mean achievement in view of the school dilemma in the United States.

Taft also learned to work well with Theodore Roosevelt when the latter succeeded to the presidency in September 1901 after McKinley's assassination. Roosevelt had learned the political lesson of the importance of the Catholic vote and was sensitive to criticism from that quarter. Throughout his career he maintained contacts with many Catholics, among both the laity and the clergy, and consistently opposed bigotry. Taft and Roosevelt saw that in the Philippines the issue of returning the friars to Spain was primarily a political and not a religious matter. The two leaders were also convinced that suitable compensation to the monastic orders for the loss of their lands could be negotiated; the sum was later fixed at $7,239,000. The Philippine Government Bill, providing for a permanent civil government until the United States deemed the Filipinos ready for self-rule, was debated in both houses of Congress largely on party and not religious lines and passed in June 1902.[26]

[26] Ibid., 60–136. See also Reuter, "William Howard Taft and the Separation of Church

Roosevelt and Taft continued to be responsive to Catholic opinion and cooperated with members of the hierarchy, particularly with Ireland and Gibbons. Reuter concluded that "the willingness of Roosevelt to practically bend over backwards in favor of Catholics in the Philippines prompted the Papacy to meet the Americans halfway. In January 1903, Leo XIII issued an encyclical directed to the Church in the Philippines."[27] It provided for a new Philippine hierarchy, separated from Spanish clerical authority. Four new dioceses were added to the existing three, all under the authority of the archbishop of Manila who was responsible to Rome. The remaining Spanish bishops resigned, and vacancies were filled by American clergymen. Continuing problems were faced openly and cooperatively on both sides. Thus, America's new role in the world had clearly involved the government in complex negotiations with the Catholic church. An expanding colonial bureaucracy in the islands became part of the governmental machinery for carrying out decisions made in Washington, Rome, and Manila. The separation of church and state was carried out, but the institutions of government and religion continued to have limited relations with each other.

Protestantism was little known in the Philippines before 1898, but representatives of both denominational and nondenominational agencies were soon on the scene. Army chaplains and YMCA leaders were conducting services within a week after the occupation of Manila. The latter first worked with troops but later reached out to American and Filipino civilians. The American Bible Society quickly spied out the land and in 1899 appointed a Methodist minister as its first official representative as it set about the work of translating the Bible into various Filipino tongues. Perhaps not surprising at the time when a Methodist was in the White House, that denomination eagerly seized the new opportunities that had opened up. The secretary for foreign missions, Adna B. Leonard, called for a massive response. In September 1898 an article in the *Methodist Review* spoke boldly: "There is no chance to shut one's eyes to the relation of missions to the success of governmental colonizing schemes."[28] The bishop of India and Southeast Asia for the (northern) Methodist Episcopal Church visited the Philippines early in 1901, opened a church, and licensed a former missionary who had already been at work there as a local preacher. Soon missionaries sent by both the woman's and the

---

and State in the Philippines," *Journal of Church and State* 24 (1982): 105–17; and Peter G. Gowing, "The Disentanglement of Church and State Early in the American Regime in the Philippines," in *Studies in Philippine Church History*, ed. Gerald H. Anderson (Ithaca: Cornell University Press, 1969), 203–22.

[27] *Catholic Influence on American Colonial Policies*, 152–53.

[28] As quoted by Frederick M. Norwood, *The Story of American Methodism: A History of the United Methodists and their Relations* (Nashville: Abingdon, 1974), 347.

general mission boards arrived, and the Methodists quickly outnumbered other Protestant bodies. At least fifty missionaries had participated in the work by 1916, when the church claimed some forty-five thousand members.

The Presbyterian Church U.S.A. sent more missionaries between 1899 and 1916, but their total church membership was much smaller. The Episcopal church under the leadership of Charles H. Brent, missionary bishop from 1902 to 1918, decided not to actively proselytize among Catholics and focused its attention primarily on the American and European communities, with some outreach among the Chinese and the non-Christian natives of the mountains. The Disciples of Christ, Northern Baptists, Christian and Missionary Alliance, Seventh-day Adventists, United Brethren in Christ, and Congregationalists were also involved in missionary outreach in the islands.

Kenton J. Clymer, whose work on *Protestant Missionaries in the Philippines, 1898–1916* is most informative and from which much of the previous paragraph has been drawn, reported that "the missionaries constituted an important and articulate segment of the American colonial population." Not only did they help shape attitudes both at home and in their chosen field about Filipino culture and about what Americans were doing there, but also "on occasion they helped shape policy as well. They helped reconcile Filipinos to their new fate and were allies of the government in what both perceived as a 'civilizing' mission."[29] The missionaries saw themselves as the conscience of the American presence and could judge others from their homeland harshly for not living up to what for them was the best in the tradition of the United States. Although missionaries held a considerable range of attitudes toward Catholicism, they generally reflected the negative views so familiar in their home constituencies and agreed that "almost no-one doubted that Catholicism, whatever its historical contributions, was a deficient form of Christianity" (96).

With some exceptions, missionaries in the early years of the century did not think the Filipinos would be ready for independence in the foreseeable future. As missionary work in the islands was part of a worldwide Christian crusade, those who served were not formally agents of the national purpose. Yet there was little doubt that most missionaries freely accepted an "ideological compatibility between church and state" and enjoyed close relations with American governmental agencies (153). A prominent Methodist, Homer C. Stuntz, believed that an interdenominational college he was planning would "be a desirable ally of the Government" (155). Most missionaries did not oppose the work of the military in deal-

[29] *Protestant Missionaries in the Philippines, 1898–1916: An Inquiry into the American Colonial Mentality* (Urbana: University of Illinois Press, 1986), 7–8.

ing with the "insurrection," though they disagreed about how widely the insurgents were supported by the Filipinos. They expressed little objection to herding civilians into "reconcentration" camps in the army's pursuit of the rebels and little patience with anti-imperialists at home. Not without some conscientious criticism of the work of certain government officials, some of whom they felt favored Catholic views unfairly, missionaries generally worked well with them.

As at home, there were tensions over the government's effort to maintain a religiously neutral school system, and missionaries often "attempted to create a Protestant presence near the public schools in the form of kindergartens, dispensaries, social clubs, and above all dormitories" (165). In the main, Clymer concluded, the missionaries applauded the civil government's attempts to remake Philippine society along American lines and helped reconcile Filipinos to the new situation. The missionary presence was appreciated by many colonial administrators, for "they, too, served the interests of the state, if not always consciously" (173). Despite some tensions, patterns of cooperation between religious and governmental agencies were being worked out under the formal recognition of the separation of church and state.

Although American missionaries were eager to spread their faith in America's new territories, their enthusiasm for work in lands under other flags was undiminished. This was especially true of China, the chosen field of many societies and individuals. By 1900 China had replaced the Near East and India as the principal target for missionary endeavors. Without the Western invasion, Christian outreach would not have been possible there, yet many missionaries sometimes seemed to critics of that time and since to be a little too ready to rely on Western arms in times of crisis. Stuart Creighton Miller has extensively documented his view that for the last sixty years of the nineteenth century "every Western invasion of China was almost unanimously conceived of by these American missionaries as an act of Providence."[30] When riots against the foreign presence erupted in the 1890s, some called outright for Anglo-Saxon armed assault to "teach the Chinese that British and American blood is *sacred*" (269).

When the Boxer Rebellion of 1900 included foreign missions as targets, missionaries welcomed the Western armies with applause as they marched on Peking.[31] Operating under protection of treaties between Western and Chinese governments, missionaries were much concerned that their rights and privileges and those of their converts be kept intact.

---

[30] "Ends and Means: Missionary Justification of Force in Nineteenth Century China," in *Missionary Enterprise*, ed. Fairbank, 254.

[31] Schlesinger, "The Missionary Enterprise and Theories of Imperialism," 357.

They were often critical of the State Department for failure to defend their treaty rights forcefully enough. Sidney A. Forsythe found that in the China sections of *Foreign Relations of the United States* for 1895 to 1905 relative to China, about half the materials were devoted to the missionaries and those they won to Christianity, but he also observed that about four times as many missionaries as other Americans were then there. A familiar Protestant bias showed in the too easy assumption of many missionaries that the Boxer uprising was anti-Catholic and not primarily anti-Western.[32]

Characteristically, missionaries avoided explicitly political questions in their efforts to win followers and improve the quality of life. "China was treated as a moral problem," wrote Paul Varg, "a country to be encouraged to adopt Christian values, technology, popular education, and constitutionalism."[33] Sure of themselves and intent on their main task, missionaries often failed to realize their actual involvement with political realities as many Chinese perceived it. M. Searle Bates analyzed the last collective theological expression of Protestant missionaries in China, produced with no significant dissent at a conference in 1907. In a memorial to the Chinese government, those present were speaking primarily of money when they proclaimed that "from our Governments we receive nothing at all." Those in the home base countries who supported missions, they insisted, prayed daily that God would bless the rulers and people of all countries not yet Christian and make them good and prosperous. They were convinced that "into all this no political or similar motive enters. . . . Devotion to Jesus Christ, a desire to see all the world worshipping the God of Heaven and to see evil practices everywhere done away, is the sole motive for the support of missions."[34] A second memorial of the conference petitioned the government for complete religious liberty for all classes of Chinese Christians. Relating the ethical argument for religious freedom to the well-being and good name of China, they argued that such liberty would promote peace, goodwill, loyalty, and patriotism throughout the empire.

What these missionaries perceived as liberating often appeared as disruptive in a traditional culture where family ties were strong and the elders revered. In the first decade of the new century, however, after the Boxer Rebellion had been put down, missionaries were at their peak of religious and cultural influence as they helped nurture a new generation of patriots and reformers in their churches, associations, schools, and

[32] *An American Missionary Community in China, 1895–1905* (Cambridge: Harvard University Press, 1971), 60–79.

[33] *Missionaries, Chinese, and Diplomats*, 324.

[34] "The Theology of American Missionaries in China, 1900–1950," in *Missionary Enterprise*, ed. Fairbank, 148.

hospitals. At home and in the field, hope for the Christianization of China seemed realizable.

Relationships between American expansionism and missionary fervor was also evident in the Near East, as it was then called, in Palestine, Syria, and Turkey. Pioneer work in Palestine was undertaken by the American Board of Commissioners for Foreign Missions (ABCFM), which had been founded in 1810. At the outset it was supported by not only the Congregational churches but also other denominations of the Reformed or Calvinist tradition, some of which, along with others, later developed their own missions in the region. It was soon discovered, after the first missionaries sailed in 1819, that maintaining missionary work among Jews in the Holy Land was difficult, but greater response was found among the Arabs, especially in surrounding areas. Various Christian missionary efforts in the region were undertaken throughout the century.

As in other parts of the world, missionaries in the Near East, according to Joseph L. Grabill, "disavowed union of Church and State, but not of Christianity and culture."[35] He also found that in the earlier twentieth century as before, their goal "was still primarily an unconscious mixture of Protestantism and Americanism" (34). Because of the tragic massacres of Armenians in Turkey in the 1890s, leaders of the ABCFM at the home base became increasingly involved with the state department, through both extensive correspondence and conferences with the secretary of state and other diplomatic personnel in Washington. The board's foreign secretary, James L. Barton, its dominant figure for thirty-five years, was especially effective in speaking for missionary interests to governmental leaders, in part because of opportunities opened through the influence of George F. Hoar, a senator who was also a board member. Candidates suggested by the board for diplomatic and consular positions were appointed in many cases. Throughout much of the 1890s the Congregationalist Josiah Strong, while still in his post with the Evangelical Alliance, worked closely with the board in organizing a "missionary lobby group that concerned itself with Turkish affairs" and served "as an ecclesiastical politician involved with the actualities of foreign policy decision-making."[36] The group's activities in Washington set precedents for continuing relationships in the twentieth century.

The Turks had long oppressed the Armenians, whose history as Christians goes back to the early centuries. Ottoman opposition to this minority, located largely in the mountainous areas in eastern Turkey, boiled over in the Armenian atrocities in the mid-1890s during which perhaps

[35] *Protestant Diplomacy and the Near East: Missionary Influence on American Policy, 1810–1927* (Minneapolis: University of Minnesota Press, 1971), 35.

[36] James Eldin Reed, "American Foreign Policy, The Politics of Missions and Josiah Strong, 1890–1900," *Church History* 41 (1972): 232.

fifty thousand lives were lost. When it was rumored during these massacres that missionaries were to be expelled from Turkey, Lyman Abbott insisted that it was the duty of the American government to protect them, "and, if necessary, to spend its last dollar and call out its last soldier for that purpose."[37] Expenditures of the ABCFM, with its chain of schools and charitable institutions in Turkey, were then larger than any American commercial investments there. In fact, the protection of missionary life and property depended on the British military presence in Turkey. "This reliance upon British power strengthened the missionaries' consciousness of a worldwide Anglo-Saxon community," Reed has concluded, "and it caused them to be ashamed of the United States and contemptuous of its policy of isolationism."[38] Strong also formed a committee of the Evangelical Alliance to coordinate the publication and political activities of the religious organizations operating in the Ottoman Empire. To some extent it "was a political front for the American Board, which preferred to stay behind the scenes" (236). American gunboats were ordered to Turkish waters, but sending troops inland was wholly impracticable.

The episode nevertheless showed that a moral crusade could effectively arouse public opinion and challenge the isolationist cast of mind. "Strong, Barton and other missionary-minded persons began to advocate an internationalist and interventionist foreign policy" (237). They lobbied in Washington on behalf of their interests in Turkey during the McKinley administration. The tension that their commitment to the principle of the separation of church and state posed for them was resolved by distinguishing between the missionaries as evangelists and citizens: in the first role they did not seek any help from their government, but in the second they expected the United States to protect life, property, and rights as defined by international treaties. Although popular concern over the Turkish situation was eclipsed for a time with the coming of the Spanish-American War, the incident showed the difficulty in separating religious from certain political concerns as the missionary crusade continued to escalate dramatically with the opening of the new century. The problem was to be demonstrated again during World War I, when a new wave of Armenian massacres dwarfed the previous one and pressed Barton and others once again into role of lobbyists.

In his book *From the Old Diplomacy to the New*, Robert L. Beisner referred to the great increase in the number of American missionaries abroad in the last decades of the nineteenth century, observed how their presence overseas helped U.S. commerce abroad, acquainted many of

---

[37] As quoted by Ernest R. May, *Imperial Democracy: The Emergence of America as a Great Power* (New York: Harcourt, Brace & World, 1961), 29.

[38] "American Foreign Policy," 234.

those back home with places they had known little about, planted the seeds of internationalism, and evoked a genuine interest in other peoples on the part of many fellow citizens. In doing these and other things, missionaries were contributing to a new sense of what their nation's mission in the world might be. "In effect," Beisner declared, "the missionaries were the first converts to a new definition of the American mission."[39] The old passive idea that the United States should be a model for other countries was giving way to a concept of an active role for the nation to further the progress of civilization. The missionary enterprise was only one factor in the development of a "new paradigm in American foreign policy" (77), but this important factor helped prepare many to welcome a larger role for their nation in world affairs. As missionary agencies went about their primary work of evangelizing, educating, and healing, a significant by-product of their activities was often the development of closer relationships between religious and governmental institutions.

An Age of Confidence

As the new century opened, though aware of growing Catholic strength, Protestant Christianity still seemed the religious persuasion most in tune with the major cultural and political opinion makers in American life. Its leaders were confident that their influence would continue to predominate. When William E. Dodge, prominent in business, philanthropy, and many Protestant causes, was helping prepare for the international conference on missions that met in New York in 1900, he expressed the mood of confidence shared by many leaders of American society as they faced the new century: "We are going into a century more full of hope, and promise, and opportunity than any period in the world's history."[40]

That sense of confidence was pervasive among the movers and shakers of the time in both religion and government. Henry Seidel Canby once reflected on the many persons growing up in the late nineteenth century who were so sure of themselves and speculated that the regularities in the pace of life of middle-and upper-class Americans during the period were responsible: "It was this familiar movement, this routine with a certainty of repetition, that inspired a confidence in a patterned universe missing today. . . . Confidence is a habit which must be acquired young and from an environment that is constant and rhythmically continuous."[41] By the time Canby penned those words, he knew that "our confidence was an

---

[39] *From the Old Diplomacy to the New, 1865–1900*, 2d ed. (New York: Thomas Y. Crowell, 1975), 76.

[40] *Ecumenical Missionary Conference in New York*, 1: 11.

[41] *American Memoir* (Boston: Houghton Mifflin, 1947), 29, 34.

illusion, but like most illusions it had many of the benefits of a fact" (129). To many leading figures in religion and government confidence seemed an assured fact when the bells rang in the new century, for many leaders had been steeped in those backgrounds of regularity that had helped develop their sense of confidence and given them a commonality of interest.

Those present at that great Ecumenical Missionary Conference in New York in 1900 could feel close to the centers of power as they were addressed by a past, present, and future president of the United States—Benjamin Harrison, William McKinley, and Theodore Roosevelt. Of those Americans who were leading the missionary crusade at the turn of the century Paul Varg wrote, "Bred in comfortable urban middle-class homes, or more often amid the happy circumstances of well-established families in small towns or on farms, this generation had no squeamish doubts about the superiority of American life. Its excellences they attributed to the influence of Protestant Christianity."[42] He added, "And it must be said that missionaries were not unique in this confidence in the universal application of Christianity and democracy—most Americans seem to have shared this faith" (76). In 1901, Woodrow Wilson, a son of the manse then serving as a professor of history before entering politics, sounded the notes of national superiority: "No other modern nation has been schooled as we have been in big undertakings and the mastery of novel difficulties. We have become confirmed in energy, in resourcefulness, in practical proficiency, in self-confidence."[43] Leaders of both religion and government knew they faced many difficulties, but they were confident they would overcome them.

Although religion and government were formally separate, there was much informal yet effective agreement between them on the goals of American life. Henry F. May has summarized the "national credo" of the time as belief in the reality, certainty, and eternity of moral values, in progress, and in culture. He concluded that more than most periods of American history, "the early twentieth century was a time of sureness and unity, at least on the surface of American life."[44] Beneath that surface were many disadvantaged people and great tensions, but at the top those guiding an aggressive, missionary-minded Protestantism and those directing the affairs of government shared much and drew strength from one another in a time of remarkable expansion. It was a time when religious leaders like Josiah Strong could quote Lyman Abbott's *Outlook* in com-

[42] *Missionaries, Chinese, Diplomats*, 3–4.

[43] "Democracy and Efficiency," as quoted by Richard M. Abrams, ed., *The Issues of the Populist and Progressive Eras, 1892–1912* (New York: Harper & Row, 1969), 274–75.

[44] *The End of American Innocence: A Study of the First Years of Our Own Time, 1912–1917* (New York: Knopf, 1969), 18.

mending the military: "The army among Anglo-Saxon peoples is no longer a mere instrument of destruction. It is a great reconstructive organization. . . . It is reorganizing society on a basis of physical health, fairly paid industry, honest administration, popular rights, and public education, in Cuba."[45]

It was a time when a justice of the Supreme Court, David Brewer, was still presenting in lectures and in print the "Christian nation" thesis of the decision he wrote for the Supreme Court in 1892 and envisioning that it would lead to peace:

> Is it not a great thing to be a leader among the nations in the effort to bring on that day when the sword shall be beaten into the ploughshare and the spear into the pruning hook, and when war shall cease? And the more thoroughly this republic is filled with the spirit of the gospel, the more universal the rule of Christianity in the hearts of our people, the more certainly will she ever be the welcome leader in movements for peace among the nations.[46]

Such expressions of confidence among religious and public leaders were quite typical as the door closed on one century and opened on another.

[45] *Outlook* 62 (July 29, 1899): 699, quoted by Strong, *Expansion*, 280–81.
[46] *The United States a Christian Nation* (Philadelphia: John C. Winston, 1905), 91. For the decision of 1892, see Chap. 1.

5

The Spirit of Reform in Politics and Religion

THE OPENING decades of the twentieth century in America are often discussed under such headings as "the progressive era" or the "progressive age." Leaders of progressivism who sang its praises at the movement's height could see it as the opening of a new epoch. Woodrow Wilson himself exclaimed in his campaign addresses of 1912, published as *The New Freedom* the following year, "Now this is nothing short of a new social age, a new era of human relationships, a new stage-setting for the drama of life."[1] Because progressivism seemed so radically new to many of its conspicuous exponents when it was politically dominant in the years 1905 to 1917, some earlier interpretations of it, by both its leaders and historians who fell under its spell, minimized the larger setting out of which it came. Because many of progressivism's promises, however, were fulfilled only in part and some not at all, its influence on later developments has also sometimes been minimized. Among the by-products of the progressive period was an increased emphasis on the positive role of the state, which had implications for the interrelationships of religion and government.

When Richard Hofstadter at midcentury wrote his widely read book, *The Age of Reform*, his interpretive analysis covered the decades from the 1890s deep into the 1930s—a considerably wider span than the years when the progressive movement was politically and culturally strong. He carefully noted how previous reforming impulses, such as the reform Republican faction of the 1880s known as the Mugwumps and the more radical agrarian Populists of the 1890s, together with the reactions to the hard times of that decade and the writings of the early muckrakers, helped shape the progressive movement. He was careful to emphasize that the latter "did not become nationwide until the years after 1901." Indeed, then it set its reformist stamp on the political parties and the national life until "participation in the war put an end" to the movement.[2] But the concern for reform did not disappear, and in the radically altered

---

[1] *The New Freedom: A Call for the Emancipation of the Generous Energies of a People*, ed. William E. Leuchtenberg (Englewood Cliffs, N.J.: Prentice-Hall, 1961), 21.

[2] *The Age of Reform: From Bryan to F.D.R.* (New York: Vintage Books, 1955), 165, 275. See also his *The Progressive Historians: Turner, Beard, Parrington* (New York: Knopf, 1968).

situation of the 1930s some legacies from the earlier movement had a continuing influence.

Various strands in the nation's religious life contributed to the rise of the progressive movement and flourished with its expanding spirit of reform. A thoughtful theological educator who lived through the period opened a chapter on "the crusading church at home and abroad":

> The first fifteen years of the twentieth century may sometime be remembered in America as the Age of Crusades. There were a superabundance of zeal, a sufficiency of good causes, unusual moral idealism, excessive confidence in mass movements and leaders with rare gifts of popular appeal. The people were ready to cry "God wills it" and set out for world peace, prohibition, the Progressive Party, the "New Freedom" or "the World for Christ in this Generation." The air was full of banners, and the trumpets called from every camp. It was a brave time in which to be alive.
>
> The churches shared the general crusading zeal and inaugurated enterprises of their own.[3]

The agencies of government and the institutions of religion were both increasing in number and scope. Although conventional understandings of their relationship outwardly changed little in the progressive years, in fact contacts were increasing in new ways. Those religious leaders who had been calling for a more positive view of the state to deal with twentieth-century crises were finding a larger following. Of course they faced sharp criticism, but they confidently believed that they were preparing the way for a better future for both church and state.

The Progressive Movement

Progressivism in politics is not easy to define, for its roots were diverse. Not only did it draw on previous reform traditions in American life, but it was also much influenced by fresh currents in the new disciplines of the social sciences, such as sociology and political science, and the stimulus of social Christianity.[4] Those who have attempted to clarify the nature of political progressivism often refer to the many strands it attempted to weave together. Walter Dean Burnham, for example, concentrating on the years from 1905 to 1915, observed that "this movement is a remarkable mixture of contradictory elements: a striving for mass democracy on the one hand and corporationist-technocratic elitism on the other."[5] This

[3] Gaius Glenn Atkins, *Religion in Our Times* (New York: Round Table Press, 1932), 156.
[4] See Chap. 3.
[5] "The System of 1896," in *The Evolution of American Electoral Systems*, ed. Paul Kleppner et al. (Westport, Conn.: Greenwood, 1981), 166.

movement of many paradoxes combined romanticism and realism, materialistic concerns with humanistic values.

Political progressivism was reformist, not radically reconstructionist. Among its followers the movement numbered many idealists, humanitarians, municipal reformers, and social Christians. Protestants were notably conspicuous in the movement. Szasz reported that a 1906 survey found that only 15 percent of a large number of social crusaders were not somehow identified as evangelical Protestants as then defined.[6] In a wide-ranging study, Robert C. Crunden has observed that, although Catholics, Jews, and people of no religious affiliation found progressive goals attractive, still "Protestantism provided the chief thrust and defined the perimeters of discourse."[7] A number of its lay and clerical figures were often busy at the firing lines: William McGuire King has noted that "Protestant reform leadership played a prominent role in municipal and civic reform during the Progressive Era."[8] And in a work focused on prominent progressive intellectuals who were foremost articulators of the movement's ideals—including such persons of Protestant background as William Allen White, Jane Addams, John Dewey, Josiah Royce, Charles H. Cooley, Robert Park—Jean B. Quandt has noted how they employed familiar religious language in their speeches and writings at that time. "Thus the modern means of communication not only became the agents of scientific reform and social harmony," she concluded, "but also the redemptive agents of the kingdom of God in America. The identification of religion and culture was nearly complete."[9]

Not only did Protestant perspectives influence progressivist thought and action, but progressivism also had an impact on many religious leaders and groups, especially those among Protestants who had affinities with liberal thinking. Thus within many denominations progressive viewpoints on culture and reform contended with older voluntaristic values and political strategies, in a number of instances making a noticeable difference in the perceptions and actions of certain communions. The process, long in the making, became especially visible in the early twentieth century. As cooperation among many denominations took a decisive new turn in that century's first decade, unitive agencies of the churches also often carried a progressive stamp.

The religious cast of progressivism, even as it enlisted the support of

[6] *Divided Mind*, 43.

[7] *Ministers of Reform: The Progressives' Achievement in American Civilization, 1889–1920* (New York: Basic Books, 1982), ix–x.

[8] "The Reform Establishment and the Ambiguities of Influence," in *Between the Times*, ed. Hutchison, 123.

[9] *From the Small Town to the Great Community: The Social Thought of the Progressive Intellectuals* (New Brunswick, N.J.: Rutgers University Press, 1970), 75.

many clergy and laity in its reforms, was generally stated in broad and nondenominational accents. Edward A. Ross, for example, had studied under Ely at Johns Hopkins but later changed his field from economics to sociology. In 1903 he published a major work, *Social Control*, and opted for a gentle approach that would persuade individuals to moderate their own ends in favor of community needs. He, too, urged the seeking of the kingdom of God—but in the context of what he called social religion, sharply to be distinguished from the conventional institutional religion he roundly criticized.[10] Agreement on generalities did not mean unanimity when it came to specific programs and solutions. Those who identified themselves as progressives primarily because of their broadly religious concerns included, but were not limited to, a number of prominent social gospel leaders. They wanted the powers of the democratic state used for the public good, with particular attention to the underprivileged.

Among others who flocked to progressivism, however, were those who did so primarily for other than humanitarian, idealistic, or religious reasons. Some historians writing since 1950 have concluded that earlier interpretations of the movement leaned too heavily on the views and claims of some of its conspicuous and articulate leaders. These more recent interpreters, who have focused more on the actual practices of economic, political, and social groups, have gathered considerable evidence to call attention to other aspects of progressivism. In a detailed study of the realities of urban reform—a primary goal for progressives—Samuel P. Hays, for example, found that "the leading business groups in each city and the professional men closely allied with them initiated and dominated municipal movements."[11] From its origins, as Richard M. Abrams has pointed out, there were two impetuses in the proposals for reform in the cities. One emanated from the settlement house and social worker movements, which stressed the needs of the poor for such services as soup kitchens, vagrants' lodgings, tenement inspection, parks, and playgrounds. "The other and more powerful impetus," Abrams concluded, "originated in boards of trade, merchants' associations, and chambers of commerce," which pressed for honesty, efficiency, and economy in urban administration.[12] In a more sweeping interpretation of progressivism,

[10] *Social Control: A Survey of the Foundations of Order* (New York: Macmillan, 1901). For an informative discussion of Ross, see R. Jackson Wilson, *In Quest of Community: Social Philosophy in the United States, 1860–1920* (New York: Oxford University Press, 1968), 98–112.

[11] "The Politics of Municipal Government in the Progressive Era," *Pacific Northwest Quarterly* 55 (October 1964): 1157–69, as reprinted in *Progressivism: The Critical Issues*, ed. David M. Kennedy (Boston: Little Brown, 1971), 91.

[12] In the introduction to chap. 3 of *Issues of the Populist and Progressive Eras*, ed. Abrams, 82.

with considerable focus on the governmental regulatory reform agencies, Gabriel Kolko declared:

> Because of their positive theory of the state, key business elements managed to define the basic form and content of the major federal legislation that was enacted. They provided direction to existing opinion for regulation, but in a number of crucial cases they were the first to initiate that sentiment. They were able to define such sentiment because, in the last analysis, the major political leaders of the Progressive Era—[Theodore] Roosevelt, Taft, and Wilson—were sufficiently conservative to respond to their initiatives.[13]

That the motivation of those caught up in progressivism was complex is clear. But the movement also incorporated several differing general approaches to reform. In the heat of political struggle, these various perspectives and the inevitable tensions among them were often obscured.

The major interpretations of progressivism put forward since the 1950s have stirred up much debate among historians, but they illustrate compellingly that the movement was indeed a web of many strands. Various passages in David M. Kennedy's useful collection of essays on the subject illustrate that some of its interpreters have emphasized its upper-class orientation, others its middle-class nature, and still others its appeal to the lower classes.[14] As James Weinstein has rightly made clear, "responsibility" was a key term in the vocabulary of progressives, but its use again showed the complexity of the movement. Some stressed society's responsibility to individuals or underprivileged classes, and others meant the responsibility of all to maintain and increase the efficiency of the existing social order.[15] The three authors of a 1977 book on progressivism shared much but disagreed sharply on some matters of interpretation. For example, John C. Burnham and John D. Buenker believed it helpful to see the progressive period marked more by the work of shifting coalitions than by a single movement; without wholly disagreeing, Robert M. Crunden thought such an emphasis concentrated too much on the political side of the wider movement and hence did not see clearly enough what he himself had discovered—"that progressivism was essentially religious."[16] But despite its inner complexities, like other such movements at critical junctures in our history, progressivism exerted pervasive influence on American life as it cut across class and party lines and won the support of large segments of the population.

[13] Reprinted from his *The Triumph of Conservatism* (Glencoe, Ill.: Free Press, 1963), in *Progressivism*, ed. Kennedy, 134.

[14] *Progressivism*, see esp. his introduction, vii–xiv, and essays by George E. Mowry, Alfred D. Chandler, Jr., J. Joseph Huthmacher, and Samuel P. Hays, 65–108.

[15] *The Corporate Ideal in the Liberal State* (Boston: Beacon, 1968), esp. x–xi.

[16] *Progressivism* (Cambridge, Mass.: Schenkman, 1977), 75; see also 5, 31, 107–9.

Gaining strength in the early twentieth century, the progressive movement became a political force that made its way up through local and
state levels to the national scene. Progressivism pressed for specific political reforms to deal with social problems resulting from the unregulated
expansion of cities and their new industries. The movement used extensively the familiar techniques of voluntary societies as it agitated for
changes at many levels through various channels. Although by no means
achieving all its ardent supporters hoped for, a number of its legislative
goals were attained. For example, it secured amendments for a federal
income tax, the direct election of senators, prohibition, and woman suf-
frage; passed antitrust legislation; formed regulatory commissions in the
areas of transportation and manufacturing; advanced the cause of con-
servation; influenced the restriction of immigration; helped to create a
juvenile justice system; and in many states instituted the direct primary,
the initiative, and the referendum.[17]

When the ambitious Theodore Roosevelt became president after the
assassination of McKinley, Roosevelt shrewdly worked to retain the support of business and financial interests while encouraging many progressive measures. A convinced Protestant himself, he increased the respect
he had earned from many Catholics because of his policies in the Philippines and through certain domestic measures, both of which enabled him
to bring prominent individuals of various backgrounds associated with
progressive causes into government service. In his victory at the polls in
1904, when he won his own term as president by a sizable plurality, he
was successful in "areas of large concentrations of Catholic voters, areas
that had supported Bryan in 1896 and 1900."[18] He took this victory as a
mandate for progressivism, at least as he interpreted it; thus, some historians date the beginning of the era as late as 1905. From then until the
election of 1920, the major presidential candidates waved the progressive
banner as the movement reached its peak.

Taft, well known for his achievements in foreign policy and carefully
chosen by Roosevelt, readily defeated Bryan as the latter made his third
try for the presidency in 1908. Although Bryan was more forthright as a
progressive, Taft was committed to a position much like that of his popular predecessor. At the outset he showed special concern for small business interests and promised to maintain the regulatory machinery for re-
straining lawbreakers and curbing the trusts. But as his term wore on he
backed away from some progressive policies favored by Roosevelt. The
latter sought the Republican nomination in 1912, but Taft, by then

[17] The literature on progressivism is vast; for a clear, compact treatment of its history and
achievements with a helpful bibliographical essay, see Arthur S. Link and Richard L. Mc-
Cormick, *Progressivism* (Arlington Heights, Ill.: Harlan Davidson, 1983).
[18] Reuter, *Catholic Influence on American Colonial Policies*, 135.

deeply entrenched among the conservative old guard, won. Thereupon, Roosevelt, placarding his progressive principles under such headings as the "new nationalism" and the "square deal" and declaring himself as fit as a bull moose, became the nominee of a third party that claimed the name Progressive but was familiarly known by the "Bull Moose" symbol. Its national convention in 1912 enthusiastically embraced many overtones of the crusading Protestantism of the time as it sang "Onward Christian Soldiers" and closed with the Doxology.

After a long struggle, the Democratic convention also produced a champion of progressivism, Woodrow Wilson, former professor and university president and current reform governor of New Jersey. Son of a Southern Presbyterian minister, he effectively appealed to moral and religious principles as he articulated his program under the banner of the "New Freedom." He attracted and held the majority of Democratic progressives and won decisively over Roosevelt, leaving Taft a poor third. Although Wilson had won less than 42 percent of the popular vote, he claimed the combined Democratic and Bull Moose votes as a clear progressive mandate for the new Democratic administration.

Wilson promptly pressed for legislation to put the progressive ideas into practice, but his first moves were somewhat cautious, in part because of the traditional Democratic concerns for state's rights. But as the election of 1916 approached and the Republicans reunited, the administration acted more forcefully on many progressive measures and enlarged the national government's regulatory functions. Wilson pointed out that in fact the Democrats had come close to carrying out not only their own platform of 1912 but also that of the fading Progressive party. As a movement, progressivism was at a point of high influence when Wilson won again in 1916 against the Republicans who had nominated Charles Evans Hughes. As former governor of New York, Hughes could point to some important reforms in the Empire state. But Wilson attracted votes from customary followers of what was then the larger party not only because of his national reform policies but also because of his role in keeping the nation out of the terrible European war—a crucial factor in a very close election.

Five months after election, however, Wilson did lead America into World War I. This turn of events posed a new set of challenges for the reforming spirit of progressivism and markedly increased the growing power of the federal government. The latter development, in part at least, was built on steps already taken under progressive leadership. During both Republican and Democratic administrations certain reforming proposals of those who had been advocating a positive state had been implemented, usually not as fully as their proponents had sought but far more than their opponents wanted. Foundations were laid for what later became known as the welfare state. The network of governmental agencies and bureaus at national, state, and local levels was spreading. Many who believed in and worked for these reforms did so on the basis of religious and moral conviction. Such emphases in the messages of the presidents and other political leaders reinforced this interpenetration of political and religious goals characteristic of the progressive era. A broad understanding of the progressive period requires that I explore a topic that illumines both the political and religious aspects of the period.

The Flowering of Social Christianity

In the exciting years of the early twentieth century, as immigrants continued to pour in and cities continued to expand, progressive politics and social interpretations of Christianity mutually reinforced each other. David B. Danbom, even adopting the term "Christian progressivism" to highlight this phenomenon, noted that for a time it "was the dominant strain of reform."[19] His usage forcefully dramatizes the ease with which many Christian individuals and groups played important roles in progressive politics. But not all those who were significantly influenced by social Christian movements of the early twentieth century and shared in the spirit of reform can properly be called political progressives. Hence this section follows the more familiar and somewhat broader heading of "social Christianity."

Social Christianity became conspicuous in the progressive period especially in what have come to be called the mainline Protestant denominations.[20] Numerically, it remained a minority movement under active and articulate leaders, but social Christianity became a pervasive force beyond those who self-consciously identified themselves with it. Its speakers were heard on many platforms, its articles and books were widely read, its teachers took places on seminary faculties. Social Christian teachings and programs were carried increasingly not only in the familiar channels of congregational and denominational life but also in certain new institutional forms that had been generated. For example, social Christianity was influential in many burgeoning settlement houses of the period, some of which had been founded in the 1890s in close relation to seminaries, such as Robert A. Woods's Andover House in Boston, Graham Taylor's Chicago Commons, and Gaylord S. White's Union Settlement Association in New York. A growing number of "institutional churches" that

---

[19] "The World of Hope": Progressives and the Struggle for an Ethical Public Life (Philadelphia: Temple University Press, 1987), 80.

[20] See Chap. 3.

conducted athletic, educational, and self-help programs along with religious ministrations in crowded urban areas further advanced its cause. Furthermore, the social spirit became a force in many of the older church-related mission and philanthropic institutions such as hospitals and homes for orphans and the elderly.

Though the term "social gospel" was not familiarly used until the twentieth century, it is sometimes applied to the whole many-sided, significant social movement of the churches since the Civil War. In his pioneering history published in 1940, C. Howard Hopkins used not only social gospel but also the term social Christianity. Henry F. May chose social Christianity to define the broader Protestant social Christian movement that he analyzed as having three main identifiable strands: conservative, progressive (the social gospel), and radical social Christianity. May's work focused on the later nineteenth century, but his typology also fits the early twentieth.[21]

The first type remained largely identified with conservative evangelical Protestants, many of whom remained within their denominational settings, where they helped support home missions and rescue mission efforts. Others became members of separate denominations engaged largely in urban religious and social work, such as the Salvation Army, the Volunteers of America, and the Christian and Missionary Alliance. Although most efforts of this type were not noted for challenging directly the individualistic social ethics inherited from the nineteenth century, they did identify with the needy, engage in social reform movements, and even occasionally and sharply criticize the social order and plead for a greater measure of justice for the dispossessed. In an important study of this extensive but long-forgotten story Norris Magnuson has emphasized "the social contributions of evangelicals during the Progressive Era."[22]

The third, quite distinctive type of social Christianity contained those of radical, reconstructionist, and socialist—rather than reformist—positions. Christian socialists adapted certain tenets of the wider socialist movement as a proper expression of basic Christian teachings while others openly espoused political socialism. In part because of the antireligious overtones sounded by so many socialists, Christian socialism was largely rejected among church people. Little groups that sought to medi-

[21] Hopkins, *The Rise of the Social Gospel in American Protestantism, 1865–1915* (New Haven: Yale University Press, 1940); May, *Protestant Churches and Industrial America* (New York: Harper, 1949), esp. part 4. See also Ronald C. White and Hopkins, *The Social Gospel: Religion and Reform in Changing America* (Philadelphia: Temple University Press, 1976), and Robert T. Handy, ed., *The Social Gospel in America, 1870–1920: Gladden, Ely, Rauschenbusch* (New York: Oxford University Press, 1966).

[22] *Salvation in the Slums: Evangelical Social Work, 1865–1920* (Metuchen, N.J.: Scarecrow Press, 1977), x.

ate between socialism and Christianity were distrusted on both sides and usually short-lived. In 1906 a concerted effort to bridge this gap was made with the formation of the Christian Socialist Fellowship, which aimed to permeate religious institutions with the social message of Jesus and demonstrate that socialism was the necessary economic expression of the Christian life. An open supporter of the Socialist party, the Christian Socialist Fellowship was centered in New York, though it had local branches in a number of cities. But after 1910 lack of support and internal dissension led to its slow decline, for it never succeeded in winning many to its view that the coming kingdom of God would be the cooperative commonwealth as envisioned by socialism.[23]

Between the conservative and radical positions as defined by May stood progressive social Christianity, the most conspicuous of the three types, which flowered in the first two decades of the twentieth century. May and I, in this study, refer to it as the social gospel. May's distinctions were based primarily on social more than theological categories, but clearly the social gospel largely rested on a liberal theological base, with but few exceptions. Most of those who fell under its spell accepted, with varying degrees of enthusiasm, an evolutionary understanding of nature and history and a critical approach to biblical study. By no means all theological liberals, however, subscribed to the social gospel. Many who remained firmly attached to the familiar individualistic ethic of the previous century cannot be identified with social Christianity. Nevertheless, those who advocated the progressive social ethic of the social gospel were primarily drawn from among those inclined to some form of theological liberalism; some preferred to be called liberal evangelical. Indeed, the majority of those leaders of the burgeoning social Christian movement in the progressive period had been inspired by the social gospel pioneers, who emphasized a positive view of the state and sharply criticized laissez-faire economics.[24]

As the social gospel flowered in the progressive period, it was reformist rather than radical. It was, however, sensitive to the critiques of socialist Christians to its left. The movement continued to stand with its nineteenth-century founders in seeking reconciliation between capital and labor, but not at the expense of the working classes, for it insisted on the right of labor to organize. This central strand of social Christianity stimulated the formation of various organizations, among them informal societies to press for certain reform causes, new denominational agencies devoted to social concern and action, and interdenominational federa-

---

[23] Hopkins, *Rise of the Social Gospel*, 233–44; Robert T. Handy, "Christianity and Socialism in America, 1900–1920," *Church History* 21 (1952): 39–54.
[24] See Chap. 3.

tions to promote cooperative efforts in applying social teachings to concrete problems of twentieth-century industrial society.[25] Just as government bureaucracies were expanded in the progressive period, so, too, did the organizational arms of the increasingly complex and multiform world of religion. Those varied agencies were often directly concerned with shaping the common welfare and joining others in pressing state agencies to deal with social inequities and injustices. The proliferation of both church and governmental organizations that was to mark twentieth-century life increased noticeably in the progressive period.

A few pioneers of the social gospel movement, as it had emerged as a recognizable force in the denominations in the last quarter of the nineteenth century, were still prominent in it flowering in the progressive period. Notable among them was Washington Gladden, who stood committed to many causes that were high among the concerns of progressivism. For example, he not only wrote and delivered sermons on municipal reform but also served for two years (1900–1902) as a member of the Columbus city council. He was an active worker for reducing fares on the street railways and improving public utilities. Along with most social gospelers, he did not favor socialism but took its arguments seriously. Characteristically, as his biographer reported, "he displayed calmness, fairness, and sympathy toward socialism that were uncommon among the Protestant clergy of his day."[26] But he stated his own views candidly: "I think that for the normal development of human character, and the stable and fruitful organization of human society, it is necessary to have private property firmly safgeguarded and private enterprise strongly encouraged by the state."[27] He thus anticipated the discussion that was to become extensive later in the century about the virtues of a mixed economy.

Gladden believed that all actual or virtual monopolies should come under governmental control and ownership and that many industries could be managed cooperatively. The growing appeal of the social gospel for his denomination was symbolized when he was elected in 1904 as moderator of the National Council of the Congregational Churches. The following year he protested against accepting a gift of $100,000 that had been solicited from John D. Rockefeller of the Standard Oil Company by the foreign mission board; in his judgment it was "tainted money," gained by unethical practices. Coming the year after Ida Tarbell's heavily documented "muckraking" *History of the Standard Oil Company*, his blast touched off a heated controversy. Portions of the gift had been spent

[25] See Chaps. 5–7.
[26] Dorn, *Washington Gladden*, 232.
[27] Gladden, *Christianity and Socialism* (New York: Eaton and Mains, 1905), 123.

before its public announcement, and in the end it was not returned. But the discussion stirred by the event gave Gladden and others the opportunity to criticize those who had secured enormous wealth by corrupt and unscrupulous means and to argue for regulating "grasping monopolies."[28] He retired in 1914 but continued to speak and write until his death four years later.

Another early leader, Josiah Strong also carried on his advocacy of the social gospel movement he had helped create. Strong worked primarily as an editor and writer who threw himself into an extensive program of popular education in public issues. Under his leadership, various periodicals, tracts, pamphlets, and Sunday school lessons were circulated, aimed at making the studies of the experts widely available in readable form to churches, YMCAs and YWCAs, colleges, and seminaries. He continued to author books, seven in all after his *Expansion: Under New World-Conditions* of 1900. The objective of his labors was to make the social gospel more widely known and better understood. In *Our World: The New World-Religion*, published thirty years after *Our Country*, he was still emphasizing the theme of American expansion. But in this last book, published only a year before his death, he focused more attention on the spread of social Christianity based on liberal theology at home and abroad and illustrated his continuing concern for the role of America in the world. Characteristically, he saw great dangers ahead, particularly the retrogression of civilization into barbarism, if right choices were not made.[29] He exemplified the growing concern of social Christianity with the importance for human good of both domestic and foreign governmental policies.

Unquestionably the most conspicuous advocate of the social gospel in the early twentieth century was Walter Rauschenbusch. He became widely known in America and abroad after the 1907 publication of the widely circulated, powerfully written *Christianity and the Social Crisis*. Actually Rauschenbusch had been active in the social Christian movement since 1886, when he had supported Henry George's run for mayor of New York.[30] Then pastor of a German Baptist Church on the edge of

[28] Gladden's forceful address before the board, "Shall Ill-Gotten Gains be Sought for Christian Purposes," originally printed in his *The New Idolatry and Other Discussions* (New York: McClure, Phillips, 1905), 57–87, is reprinted in *Social Gospel in America*, ed. Handy, 119–34; see also Dorn, *Washington Gladden*, 240–67.

[29] Hopkins, *Rise of the Social Gospel*, esp. 258–63; Strong, *Our World: The New World-Religion* (New York: Doubleday, Page, 1915); Paul R. Meyer, "The Fear of Cultural Decline: Josiah Strong's Thought about Reform and Expansion," *Church History* 42 (1973), 396–405.

[30] Eileen W. Lindner has concluded that Henry George should be accounted not only as a forerunner of the social gospel but also as a participant in the movement; see her article, "The Redemptive Politic of Henry George: A Legacy to the Social Gospel," *Union Seminary*

Manhattan's Hell's Kitchen, Rauschenbusch soon became acquainted with Richard T. Ely, from whom he learned much. The young minister was a principal founder in 1892 of the Brotherhood of the Kingdom, an inner circle of prominent reformers, including both ordained and lay persons, some of them already well known. It met annually for more than twenty years for mutual instruction, support, and inspiration.

In 1897 Rauschenbusch was called back to Rochester Theological Seminary, from which he had graduated eleven years before. He was soon named professor of church history, but he could not forget his commitment to the social gospel and his concern for the plight of the people among whom he had labored as pastor for eleven years. Accordingly, he wrote Christianity and the Social Crisis "to discharge a debt" to them; he hoped that the book might help "to ease the pressure that bears them down" and increase the forces that bear them up.[31] Before its publication, he thought that his outspoken book might get him into trouble and even lead to his dismissal. But it appeared following a bitter coal strike in 1905 that had focused attention on the problems of labor and in a year during which a financial panic pointed to the need for reform. As Rauschenbusch later interpreted the success of his book, "the social awakening of our nation had set in like an equinoctial gale in March," and it "drew me, in spite of myself, into the public discussion of social questions."[32]

Thrust into the intellectual leadership of the social gospel as it burgeoned in the progressive period, he was invited to speak frequently from coast to coast. Concurrently he produced six more books, two of them major works. Thus Rauschenbusch became America's best-known Christian social prophet at the height of the progressive period. He was frequently consulted on many public issues. In his early ministry, he had largely adhered to a strict separationist position in matters of religion and government, a view consistent with prevailing opinion in his denomination. But he was not wholly comfortable with that view even then, for in remarks before the Baptist Congress in 1889 he declared:

> Brethren, I feel sometimes that in our strong statements of the separation between Church and State, we have come to gather up our skirts and act as if the State had no more claim on us; that somehow our life as christians and as citi-

---

Quarterly Review 42 (1988): 1–8. An older biography of Rauschenbusch still has value because it was written by one of his student secretaries and close friends: Dores R. Sharpe, Walter Rauschenbusch (New York: Macmillan, 1942). But the definitive study is Paul M. Minus, Walter Rauschenbusch: American Reformer (New York: Macmillan, 1988).

[31] Rauschenbusch, Christianity and the Social Crisis (New York: Macmillan, 1907), xv. The book has been reprinted many times, and parts have appeared in many anthologies; see, e.g., Walter Rauschenbusch: Selected Writings, ed. Winthrop S. Hudson (New York: Paulist Press, 1984), 144–66.

[32] Christianizing the Social Order (New York: Macmillan, 1912), vii.

zens can be cut asunder; that on one side we can be christians and on the other side we can be citizens. It is not true. We must be the two things at the same time, and we can be that in just one way—by being animated by the life of Jesus Christ, and by carrying that life into the State in every direction.[33]

He went a step beyond that in his book of 1907 when he explained that "historical experience has compelled us to separate Church and State because each can accomplish its special task best without the interference of the other. But they are not unrelated." Rauschenbusch thought they could cooperate with each other, for "the output of each must mingle with the other to make social life increasingly wholesome and normal." For Rauschenbusch at that turning point in his career, "church" and "state" were to be seen as but partial organizations of humanity for special ends; their common aim "is to transform humanity into the kingdom of God."[34] He was restating the familiar hope for a Christian America in a way that legitimated both social gospel and progressive aims for many of his readers.

Christianity and the Social Crisis was a broad, rather general appeal for attention to the evils and problems of modern society. As he became a prominent Christian reformer, Rauschenbusch increasingly sought to explicate some practical ways to move the country nearer to his vision of the kingdom of God. In undertaking this task, he adopted many suggestions from the growing volume of progressive, reformist, and socialist writings of his time. Much of the content of his most programmatic book, *Christianizing the Social Order*, was drawn from such materials and often expressed in the language of the current democratic idealism. In his book of 1912 he illustrated the tendency of many progressive social gospel leaders to take socialism seriously. Although he sometimes called himself a Christian socialist, he was not affiliated with socialist political organizations; and he both criticized aspects of their overall programs and explicitly disavowed revolutionary action.[35]

Rauschenbusch's thinking about the relationship of religion and government also shifted as he approached an emphasis on the positive view of the state earlier articulated by Ely and others. Caught up in the hope and enthusiasm that accompanied progressive reform movements as he was preparing his second major book for the press, he made the controversial claim, later to be sharply criticized, that four great sections of the social order—family, church, education, and the political organization of the nation—"have passed through constitutional changes which have made them to some degree part of the organism through which the spirit

[33] *Proceedings of the Baptist Congress* (1889), 140.

[34] *Christianity and the Social Crisis*, 380.

[35] Minus, *Rauschenbusch*, 91, 100, 192.

of Christ can do its work in humanity."[36] He knew that to include politics in the list was challenging:

> To Americans this may seem a staggering assertion, for of all corrupt things surely our politics is the corruptest. I confess to some misgivings in moving that this brother be received among the regenerate, but I plead on his behalf that he is a newly saved sinner. Politics has been on the thorny path of sanctification only about a century and a half, and the tattered clothes and questionable smells of the far country still cling to the prodigal.

> He added that "the fundamental redemption of the state took place when special privilege was thrust out of the constitution and theory of our government," allowing it to be based on the principle of personal liberty and equal rights (148).

In 1912—the year when the major contenders in the three-cornered presidential race put forward progressive platforms in varying accents— Rauschenbusch along with many others could hope that the promises of democracy were on their way to fulfillment. For him, the essentially redeemed state should now move into the fifth and unregenerate section of the social order, business, "the seat and source of our present troubles" (156). In a familiar progressive strategy he advocated the use of the channels of government to help correct economic abuses. He interpreted events of the times as evidence that the democratic state "had to step in with its superior Christian ethics and put certain limits to the immoralities of Capitalism" (239). Here he clearly challenged the individualistic ethics that many had long assumed consistent with biblical faith. In taking such a strong position, this Christian reformer epitomized the effort of the social gospel to magnify the positive role of the state in the struggle against social evil and injustice.

For Rauschenbusch and others who believed that the kingdom of God was near, the recovery of a truly Christian social faith was a possibility, and with it could come a vastly improved if not perfect social and economic order. At the end of the long book in which he devoted so much attention to public affairs, he sensed that many might feel it paid too little attention to religion and dealt too much with economics and politics. He concluded by insisting that the sole concern of the book was "for the kingdom of God and the salvation of men. But the kingdom of God includes the economic life; for it means the progressive transformation of all human affairs by the thought and spirit of Christ" (458). Many could not understand how a Christian could face the social questions of the time seriously without seeming to forsake faith. The consequent isolation experienced by Rauschenbusch, both early and late in his career, was the

---

[36] *Christianizing the Social Order*, 154.

primary reason Winthrop S. Hudson so perceptively called him "a lonely prophet." Although Rauschenbusch once mentioned that because of early deafness his life had been "physically very lonely," the loneliness caused by failed understandings of the way that his religious faith undergirded a social vision especially troubled him.[37] But the confident hope that the kingdom of God on earth was coming at last buoyed up the social Christians in the heyday of progressivism.

Institutionalizing the Social Gospel

As the social gospel flowered in the century's first decade, its causes were taken up by many leaders and followers, the majority working primarily within their own denominational frameworks. When we look back at such a movement, our attention easily focuses on only a few of its outstanding thinkers and doers, but figures prominent and well-known in their time, and especially within their own denominations, are overlooked. As the denominational spectrum continued to widen in this period, those who labored chiefly within their own communions were often highly influential there but did not draw the attention attracted by a few of the more widely known speakers and writers. One clear sign of the growing impact of the social gospel was the way it became recognized and to some degree institutionalized within a number of the denominations. It also became important in the life of the growing network of interdenominational agencies, especially the Federal Council of the Churches of Christ in America, but those organizations depended heavily on the goodwill and support of their member communions. The spread of the social gospel through these many channels helped raise the awareness of growing numbers of people with regard to pressing public issues of the time. Donald K. Gorrell has traced in considerable detail "the way Protestant denominations, challenged by the needs of a changing social order, accepted responsibility for the welfare of a nation" in the first two decades of the twentieth century.[38]

The (northern) Presbyterian Church in the United States of America was the first denomination to appoint an official agency with paid staff to extend and act on social gospel concerns; in 1903 its Board of Home Missions founded a Department of Church and Labor. The work was headed by Charles Stelzle, whose background was unique among social

[37] Hudson, *The Great Tradition of the American Churches* (New York: Harper, 1953), 226–43; for the source of Rauschenbusch's comment about his loneliness, see *Rauschenbusch*, ed. Hudson, 45.

[38] *The Age of Social Responsibility: The Social Gospel in the Progressive Era, 1900–1920* (Macon, Ga.: Mercer University Press, 1988), ix.

gospel leaders. Raised on Manhattan's lower East Side, he had dropped out of school at eleven to begin working to help his widowed mother take care of his younger sisters. Later he attended night school and became a machinist and also an ardent union member. Deciding to enter the ministry, he was privately tutored, then attended Moody Bible Institute for ten months, and was finally ordained during his third pastorate. Named as superintendent of the newly formed department, Stelzle wrote many articles and books and traveled widely as he interpreted the labor movement to the churches and the churches to working people. He popularized the observation of Labor Sunday, served as the first fraternal delegate of the churches to the American Federation of Labor, and in 1910 founded New York's Labor Temple, a church with an outreach among laboring people. His theology remained broadly conservative. But as he focused on the practical application of the gospel to contemporary problems, Stelzle became a prominent voice in social gospel circles. Somewhat ironically, conservatives in his own denomination criticized his work so sharply that he resigned his position after ten years but continued his active career largely on a free-lance basis.[39]

"Methodism in 1900 shared many of the characteristics of American society," Robert Moats Miller has remarked. "By every statistical measurement, the Methodist bodies were the largest, wealthiest, and most powerful of all Protestant denominations."[40] Members of that denominational family first developed informal organizations, then official statements, and finally departments devoted to social problems in the progressive period; all measures demonstrated the penetration of the social gospel into its structures. The lead was taken by the (northern) Methodist Episcopal Church in 1907 when a group of ministers, educators, and public figures formed a voluntary society, named it the Methodist Federation for Social Service (MFSS), and chose Herbert Welch, president of Ohio Wesleyan, as its president. A key member of the founding group was English-born Harry F. Ward, graduate of Northwestern University and former settlement house head resident, who then served several churches in slum areas of Chicago. Hoping to win the attention of the denomination's quadrennial General Conference, Ward took the lead at an informal meeting of a few MFSS members in drafting a statement of what Methodists stood for on social issues. In revised form it was passed unanimously without debate as part of a report on the State of the Church and soon became known as the "Social Creed of Methodism." It was really

[39] Charles Stelzle, A Son of the Bowery (New York: Doran, 1926). For a brief introduction to his career with selections from his writings, see White and Hopkins, Social Gospel, 51–54, 65–69.

[40] "Methodism and American Society," in The History of American Methodism, ed. Emory S. Bucke (New York: Abingdon, 1964), 3: 328.

more a statement of principles and goals, but the word "creed" caught on.

The creed was destined to be a major expression of the social gospel. With various changes and additions through the years it was endorsed by other Methodist bodies, for example, by the Methodist Episcopal Church, South, in 1914 and the smaller Methodist Protestant Church two years later. It was also adopted as the "Social Creed of the Churches" by members of some other denominational families—such as the Congregational, Baptist, Presbyterian, Episcopal, Reformed, and Quaker—and interdenominational movements, especially the Federal Council of Churches.[41] The original statement affirmed several specific points that Methodists stood for: equal rights and complete justice for all, the principle of conciliation and arbitration in industrial dissensions, the abolition of child labor, the regulation of the conditions of toil for women to safeguard the physical and moral health of the community, a living wage in every industry, and the most equitable division of the products of industry as can ultimately be devised.[42]

At the same time that the creed was adopted in 1908, the General Conference noted with satisfaction the formation of the MFSS and approved its objectives. But the conference did not financially support it, then or later, for the federation preferred to be "unoffical" to allow its offering of "prophetic" statements. In 1912 the MFSS was recognized as an independent agency of the church. Ward was called to teach at Boston University School of Theology the next year and served also as part-time secretary for the MFSS. In prodding its denomination to pay official attention to social, civic, and moral conditions and issues, the federation was instrumental in getting Methodists more deeply involved in public action for the common good.

In the Episcopal church, then formally the Protestant Episcopal Church, two voluntary organizations devoted to the perplexing problems of modern society had been founded. These were the Church Association for the Advancement of the Interests of Labor (CAIL), founded in 1887, which focused largely on practical social activities, and the Christian Social Union (CSU), formed four years later primarily as an educational ef-

[41] See Chap. 6.

[42] The story of the framing of Methodism's social creed has been told many times. See, e.g., two articles by Donald K. Gorrell, "The Methodist Federation for Social Service and the Social Creed," *Methodist History* 13 (January 1975): 3–32, and "The Social Creed of Methodism through Eighty Years," *Methodist History* 26 (July 1988): 213–28, and also his *Age of Social Responsibility*, 100–104; Eugene P. Link, *Labor-Religion Prophet: The Life and Times of Harry F. Ward* (Boulder, Colo.: Westview Press, 1984), 38–54; Creighton Lacy, *Frank Mason North: His Social and Ecumenical Mission* (Nashville: Abingdon, 1967), 129–45. For the general setting, see Walter G. Muelder, *Methodism and Society in the Twentieth Century* (New York: Abingdon, 1961).

fort to broaden understandings of the relationship of faith to pressing economic and social issues. At the church's General Convention of 1901 a commission of nine members was appointed to become a reconciling force in industrial conflict. The new commission also sought to play a coordinating role among the various groups in the church concerned with social questions, including the two just mentioned and others more local in orientation. In 1910 the original commission was expanded as a "Joint Commission on Social Service," which by 1912 appointed Frank M. Crouch as full-time field secretary—an important step in the process of the institutionalization of social and reform concerns in a denomination. Eventually, CSU and CAIL disbanded, when satisfied that their work was being properly carried on under official church auspices. Several Episcopal groups devoted to Christian socialism—notably the Church Socialist League formed in 1911—also pressed the church to be more fully involved in social issues. Supported by several prominent bishops, its views were eloquently presented by Vida D. Scudder, a professor at Wellesley and well-known author, some of whose writings were devoted to social issues.[43]

Despite the prominence of such social gospel leaders as Gladden and Strong in its ranks, Congregationalism was slow in taking strong official action on the social issues of the day. The National Council of the Congregational Churches named an Industrial Committee in 1901, but not until 1910, following a challenge by Graham Taylor, professor at Chicago Theological Seminary and director of the Chicago Commons settlement, did the denomination appoint Henry A. Atkinson as secretary of labor and social service and launch an aggressive progam of social action.[44]

After the Southern Baptist Convention had been founded in 1845, the predominantly white Baptists in the North maintained the older societies for mission, publication, and education, but as that proved insufficient to provide a principle of unity for the northern congregations, it was decided in 1907 to form the Northern Baptist Convention (later known as the American Baptist Churches). A constitution and bylaws were adopted the next year at its first annual meeting in Oklahoma City. Perhaps because of Rauschenbusch's fame, his name is often linked to the social gospel movement among Baptists. But also very well known at the time and

[43] On CAIL, see White and Hopkins, *Social Gospel*, 70–72; for greater detail consult Spencer Miller and Joseph F. Fletcher, *The Church and Industry* (New York: Longmans, Green, 1930). On Christian socialism, see Vida D. Scudder, *Socialism and Character* (Boston: Houghton, Mifflin, 1912), and her mature reflections on Christian socialism in her autobiography, *On Journey* (New York: E. P. Dutton, 1937).

[44] Hopkins, *Rise of the Social Gospel*, 288; Gorrell, *Age of Social Responsibility*, 80–81, 139–42.

more directly related to its institutionalization in the northern denomination was Samuel Zane Batten. Long a close friend of Rauschenbusch and fellow founder of the Brotherhood of the Kingdom, Batten moved at the convention's 1908 meeting that a committee be named to investigate and report on the social service work of its churches. In its report the next year, the committee outlined plans for a series of educational pamphlets on social issues, recommended the adoption of the social creed of the churches, and urged that an official Social Service Commission be developed to coordinate and pursue an aggressive program. These steps were taken, and Batten, who soon became a professor of social science at Des Moines College, chaired the new commission. In 1913 the denomination's publication society created a Department of Social Service and Brotherhood and elected Batten as its secretary.[45]

Batten was both activist and thinker; one of his books, *The Christian State*, focused on the interrelationships between the state and religious institutions and amplified themes that social Christian leaders in the 1890s had articulated as increasingly reflective in the religious reformism of the progressive period. The three great facts of the modern world, he declared in 1909, were the state, democracy, and Christianity; the latter was "the most potent force in our modern civilization."[46] Here he concisely stated a major emphasis of the social gospel, one that drove its concern with the full life of society; therefore, the social gospel became involved with governmental agencies as they carried out their growing societal responsibilities in the progressive era.

Batten's view of Christianity as "the most potent force" reflected the anthropocentrism of much liberal theology: "Christianity, in its first article, is confidence in men; it is a passion for the downmost man; it is a missionary enterprise seeking to help the other man and to create in him a full consciousness of his worth" (178). But the state, originating in the nature of humanity and the purpose of God, was also heavily emphasized, for it was "the one organ great enough and varied enough to express and correlate the varied powers and talents of mankind, the one medium through which all men can cooperate in their search after social perfection" (31). He agreed that persons could not be made good by the law, but he nevertheless insisted that the state could do many things "in behalf of the moral life of the people," for example, by clearing away artificial social barriers (76). At a time when progressivism and the social gospel were both deeply committed to the democratic ideal, Batten added his

[45] Several of Batten's reports on the work of the Social Service Commission are reprinted in part in William H. Brackney, ed., *Baptist Life and Thought: 1600–1980, A Source Book* (Valley Forge, Pa.: Judson Press, 1983), 270–74.

[46] Samuel Zane Batten, *The Christian State: The State, Democracy and Christianity* (Philadelphia: Griffith and Rowland, 1909), 31.

endorsement to the chorus: "Democracy is the one idea of human society that is befriended by the universe, legitimated in history, in accord with the Christian spirit, and inevitable in the future. Democracy is inevitable where Christianity is regnant and men know one another as brothers" (165). For him, democracy was "less a form of government than a confession of faith," a confession of human brotherhood based upon the divine Fatherhood (253).

Batten was reaching for a comprehensive synthesis of church and state, and for him the central social gospel doctrine of the kingdom of God provided "a great social synthesis that includes within its scope the whole life of man" (288). Though church and state are both institutions of the kingdom and must sustain a vital relation to one another, yet they are separate and not to be confused. Keenly aware of the tensions between Catholic and Protestant, he sought to identify respective strengths and weaknesses in their positions on religion and government as he understood them:

> The Romanist is eternally right when he claims that the State must be subordinate to Christ, and must seek his kingdom in the world; but he is as eternally wrong when he claims that Christ has delegated his authority to another, be that a man or an institution. The Protestant is eternally right when he demands the separation of Church and State in the interests of both, but he is as eternally wrong when he construes this separation to mean the divorce of religion from civil affairs and the abandonment of the State as a secular institution [291].

Social gospel idealism and optimism were vividly expressed in Batten's as in so many other writings of the Christian progressives, for as he saw it, "in the religion of Christ we have everything that the State can need, both to ensure its perpetuity and to promote its progress. We have in it the supreme ideal which shines before men to lure them upward and onward" (322). He was sure the state could become more Christian and exert increasing pressure against evil and a steady purpose in behalf of virtue. Christian aims, Batten was convinced, were already partly recognized in the legislation and policy of the "more advanced nations," such as Germany, Great Britain, and the United States (393–94). In *The Christian State* he clearly expressed the convergence of kingdom of God theology and progressive reformism as it stressed the positive role of the state in dealing with social and economic problems but affirmed the familiar goal of Christianizing America while keeping the institutions of religion and government separate but cooperating.

As the controversial social gospel movement found official acceptance in a number of major Protestant communions, so also did the drive for cooperation among them. The two trends were mutually supportive. Such formative social Christian figures as Gladden and Strong had long favored the unitive trend, and most of those of progressive cast in the twentieth century saw the two movements as complementary. With few exceptions, nineteenth-century patterns of Protestant unity had been voluntary, as individuals of various denominational backgrounds worked together in common efforts for evangelism, mission, education, and publication: the Evangelical Alliance, the American Bible Society, the American Sunday School Union, and the Religious Education Association (REA) are illustrations. The latter, although not a formal Protestant organization, was dominated at the time of its founding in 1903 and in its early years by progressive Protestant educators. In a 1914 statement of its principles the REA, characterized by Gorrell as a barometer of Protestant social Christianity, declared its belief that "the age of sheer individualism is past and the age of social responsibility has arrived."[47]

A new direction in Protestant organizational history was taken in 1893 when sixty-eight persons, meeting to further cooperation in foreign missions, were present not as individuals only but as officers and representatives of denominational boards. The first gathering proved so helpful that it was continued annually; by 1911, it had matured into the Foreign Mission Conference of North America, by then representing fifty-five boards and societies. The women of many denominations had organized their own missionary societies in the later nineteenth century; in 1897 they also undertook interdenominational meetings, which by 1916 became regularized as the Federation of Woman's Boards for Foreign Missions in North America with fifteen members.

The home mission boards followed the same path in 1908 as they organized the Home Missions Council and the Council of Women for Home Missions. These two councils, which worked closely together, did much to encourage the spread of the social spirit in the home missions work of the churches. In the nineteenth century the emphasis had been heavily on evangelism and the building of new churches, but now came increasing concern for missions in urban areas and among immigrants. Christian centers, institutional churches, and rescue missions mingled the social with the evangelical approach as they extended work in the slums and among those newly arrived from abroad. The new social emphases also informed many missions in rural areas and among the Indian tribes.

These developments helped pave the way for what many had long desired: an agency that would formally and regularly bring responsible representatives of denominations together in a cooperative agency officially supported by many communions. That finally came about in December

[47] *Age of Social Responsibility*, 248–50, 339–41. On the REA, see Stephen A. Schmidt, *A History of the Religious Education Association* (Birmingham, Ala.: Religious Education Press, 1983).

1908 with the founding of the Federal Council of the Churches of Christ in America (FCC). Many of the larger and some of the smaller denominations became members—thirty-three in all.[48] The council had no authority over its members, but it encouraged and supplied channels for cooperation in evangelism, education, missions, and social service. In the welcoming address to the delegates at the founding meeting, Presbyterian leader William H. Roberts neatly conjoined the historic church interests in evangelism and missions at home and abroad with social gospel emphasis on "the thorough Christianization of our country":

> The essential spirit of our Nation is thus that of Jesus Christ, and it is the duty of the American Churches to make that spirit more Christian, to awaken yet greater national interest in the welfare of all earth's peoples, to provide men and means in increasing ratios for the work of spiritual salvation, and to hasten the day when the true King of Men shall everywhere be crowned as Lord of all. This council stands for the hope of organized work for speedy Christian advance toward World Conquest.[49]

A number of the characteristic themes of the cooperative Protestant movement in the progressive period were woven together in that concise summary.

Without neglecting the historic concerns of cooperative Protestantism for unity and mission, the council in many ways embodied the social gospel. At the founding meeting it accepted a strongly worded report on "The Church and Modern Industry," ably presented by Frank Mason North. Secretary of the New York City Church Extension and Missionary Society and member of the executive committee of the MFSS, North had been present some of the time when Ward with the help of others had drafted the original, Methodist version of the social creed in May 1908. He now incorporated in the conclusion of his report a revised version of Methodism's social creed, which added four articles. The document, soon known as the "Social Creed of the Churches," was widely adopted by many denominations, as mentioned above. Slightly revised by the council in 1912, it stood as its official position until 1932. Hence the FCC was a strong influence in the spread of progressive patterns of social thought and action in the churches. Yet the member denominations had large

---

[48] For full treatments of the complex history of the founding and development of these cooperative agencies, see Samuel McCrea Cavert, *The American Churches in the Ecumenical Movement, 1900–1968* (New York: Association Press, 1968), esp. 34–87, and *Church Cooperation and Unity in America, A Historical Review: 1900–1970* (New York: Association Press, 1970), esp. 34–76. For more on cooperation among the woman's foreign boards, see also Hill, *The World Their Household*, esp. 143–91.

[49] As quoted by Elias B. Sanford, ed., *Federal Council of the Churches of Christ in America: Report of the First Meeting . . .* (New York: Revell, 1909), 323.

numbers—probably majorities in most cases—who were committed to neither liberal nor social causes and some who opposed them. Hence both denominational and interdenominational agencies had to move somewhat cautiously as they sought to educate their constituencies. But the progressive spirit of the times was favorable for such efforts and the causes for which the social gospel stood.

Social Christianity was much stronger in the North than in the South; for example, the northern branches of Baptist, Methodist, and Presbyterian denominations pioneered its spread, and the Congregational churches were largely located in that region. Kenneth K. Bailey observed that at the dawn of the century "the rural homogeneity of the South was little disturbed by immigration, industrialization, new intellectual currents, and all those other forces which were elsewhere transforming society."[50] The changes were beginning to come, however; as progressivism became a national movement politically, its ideas and approaches became increasingly familiar in the South. While it was not entirely absent, during that period liberal theology did not get a foothold there, but more conservative forms of social Christianity that espoused reformist aims did. "An important characteristic of Southern reform," wrote John Lee Eighmy, "was the broad range of causes it embraced—causes which, by reason of the humanitarian zeal with which they were promoted, became something of a counterpart to the social gospel in the North."[51]

There was less attention to the problems of capital and labor and the evils of the slums than in the North; the South, however, favored such causes as prison reform, public health, organized charities, child labor, the regulation of business, and improved education. Although lynching was increasingly opposed, only a few gave much attention to the issues of racial justice. Some pioneers began to raise that matter in the progressive period, but on the whole that concern was neglected. As the North was much concerned with widening its alliances in the South, the issue was also largely neglected in the northern states, in both church and political life. Some courageous pioneers stated their increasing distress with that situation;[52] in general, as Robert Moats Miller has put it: "It is one of the

---

[50] *Southern White Protestantism in the Twentieth Century* (New York: Harper & Row, 1964), 4.

[51] "Religious Liberalism in the South during the Progressive Era," *Church History* 38 (1969), 362. On the spread of liberalism in the South, see Hugh C. Bailey, *Liberalism in the New South: Southern Social Reformers and the Progressive Movement* (Coral Gables, Fla.: University of Miami Press, 1969). There is a chapter on "Voices from the New South" in White and Hopkins, *Social Gospel*, 80–97.

[52] E.g., on Gladden's awakening to the race problem after reading W.E.B. Du Bois's *The Souls of Black Folks* (Chicago: A. C. McClung, 1903), see Dorn, *Gladden*, 298–302; on Rauschenbusch's troubled reflections on the issue, see Max Stackhouse's "Introduction" to Rauschenbusch's hitherto unpublished manuscript, *The Righteousness of the Kingdom*

supreme ironies of American history that the Populist-Progressive era—
an age which saw every other cancerous social growth undergo surgery—
coincided with the crest of the wave of racism. In fact, many progressive
reformers, including leaders of the social gospel, were either indifferent
to the Negro's plight or actually hostile to his aspirations."[53]

Of the major southern denominations, the Methodist Episcopal
Church, South, was perhaps the most open to social gospel influence. A
charter member of the FCC, its Bishop E. R. Hendricks served as the
council's first president, and it affirmed the social creed in 1914. A study
of its woman's home mission movement showed that it accepted social
emphases in a moderate form, with little attention to labor unions and
tenant farmers, and was led by comfortably situated persons who only
gradually moved from a patronizing condescension toward those whom
they sought to "uplift"—a favorite word of the period.[54] Ronald C.
White, Jr., however, has carefully documented that there was considerably more attention given to racial justice in social gospel thought and
action, both in the North and the South, than has generally been recognized.[55]

Concern for temperance and prohibition was especially evident among
southern Protestants, and in this matter they were united in a common
cause with their northern counterparts and most progressive reformers.
"Southern churches made their most direct contribution to Progressivism
through the prohibition movement," Eighmy declared.[56] It has been difficult for Americans raised since the Eighteenth Amendment prohibiting
the manufacture, sale, or transportation of intoxicating liquors went into

---

(Nashville: Abingdon, 1968), 33 n.26; see also Rauschenbusch's "Belated Races and Social
Problems," *Methodist Review Quarterly* 63 (April 1914): 252–59, which was published by
the American Missionary Association in the same year as a pamphlet.

[53] "Methodism and American Society," in *History of American Methodism*, ed. Bucke, 3:
360.

[54] John P. McDowell, *The Social Gospel in the South: The Woman's Home Mission
Movement in the Methodist Episcopal Church, South, 1886–1939* (Baton Rouge: Louisiana
State University Press, 1982). On southern Presbyterians and Baptists, see, e.g., Ernest Trice
Thompson, *Presbyterianism in the South*, vol. 3, *1890–1972* (Richmond: John Knox Press,
1972), esp. chap. 10, "The Church and Its Mission," 250–73; John Lee Eighmy, *Churches
in Cultural Captivity: A History of the Social Attitudes of Southern Baptists* (Knoxville:
University of Tennessee Press, 1972), esp. chap. 4, "The Social Gospel Moves South," 57–
71; and David Brian Whitlock, "Baptists and Southern Culture: Three Visions of a Christian America" (Ph.D. diss., Southern Baptist Theological Seminary, 1988), esp. on Charles
S. Gardner, author of *The Ethics of Jesus and Social Progress* (New York: Doran, 1914).

[55] *Liberty and Justice for All: Racial Reform and the Social Gospel (1877–1925)* (San
Francisco: Harper & Row, 1990). His chapter on "Edgar Gardner Murphy: A Southern
Case Study," 148–65, provides insights into regional concern for racial reform, with partic-
ular attention to the Episcopal Church.

[56] "Religious Liberalism in the South," 363.

effect in 1920 and its repeal thirteen years later to understand how important to the reforms of the progressive period temperance was. In fact, as Paul A. Carter has carefully explained, prior to the passage of the Volstead Act—which defined intoxicating liquors as having more than one half of one percent of alcohol—in 1919, "the dry crusade spoke the language of social and humanitarian reform—and had the profoundest kinship with the Social Gospel." He emphasized that, only with the exception of the Protestant Episcopal, "all the churches which had been permeated by the Social Gospel *were also officially committed to Prohibition.*"[57]

K. Austin Kerr has pointed out that the Eighteenth Amendment was not an *experiment*, as it later came to be called, but in the progressive mind a *reform*, aimed primarily at controlling the liquor traffic by striking at the brewers and saloon keepers. The climactic drive for prohibition drew on the experience of its nineteenth-century predecessors even as it exhibited certain characteristics of progressivism: idealism, evangelism, moralism. The crusade was led by the Anti-Saloon League, founded in Ohio in 1893 and nationally two years later. It differed from some other organizations concerned with temperance by being politically astute but nonpartisan and focused on its single issue. A number of Protestant ministers were among its founders and central leaders. Although it was rather tightly controlled from the top, the league saw itself as the political arm of the churches on the temperance question, as "the church in action."[58] Prohibition was a cause that drew the support of many kinds of Christians, liberal and conservative, black and white, northern and southern. It caused a proliferation in the size and number of voluntary associations related to religion, some denominational, others "independent" but drawing primary support from church people. It also sought to use the powers of government to attain its reformative goal. Once that was attained, the character of the movement changed as the "law and order" issue became primary. But at the peak of progressivist enthusiasm, prohibition was part of the reform program of large numbers of participants in the movement and a favorite cause of its Protestant supporters—and not a few Catholics.

Among Protestants the social gospel and liberal theology were, with few exceptions, closely linked. In Roman Catholicism a strong social Christian movement also flowered but on different theological premises. In his *The American Catholic Experience*, Jay Dolan entitled a long chapter "Toward a Social Gospel." After tracing the background for this in

[57] *The Decline and Revival of the Social Gospel: Social and Political Liberalism in American Protestant Churches, 1920–1940*, rev. ed. (Hamden, Conn.: Archon Books, 1971), 32–33 (emphasis his).

[58] *Organized for Prohibition*, 126.

nineteenth-century conditions and the writings and actions of Pope Leo XIII, he showed how conservative social and theological trends checked the growth of the social movement as interest focused more on the practice of charity than on the concepts of justice. But the tide began to turn early in the progressive period, in part because the reformist mood of the times prevailed; in part because a number of priests ministering in working-class parishes became active supporters of the labor movement. The network of Catholic charitable institutions—including hospitals, orphanages, and settlements—continued to grow impressively, increasingly permeated with the social spirit. In 1901 a group of organizations composed largely of laypersons concerned with charitable, educational, and social efforts formed the American Federation of Catholic Societies, which became "a clear-cut example of Catholic progressivism."[59] In pursuing its goal to build a Christian America on Catholic principles, it sought the moral reform of society and by 1910 advocated a labor-centered program of social reform. The leader in the latter efforts was Peter E. Dietz, a labor priest who served as executive secretary of the Federation's Social Service Commission from 1911 to 1915 and (in a way paralleling the work of Charles Stelzle) strengthened its ties with the American Federation of Labor.

It was John A. Ryan, however, who showed the way to relate progressivism's spirit of reform with Catholic social thought. A child of immigrant Irish parents in Minnesota, he became an early devotee to the cause of economic justice, and after ordination he completed his doctoral studies at Catholic University and then taught at Archbishop Ireland's St. Paul Seminary. His book *A Living Wage*, highly commended in an introduction by Richard T. Ely, affirmed that justice required that workers be paid a wage adequate to maintain their families in decent comfort and advocated a full circle of progressive causes as he promoted economic democracy. In this and later writings he drew on the natural law tradition so emphasized by Pope Leo XIII, an emphasis that contributed to renewed interest in the encyclical *Rerum novarum*. He moved freely in reform circles, helped to write a new minimum-wage law in his native state, and became a well-known speaker and writer on such themes. In keeping with much progressive thought, he stressed the necessity of state intervention for reforming the social order. He based his program not on progressivist philosophy but on principles of Catholic theology and thereby helped give his church "the foundations of a social gospel."[60]

[59] Dolan, *American Catholic Experience*, 341; for the earlier period see Chap. 3.

[60] Ibid., 343; on Ryan, see his *A Living Wage: Its Ethical and Economic Aspects* (New York: Macmillan, 1906), and Francis L. Broderick, *Right Reverend New Dealer: John A. Ryan* (New York: Macmillan, 1963). Selections from *A Living Wage* and its Introduction by Ely are reproduced in White and Hopkins, *Social Gospel*, 220–26.

The percentage of church members, both Catholic and Protestant, in the rapidly growing population was steadily increasing in the progressive period; thus, the network of such church-related institutions as orphanages, homes for the elderly, hospitals, and social settlements was also expanding. As has been observed, contemporary prevailing interpretations of the separation of church and state had heightened the wall between the government and denominations and their educational institutions. With very few exceptions, as for some schools on Indian reservations, this meant that public funds were simply unavailable for church-sponsored education.[61]

For church-related agencies concerned with the public good, however, the same rules did not apply. An important Supreme Court decision of 1899, *Bradfield* v. *Roberts*, found that religious institutions performing welfare services were eligible for government assistance. A group named "The Directors of Providence Hospital" had been incorporated by an act of Congress in 1864 to operate a hospital in the nation's capital, with no reference to the religious faith of the incorporators. When, later in the century, Congress authorized the commissioners of the District of Columbia to provide funds to erect new buildings to this and another private hospital, an injunction was granted by the supreme court of the district on the grounds that Providence was a Catholic hospital, run by Catholics and owned by the Sisters of Charity of Emmitsburg, Maryland. The injunction was overruled by the court of appeals, and the Supreme Court of the United States affirmed that judgment. The character of the corporation, it was declared, was legal, and the facts that its members were said to be members of a monastic order or sisterhood of the Roman Catholic Church and that the hospital was conducted under church auspices "are wholly immaterial, as is also the allegation regarding the title to its property." The court said:

> Whether the individuals who compose the corporation, under its charter, happen to be all Roman Catholics, or all Methodists, or Presbyterians, or Unitarians, or members of any other religious organization, or of no organization at all, is of not the slightest consequence with reference to the law of its incorporation, nor can the individual beliefs upon religious matters of the various incorporators be inquired into. Nor is it material that the hospital may be conducted under the auspices of the Roman Catholic Church.[62]

---

[61] The most notable exception was for grants for Catholic Indian schools, which came out of Trust and Treaty funds set up when the government bought land from the Indians or were provided by formal treaty. This money was made available when the Indians themselves petitioned for it, as was done by the Sioux. The Supreme Court affirmed their right to the funds in *Quick Bear* v. *Leupp*, 210 U.S. 50 (1908). The case is discussed and much of it reprinted in Noonan, *The Believer and the Powers That Are*, 214–17.

[62] *Bradfield* v. *Roberts*, 175 U.S. 291 (1899) at 298. See Stokes, *Church and State*, 2: 730–33.

The incorporation as such was for certain defined purposes and with clearly stated powers; hence, it was a secular institution under the law by which it existed. It was not transformed into a religious or sectarian body by whoever happened to be its directors.

"Here was the beginning of legal reasoning on the role of religious welfare in modern society," Bruce Nichols has commented. "Religiously based services were welcomed on the basis of their ability to provide a service with clear secular purpose."[63] Although disputes about defining a sectarian agency continued to erupt, in the progressive period the spreading network of church-related agencies of charity and social service proceeded apace. As governmental bureaucracies were being multiplied in the same period, clashes over how to handle relationships between the expanding institutions of churches, including "related" ones, and governments were to escalate long after the period was over.

In summary, during the late nineteenth and early twentieth centuries the pressures of rapid increases in population and rising religious tensions had somewhat heightened the wall of separation between church and state. But the evils that accompanied industrialization and urbanization had evoked closely related political and religious concerns for social justice. Both the progressive movement and social Christianity recognized the need for the state's increased role in dealing with twentieth-century problems. By the early years of the century, a number of the churches had developed, within themselves and in cooperation with others, voluntary movements and official agencies that had strong concerns for the health of public life. Although they were often controversial, many of those involved with them witnessed and acted on behalf of their concerns in both church and the larger public. They experimented with strategies—whose longevity has proved their efficacy—by which to influence public opinion. They struggled to remain faithful to their religious traditions while serving an industrialized, urbanized, religiously pluralistic nation. How well they succeeded soon became a matter of controversy that continues to the present.

[63] Nichols, *Uneasy Alliance*, 28.

6

Unitive and Divisive Forces in Religion during the Progressive Period

IN AN ESSAY on "The Intellectual Temper of the Age" published in 1913, George Santayana, who had been teaching philosophy at Harvard for nearly a quarter-century, offered a penetrating observation of the time in which he lived:

> The present age is a critical one and interesting to live in. The civilisation characteristic of Christendom has not disappeared, yet another civilisation has begun to take its place. We still understand the value of religious faith; . . . . On the other hand the shell of Christendom is broken.[1]

To interpret his observation from a later historical perspective, certain aspects of traditional Christendom had persisted in its voluntary Protestant form into the twentieth century, despite the fact that decisive changes, such as the rapid growth of Catholicism and Judaism through immigration, had taken place. Although tensions were increasing within Protestant ranks and challenges were mounting from those outside its sphere of direct influence, an unofficial, diversified establishment of religion continued to operate effectively in the society.

Santayana was keenly aware of shifts in the intellectual climate. The importance of the Christian faith and its churches was still generally recognized throughout American culture, even though critical minds, influenced by the Enlightenment, Romanticism, pure and applied science, historical method, and the increasing pluriformity of religion were questioning long-accepted views. The familiar assertion that America was a Christian nation, for example, was being looked at critically.

The emergence of empirical trends in philosophy and the rise of naturalistic strains in literature were foreshadowing the end of the cultural dominance of Christendom, even in its mild, voluntary form in American life. Although the tension between faith and doubt has been a factor in many chapters of religious history, some periods show such a preponderance of belief that they can be characterized as ages of faith. The middle third of the nineteenth century in the United States has often been described as such a time in Protestant history, for then the rapidly growing

---

[1] *Winds of Doctrine: Studies in Contemporary Opinion* (New York: Scribner, 1913), 1.

evangelical denominations were a dominant force in religion and culture.[2] The first two decades of the twentieth century, however, were quite different. They were years in which questionings of the very ground of belief systems were increasing, even as strong faith seemed to be holding its own. The Christian believers were many, and the critical questioners few. But the very fact that the latter's doubts were publicly expressed and seriously debated meant that alternatives to theistic belief, alternatives that claimed scientific and philosophical justification, were increasingly pressing those who held traditional views about God and the institutions based on them toward a more marginal role in the larger society.[3] Even as religious institutions continued to grow and flourish internally, their public visibility was beginning to decline because it was increasingly evident that individuals and groups could opt for one religious position or another— or none at all—as they chose.

The early years of the twentieth century, prefiguring patterns that were to mark its continuing religious history, were times of commingled faith and doubt. Faith in God, faith in progress, faith in humanity, faith in democracy, faith in freedom were eloquently expressed by both laity and clergy, by those both inside and outside the churches. But the authorities invoked for many such statements of faith were often not those that had the ring of Christendom, classic or voluntary, even when cited by prominent ministers. Although many expressions of faith were offered forcefully, the period could no longer be typified as an age of faith. Externally the churches were flourishing, for they continued in a remarkable way to maintain closely their percentage of members in a still rapidly growing population. Estimates based on the federal religious censuses of the United States for 1906 and 1916 showed that the increase of adult church members (thirteen years old and up) was 18.6 percent at a time when the adult population increased by 19 percent.[4]

Many developments of the preceding century, especially its latter half, had left their marks on the new one. Critical study of the Bible had suggested to many that, while that holy book was still an authority in matters of the spirit, it was not necessarily an authority in matters of geology, geography, and science. Historical examination of creeds had convinced

[2] See, e.g., Robert T. Handy, "The Protestant Quest for a Christian America," *Church History* 22 (1953), 8–20, where such contemporary observers as Alexis de Tocqueville and Robert Baird were cited; the point is further stressed in Handy, *A Christian America: Protestant Hopes and Historical Realities*, 2d ed. (New York: Oxford University Press, 1984), esp. chap. 2, "A Complete Christian Commonwealth" (1800–1860), 24–56.

[3] For the background of this development in the later nineteenth century, see James Turner, *Without God, Without Creed: The Origins of Unbelief in America* (Baltimore: Johns Hopkins University Press, 1985).

[4] C. Luther Fry, *The U.S. Looks at its Churches* (New York: Institute of Social and Religious Research, 1930), 108–9.

growing numbers that those texts were products of a particular time and place and that familiar and popular understandings of them lacked their former power. Once such questions had been raised, they could not easily be put down; many traditional beliefs about biblical interpretation and denominational claims fell under scrutiny. As Henry Van Dyke pictured the situation just prior to the turn of the century in his significantly entitled *The Gospel for an Age of Doubt*, "the questing spirit is abroad, moving on the face of the waters, seeking rest and finding none."[5]

The questioning did not diminish in the new century; in the heart of the progressive period Washington Gladden observed that "the sound of inquiry was abroad."[6] From the point of view of many of the traditionally minded who were accustomed to identifying faith with the voluntary Christendom in which they had been nurtured, it was an age of doubt that threatened the faith to which they clung. For those trying to mediate between Christian faith and culture rapidly changing by the force of both democratic and intellectual pressures, it was a time of challenge and experimentation. In opening themselves to some trends of their time in an effort to reconcile them with their received religious traditions, many were satisfied that their reinterpretations were helpful, even necessary, for seeing faith in a new light while remaining true to it. But some were moving or drifting away from a recognizable and active Christian connection, and others were resisting all efforts to mediate between a changing culture and inherited religious teaching as a dilution of faith.

In such a time of transition, dominant groups are especially vulnerable. As we look back to the pre-World War I days with some knowledge of how the multiplying pressures of those times were beginning to affect Protestant life and thought, we may wonder that so few then perceived how deep the challenges were. Denominational and interdenominational leaders seemed to remain superbly confident that their dominance in the culture would hold, that their understandings of the relationship between religion and government would not be shaken, and that the twentieth would indeed be a "Christian" century as they defined it. It took a Catholic layman like Santayana to see that another civilization was beginning to displace the one in which American Protestants had been so strongly entrenched.

Why could so few of them see it then? Later in the century, as consciousness of the meaning of the ever-widening pluralization of religion spread and the Supreme Court began to reinterpret long-dominant definitions of church-state relations, many became aware of what had been

[5] *The Gospel for an Age of Doubt: The Yale Lectures on Preaching, 1896* (New York: Macmillan, 1897), 7.
[6] *Recollections* (Boston: Houghton Mifflin, 1909), 262.

happening over a long period of time. But it requires a closer look at major and some smaller Protestant bodies in the years prior to World War I to understand why they could then expect to retain their accustomed position in American life in the face of sweeping demographic, intellectual, and religious changes.

Centripetal and Centrifugal Forces in the Protestant World

A growing number of churches in the United States, large and small, were normally classed as Protestant in this as in other periods of American life. The more conspicuous and influential denominational families in the progressive period were the eight largest ones, which had memberships ranging from some half a million to six million. The colonial period had seen three giants: Congregational, Episcopal, Presbyterian. But two other denominational families, Baptist and Methodist, grew to be the two largest American Protestant groupings in the first half of the nineteenth century and have remained so ever since. The Disciples of Christ or Christian churches emerged indigenously in the same period, eventually subdividing into several major branches. All these had historical roots in British Protestant traditions, and their theological histories were marked in varying degrees by ongoing tensions between Calvinism and Arminianism. The Reformed churches, Dutch and German, also had deep historical roots in the colonial period and with the Calvinist tradition, but had remained comparatively much smaller bodies. The other large (and rapidly growing) denominational family, the Lutheran, stemmed largely from the European continent as various branches of that tradition came primarily from Germany and Scandinavia over three centuries. In the early twentieth century many languages continued to be used in some of these bodies, but the increasing use of English contributed to the unitive trends among the various branches most akin ethnically and theologically.

Although some strands of Lutheranism underwent unification in 1917 and 1918, all these eight denominational families were divided along sectional, ethnic, and racial lines. The illustrations are familiar: for example, there were northern and southern branches of Baptist, Methodist, and Presbyterian churches; both Dutch and German Reformed communions; a variety of Lutheran synods; and separate African American denominations, especially among Baptists and Methodists.[7] In American culture at that time, the predominantly white, English-speaking denominations were especially influential as they continued to hope and work for a more

[7] For the general background, see Gaustad, *Historical Atlas of Religion in America*, Part 2. For extended treatments, see Piepkorn, *Profiles in Belief*, vol. 2.

fully Christian America, although many smaller bodies also exhibited similar characteristics.

There were, however, sharp tensions within most of these denominational groupings, large and small—sometimes because of the differing ethnic and racial stocks within a given body, also because of theological disputes within various communions. In view of the intense bitterness of the fundamentalist/modernist controversies of the 1920s, especially among Baptists and Presbyterians but certainly elsewhere too, it has been convenient to interpret Protestant history in the period before World War I back through those struggles in a way that distorts an interpretation of the prewar period. It has been presented as a battle between two armies, thus obscuring how much the churches had in common and minimizing the considerable amount of cooperation most of them practiced. In fact, the fundamentalist/modernist controversy erupted after the Great War, when military language was all the more readily transferable to other kinds of human conflict, including the religious. In his study of the post-Darwinian controversies in Great Britain and America in the later nineteenth century, James R. Moore has richly illustrated the dangers of using the imageries and concepts of war in portraying the religious past, not least because it so easily traps the interpreter in false polarizations. He observed that "the military metaphor must be abandoned by those who wish to achieve historical understanding."[8]

Because struggling groups use history to justify themselves and criticize their opponents, they easily assume that the conflict of their time was also a feature of the past. This was often so in the heat of the Protestant theological struggles of the 1920s and what followed. As a consequence, interpretations of the prewar period were often distorted, and the terms fundamentalism (coined in 1920) and modernism were incorrectly applied to earlier conservative and liberal religious movements. The actual spectrum of theological parties in the early twentieth century has thus too often been obscured by an oversimplified liberal/conservative dichotomy. George M. Marsden has observed that before World War I, "the emerging fundamentalist coalition was largely quiescent. Few could have predicted the explosion that followed."[9] Now after a half-century of various

[8] *The Post-Darwinian Controversies: A Study of the Protestant Struggle to Come to Terms with Darwin in Great Britain and America, 1870–1900* (Cambridge: Cambridge University Press, 1979), 76.

[9] *Fundamentalism and American Culture: The Shaping of Twentieth-Century Evangelicalism: 1870–1925* (New York: Oxford University Press, 1980). Marsden notes that the word "fundamentalist" was invented by Curtis Lee Laws in 1920 (ibid., 107). The term "fundamental" as applied to religion, however, became well known earlier, especially through the circulation of twelve small volumes entitled *The Fundamentals: A Testimony to the Truth* (Chicago: Testimony Publishing Co., n.d. [1910–15]). The fundamentalist movement emerged out of a complex historical rootage; see, e.g., Ernest R. Sandeen, *The*

attempts to understand those intense controversies and perceptive efforts to analyze what led up to and followed from them, we can see the facts more clearly: parties that, it is claimed, waved the banners of fundamentalism and modernism tended to be the extremes of the larger complex movements of conservative, moderate, and liberal evangelical Protestants.[10]

That there were some sharp differences among Protestants during the progressive period is true enough. Yet there was also a strong sense of a larger unity and considerable practical cooperation among the communions, especially those steeped in the British Protestant traditions. Although there were divisive centrifugal forces at work within and between denominations, strong countering centripetal tendencies also held them in check. Hence outwardly the pattern of the familiar united Protestant front remained intact despite its inner tensions and differences. Not only did evangelical claims that the United States was a Christian nation continue to be highly influential, but also the consonance of such views with many progressive aims seemed to many Protestants to promise that the country would come even closer to attaining their ideals. While emphasizing the separation of church and state, they hoped and expected that the familiar methods of voluntaryism and persuasion would work for the still fuller Christianization of the culture. In the following analysis I illustrate these generalizations by showing that the centripetal, unitive forces seemed to be gaining ground against the centrifugal, divisive ones among Protestants in the progressive period.

Centrality of the Bible

With few exceptions, Protestants shared a common devotion to the Bible, as was evident in their patterns of preaching, worship, and Sunday school teaching. Familiar biblical phrases and cadences informed the way they spoke and wrote. They could and often did disagree about how to interpret "the word of God" because they were informed by differing theological parties and denominational traditions. In some seminaries biblical criticism was taught routinely, while others resisted that trend. But the Bible continued to serve as the central point of reference for Christian life

---

Roots of Fundamentalism: British and American Millenarianism, 1800–1930 (Chicago: University of Chicago Press, 1970).

[10] Important works for understanding these movements historically, in addition to those by Marsden and Sandeen, include Kenneth Cauthen, *The Impact of American Religious Liberalism*, 2d ed. (Washington, D.C.: University Press of America, 1983); Hutchison, *Modernist Impulse*; C. Allyn Russell, *Voices of American Fundamentalism* (Philadelphia: Westminster, 1976); Szasz, *Divided Mind*.

in church and world. The major denominations carried into the progressive period the views and practices that they had developed in the latter nineteenth century when, as David Danbom puts it, they "served as truly national institutions," helped by the fact that they "spoke a common language, among themselves as with the citizenry as well," for despite divisions "they shared a broad ethical foundation and a collection of sacred literature." Biblical imagery not only served as a cohesive force among the denominations, in their environing culture, but it also enabled the churches to speak "to an out-of-church citizenry that was more familiar with the ethics, myths, traditions, and literature of Christianity than is the unchurched population today."[11] Such famous political figures of the progressive period as Bryan, Roosevelt, and Wilson knew well how to appeal to idioms, rooted in biblical materials, common in both churches and, to a considerable degree, the larger society.

Christocentrism

Protestant piety, theology, and practice was prevailingly rooted in devotion to Jesus Christ. With few exceptions, belief that God was in Christ, that the Eternal was revealed in the person and work of Jesus Christ as Lord and Savior was normative. When this common orientation was articulated in sermonic and theological discourse in pulpits, prayer meetings, Sunday school classes and seminary lectures, differences of interpretation did emerge; they reflected the pluralistic nature of the Protestant tradition with its criss-cross of denominations, renewal movements, and various enthusiasms. Those attached to historic confessionalist bodies often tended to express their Christocentrism in traditional terms, as did those stemming from revivalistic pietism, although the vocabularies disclosed the variations in heritages. As evangelical liberals affirmed their belief in the unique divinity of Jesus Christ, they often sought to ground that faith more philosophically in the ontological being of God than did some of their conservative coreligionists, but they were troubled when a few of their number showed inclinations toward more naturalistic or humanistic positions—only a small cloud on the horizon at that point. As Hutchison has concluded, "Few, if any, Protestant liberals—modernistic or otherwise—denied normative status to Christ and to the Christian tradition."[12] The pervasive recognition of the centrality of Christ served as a strong unitive force across the wide Protestant spectrum.

[11] "The World of Hope," 21.
[12] Hutchison, Modernist Impulse, 8. See also H. Shelton Smith's chapter, "The Christocentric Liberal Tradition," in American Christianity: An Historical Interpretation with Rep-

The Kingdom of God

The use of the language and theology of the coming kingdom of God also provided a centripetal check on disruptive centrifugal tendencies in this period. Many relevant biblical passages were regularly invoked when this theme was used in sermon, lesson, lecture, journal, and book. Although some dwelt on the eschatological, end-of-time aspects of the kingdom's coming and expected it soon, others referred more freely to the "building of the kingdom" on earth as they sought a fully committed adherence to God's will in human affairs of the day. Szasz has aptly noted that the "vagueness of the Kingdom ideal . . . allowed for varying interpretations."[13] Partly because of the varied biblical contexts in which references to the kingdom of God appeared, this formulation remained highly effective in encouraging leaders of congregations and denominations to work together as they appealed to their constituencies. The term had considerable resonance with the wider public, for, as Washington Gladden emphasized, it was prominent among the ruling ideas of that age.[14] Though often not explicitly expounded in religious utterance, the political undertones of "kingdom," often referred to as "reign" or "rule," provided a favorable climate for those advocating a more positive role for the state.

Foreign Missions

With few exceptions, the Protestant churches wholeheartedly backed the foreign missionary movement, then one of their principal causes, for which the general and woman's boards of the denominations, with the help of various interdenominational and nondenominational agencies, maintained extensive home bases, raised vast sums, and sent thousands of missionaries abroad. Noting that by 1910 Americans had surpassed the hitherto dominant British in the numbers sent out and in the sums raised for the missionary cause, Hutchison observed that Protestant leaders

> spoke with remarkable unanimity across the theological spectrum. . . . In view of the bitter falling-out that was to come after 1920 between liberal Protestants and their biblically-conservative brethren, the extent of this earlier collaboration is striking. Opposing forces could collaborate because the principal common enterprise, converting the world to Christ, seemed more compelling than

---

resentative Documents, ed. Smith, Handy, and Lefferts A. Loetscher, vol. 2 (New York: Scribner, 1963), 255–308.

[13] *Divided Mind*, 44.

[14] *Ruling Ideas of the Present Age* (Boston: Houghton Mifflin, 1895), 13.

any differences; but also because they shared a vision of the essential rightness
of Western civilization and the near-inevitability of its triumph.[15]

The roots of this agreement were not wholly biblical or theological, for
the "gospel of Christian civilization" (95) was an accepted tenet, among
both liberals of various stripes whose hopes were invested in a coming
kingdom on earth and conservatives, including the growing number of
premillennialists who expected the Second Coming of Christ to bring the
heavenly kingdom to earth at any moment. So, Hutchison concluded,
"with the help of conciliatory attitudes among missionary statesmen, and
with just a little obfuscation (on both sides) of theological issues, premillennialists for some fifty years seemed able to march in step with liberals
and moderates in the exultant campaign for speedy world evangelization" (112). The mounting concern for the quality of civilization at home
and abroad, expressed in expanding institutional networks for missions,
increased contacts between church and governmental agencies, especially
the state department.

Reformism

Because of the attention given to the rapid expansion of the social gospel
in the progressive period, it has been easy to overlook the social concerns
and activities of those not directly related to that movement. But others
across the religious spectrum were prepared to speak and act on behalf of
social reform in the earlier years of the twentieth century. It often comes
as a surprise to find that in the progressive period many now remembered
as prominent fundamentalists contributed to reform efforts, including as
Mark A. Matthews, William Bell Riley, John Roach Straton, and Billy
Sunday.[16] Magnuson has documented how various representatives of revivalistic and holiness faiths "produced extensive social programs and
close identification with the needy."[17] Although the tensions between the
advocates of the social gospel, who in most cases adhered to some form
of theological liberalism, and Christian reformers of other rootage were
increasing, the wider concern for overcoming social evils kept the discussion open and encouraged some mutual cooperation. This is especially
clear in the case of the drive for prohibition, which was a major reform
movement in the progressive era, one that most Protestant bodies

---

[15] *Errand to the World*, 95.

[16] Russell has chapters on Straton and Riley in *Voices of American Fundamentalism*, and
an article on "Mark Allison Matthews: Seattle Fundamentalist and Civic Reformer," *Journal of Presbyterian History* 57 (1979): 446–66.

[17] *Salvation in the Slums*, 178.

strongly supported, some very vigorously, and one that involved churches in political action. The cause of temperance provided many cooperative ties among the churches across sectional, racial, and theological lines.[18] On the whole, concern for reform, broadly understood, exerted a generally unifying influence among the denominations in the progressive period even as it directed attention to public questions.

Cooperative Movements

In view of later developments within and against movements for cooperation among the denominations that have come to be called ecumenical, few may now realize how far it reached across the Protestant spectrum in the years prior to World War I. The origin of agencies representing various denominational boards, councils for foreign and home missions and missionary education, and the formation of the Federal Council of the Churches of Christ in America have already been discussed with particular reference to their role in the social Christian movement, but the FCC especially was equally concerned with promoting wider general cooperation among the original thirty-three churches that had officially joined it in 1908. Among its members were many larger evangelical denominations, including those from both the North and the South, a major Lutheran synod, and two large black Methodist communions.[19]

The FCC shared the enthusiasm for missions characteristic of its times and allied itself with the interdenominational mission agencies; thus it combined concern for cooperative, social, and missionary Christianity. The young council succeeded in holding the support of denominations in which vast groups—probably majorities in most cases—leaned toward religious conservatism. In 1919 William Jennings Bryan, now remembered as a champion of fundamentalism, called the Federal Council "the greatest religious organization in our nation" and served on its commission on temperance.[20] The participation of some black denominations in the work of the cooperative agencies at a time of increasing national segregation helped provide some effective links between black and white Protestants. In 1904, when the movement for closer cooperation among

[18] See Chap. 5.

[19] Cavert, *American Churches in the Ecumenical Movement*, 44, 52. The Episcopal Church was represented by its Commission on Christian Unity and did not become a full member until much later (1940). Although three Baptist denominations were members, the large Southern Baptist Convention was not.

[20] As quoted by Szasz, *Divided Mind*, 113, referring to Bryan's *Commoner* 19 (May 1919). This weekly newspaper was edited by Bryan with the help of his brother for twenty-two years following his defeat in 1900.

the denominations was rapidly developing, the episcopal address of the African Methodist Episcopal Church welcomed the trend: "The pronounced tendency to unity of spirit and cooperation in Christian work, and, indeed, to organic union, is hailed with delight."[21] Although unevenly, the centripetal forces seemed to be winning over the centrifugal, which had so often led to disruptions and schisms in American Protestant history. All this encouraged the churches' leaders to hope for both continued expansion of Protestant influence in the larger society and maintenance of patterns of church-state relations favorable to them.

Anti-Catholicism

Efforts to list the forces of cohesion in a many-sided movement tend to focus on those that can be described as positive, but the essentially negative power of anti-Catholicism persisted through the progressive period to strengthen bonds of unity across the denominationally divided Protestant ranks. To be sure, the extremism of the 1890s as promoted by the American Protective Association had faded, but the Catholic/Protestant stalemate over the public school issue not only persisted but increased as the influx of European immigrants, vast numbers of them Catholics, came to a peak. To hold off a perceived Catholic threat, the "wall of separation" became more strictly interpreted by many Protestants. In his *Church and State in the United States*, published in 1888, Philip Schaff had clearly stated his understanding that there could be no complete disjunction between church and state, for "an absolute separation is an impossibility."[22] But when his son David S. Schaff, also a church historian, wrote on "The Movement and Mission of American Christianity" in 1912 he put it differently. Interpreting Christianity in the United States chiefly in Protestant terms, he emphasized that "its mission seems plainly to be to demonstrate that the complete separation of church and state, as we have practiced it, is the principle most favorable for the development of the Christian religion."[23] His own hopes for that development were not far from the surface when he exclaimed, noting that the patterns of immigration were bringing in such groups as Bohemians, Italians, and Poles, "there could be no nobler task, no more brotherly task, no more patriotic task for the American churches than to bring to living embodi-

[21] *Journal of the Twenty-second Quadrennial Session of the African Methodist Episcopal Church . . . 1904* (Nashville: African Methodist Episcopal Church Sunday School Union, 1905), 74.

[22] See Chap. 1.

[23] "The Movement and Mission of American Christianity," *American Journal of Theology* 16 (1912): 63.

ment in these peoples, the spirit of John Huss and Savonarola and John à Lasco, whether they remain in their mother churches or make the transition to the Protestant communions" (69).

Protestant missionaries working with immigrants were usually much less veiled. Even a man of ecumenical spirit, Howard B. Grose, called by Martin E. Marty "the least anti-foreign and anti-Catholic among Protestant experts" in the church extension field, could argue for the conversion of Catholics because "the foundation principles of Protestant Americanism and Roman Catholicism are irreconcilable."[24] Protestants generally dismissed as misleading or deceitful such claims as one made by the titular head of American Catholicism, James Cardinal Gibbons, that "American Catholics rejoice in our separation of Church and State; and I can conceive of no combination of circumstances likely to arise which should make a union desirable either to Church or State."[25] The awareness of what was conceived as a common enemy served as a unifying force among Protestants of many types. In general, they interpreted the wall of separation as standing against any effort of the Catholic church to overly influence or control the state.

Patriotism

The spirit of patriotism that surged through American life at the opening of the twentieth century following the Spanish-American War was widely shared in the Protestant churches, which for the most part prided themselves on the close affinity between their faith and their nation. It was never more clearly put than by the Northern Methodists in 1900 when they voted permanently to display the American flag on the platform of their quadrennial General Conference; the Methodists claimed that their church "has ever been loyal and true to the government of the United States" and affirmed that "we believe that our devotion and loyalty thereto should be manifested and emphasized by this General Conference in order that with our loyalty to the King eternal may be advanced our love of country and its institutions."[26] Similar patriotic sentiments could also be sounded among Southern Methodists; the famous revivalist Samuel Porter Jones, often called "the Moody of the South," declared in a letter to the press in 1901 that "God has given us the greatest country the

[24] *Modern American Religion*, 1: 155. Grose is quoted from his *The Incoming Millions* (New York: Revell, 1906), 99.

[25] "The Church and the Republic," *North American Review* 189 (March 1909): 336.

[26] David J. Monroe, ed., *Journal of the General Conference of the Methodist Episcopal Church . . . 1900* (New York: Eaton and Mains, n.d. [1900]), 186–87.

sun shines on."[27] Ministers of many other denominations and roles wove the theme into their messages. Congregationalist Washington Gladden, for example, preached that "the nation is a divine institution. . . . Love of the nation, in its true conception, is a religious devotion."[28] A chapter by McLoughlin on Presbyterian revivalist Billy Sunday treated his whole career under the caption "Christianity and Patriotism Are Synonymous."[29] Many Protestants were less bombastic about it, but for them, too, Christianity meant primarily their "reformed" tradition, which they often associated with their Americanism.

Public Schools

Closely related to the unifying bond of patriotism for the great majority of American Protestants was their continuing devotion to the public school. The anti-Catholic aspect of this attitude has been mentioned, but the Protestant vision of public education operated internally as an effective binding force. John E. Smylie has observed that, because of the divided state of the churches, the nation absorbed a classic function of "the church" in Western civilization by becoming the primary society through which individuals, Christian and non-Christian alike, found personal identity. "Thus the unity which theology would localize in Christ and his church was actually realized in the American experience in the nation," Smylie explained. He added that "the public school system forged this unity."[30] Sidney E. Mead has perhaps overstated the point in saying that "the public schools in the United States took over one of the basic responsibilities that traditionally was always assumed by an established church. In this sense the public school system of the United States *is* its established church."[31] But his remark does fit the opening decades of the twentieth century, when many Protestants—and some other Americans—viewed the common schools with religious and patriotic fervor because they filled a gap in an increasingly pluralistic culture and provided a unifying force.

These various tendencies provided a certain cohesiveness for American Protestants across their many lines of division and assured them that their prominence in the culture was secure despite the society's vast changes.

[27] As quoted by William G. McLoughlin, *Modern Revivalism: Charles Grandison Finney to Billy Graham* (New York: Ronald, 1959), 310, 454.

[28] As quoted by Gorrell, *Age of Social Responsibility*, 125.

[29] McLoughlin, *Modern Revivalism*, 400–54.

[30] John E. Smylie, "The Christian Church and the National Ethos," in *Biblical Realism Confronts the Nation*, ed. Paul Peachey (Scottdale, Pa.: Herald Press, 1963), 39.

[31] Mead, *Lively Experiment*, 68.

The voluntary patterns of relating religion and government, tested for more than a century under the rubric of the separation of church and state, seemed to be working well for Protestants. Many were worried about the growing numbers of Catholics, but for the most part they were confident that the "wall of separation" would protect their free state and democratic ways from a hierarchical church that seemed to them so "foreign." When William Adams Brown undertook soon after World War I to assess the religious situation as it had been just before American entry, he observed that "while jealously guarding the principle of the separation of state and church, the American people are equally insistent upon the fact that their country is a Christian nation."[32] His evidence was similar to that of Philip Schaff and David A. Brewer some thirty years before. The great majority of Americans continued to accept the patterns of voluntary Christendom that had been shaped in the nineteenth century.

Deepening Tensions among Protestants

By the second decade of the twentieth century, however, some indications showed those patterns beginning to wear thin, especially among some educated clergy and lay leaders. A central thesis of Danbom's *"The World of Hope"* is that what he styles the "Christian progressivism" of the century's first decade was being "challenged by more scientific reformers who judged truth empirically and valued efficient behavior more highly than individual character."[33] Both types worked well together, for there was general agreement on the main concepts stressed by the Christian reformers: justice, duty, character, service, the golden rule, brotherhood, the law of love. In a more homogeneous society such constructs could guide public policy. But when it came to applying them to specific problems in an increasingly heterogeneous society, their very vagueness and comprehensiveness—one reason they were so widely appealing—also proved to be their weakness. Some progressivist Christians were tending to believe that hortatory and moralistic approaches were not enough and willingly sought more scientific and efficient guides for reform. Thus, a growing group of scientifically minded progressives "who looked for solutions to public problems that transcended Christianity seemed to gain strength and confidence" (132). They influenced the way some social gospel reformers shaped their appeals by stressing the role of expert administrators in finding better ways of solving social problems and emphasiz-

---

[32] *The Church in America: A Study of the Present Condition and Future Prospects of American Protestantism* (New York: Macmillan, 1922), 80.

[33] *"The World of Hope,"* viii.

ing the regulatory role of governmental agencies in moving toward a more just society. "Social Gospelers, such as Graham Taylor and Washington Gladden," Danbom declared, "integrated concepts of empiricism and efficiency into their messages with little difficulty" (146). He has admitted that the distinctions are clearer looking back than they were at the time, when "Christian and scientific reform concepts were mixed rather promiscuously by all sorts of progressives" (146).

The two basic types of reformers worked together in the teens; meanwhile, the intellectual differences between their approaches were widening. The concern for both personal and social regeneration, so important to social Christians, was of less importance to the scientific progressives who focused more on helping people by improving their environment. While the former continued to emphasize the importance of character, the latter were more interested in functional behavior that was measurable as efficient. But prominent social gospel leaders, characteristically drawing on the mediating style of the evangelical liberal theology that informed them, insisted that the individual and social gospels were one and that evangelism and social service belonged together. For example, Shailer Mathews, dean of the University of Chicago's divinity school and at one point president of both the FCC and the Northern Baptist Convention, and Harry F. Ward of Boston University's school of theology and the MFSS both stressed the inseparable complementarity of individual and group in Christian life—Mathews in *The Individual and the Social Gospel* (1914), and Ward in *Social Evangelism* (1915).[34] In his last book, based on lectures delivered in April 1917, Walter Rauschenbusch discussed the tension in the context of history and theology in "The Social Gospel and Personal Salvation" chapter. Affirming that "the salvation of the individual is, of course, an essential part of salvation,"[35] he also found that "the fundamental theological terms about the experiences of salvation get a new orientation, correction, and enrichment through the religious point of view contained in the social gospel" (105). Such changes led not away from but to the heart of the faith, for they "would effect an approximation to the spirit and outlook of primitive Christianity, going back of Catholicism and Protestantism alike" (105). Although the Christian progressives thus justified their own position, on the whole the progressive movement in the years just prior to the war was significantly influenced by the more secular emphases of the scientific approach and the need for businesslike efficiency.

At the same time, tension between parties in Protestant churches that

---

[34] These study books and other similar materials are discussed by Gorrell, *Age of Social Responsibility*, 230–41.

[35] *A Theology for the Social Gospel* (New York: Macmillan, 1917), 95.

accepted liberal trends in theology and social thought and those that resisted them was steadily increasing. For the most part, the snapping of
bonds that had long allowed those of various theological alignments and
practical commitments in the major denominations to work together still
lay ahead, but sharper lines between differing positions were being
drawn. Tensions, more fully revealed during World War I and its aftermath, were already surfacing. In the last chapter of the last volume of *The
Fundamentals*, Charles R. Erdman of Princeton Theological Seminary
sharply criticized the "so-called 'social gospel' which discards the fundamental doctrines of Christianity and substitutes a religion of good
works."[36] He was dismayed by those who "in the name of Christianity,
have been promising a new social order, a kingdom of God, which they
declare the Church will introduce," for they thus occasioned sharp criti-
cisms of the church and subjected it to "being held responsible for social
sins and injustices, for the wrongs and grievances of the age" (118). In his
view, the church had arrogated to itself improper functions and promised
action for which there was no written word of scripture—it had tres-
passed into the work of the state, which "is quite as purely a divine institution as is the Church" (119). It was the task of the state, not the church,
to undertake social reconstruction when necessary and to secure by legal
enactments and legislative processes the abolition of abuses. He concluded by challenging the postmillennial views of the liberal social gospel
by appeal to biblical prophecy: "The hope of the world is not in a new
social order instituted by unregenerate men; not a millennium made by
man; not a commonwealth of humanity organized as a Socialist state; but
a kingdom established by Christ which will fill the earth with glory at the
coming of the King" (119).

In assessing the reasons for the dramatic disappearance or at least the
severe curtailment of the interest of conservative evangelicals in social
issues by the 1920s, George Marsden has observed that social gospel leaders' efforts to hold the reforming and evangelistic implications of the gospel together in a viable relationship did not seem to be working well in
the years just prior to the war. "The Social Gospel was presented, or was
thought to be presented, as equivalent to the Gospel itself," he concluded,
also noting that "the liberal and Social Gospel emphasis on the kingdom
of God as realized in the progress of civilization was readily contrasted
with premillennialist eschatological hopes."[37] The shell of voluntary Protestant Christendom, to paraphrase Santayana, was close to breaking;
centrifugal forces were rising against those that had long and successfully
kept an evangelical united front intact. The familiar agreements that had

---

[36] "The Church and Socialism," *The Fundamentals* 12 (1915): 116.
[37] Marsden, *Fundamentalism and American Culture*, 92.

been holding together the Protestant establishment, especially as represented by the large denominational families, were being strained from within.

Protestant Proliferation

By the early twentieth century, though not then taken very seriously by most of the larger denominations, new movements within the Protestant world were widening the denominational spectrum, often at the expense of what are now called the larger mainline churches. At the time they seemed small and inconsequential, not threatening to the prestigious giants. The Holiness movement, drawing on previous perfectionist trends in the Wesleyan tradition and in the revival theology of Charles Finney and Asa Mahan at Oberlin, began to grow into a visible force for renewal in the churches soon after the Civil War. Troubled by the accommodation of churches to the culture, the new movement, committed to revivalism and missions, put emphasis on a strict personal moral code. Holiness views, strong among Methodists, also gained support among Presbyterians, Baptists, and Congregationalists. At first Holiness leaders, especially among Methodists—for John Wesley had put considerable stress on Christian perfection—disavowed any intention of leaving their denominational homes. They developed a spreading network of associations of those seeking perfection and multiplied their own "faith missions." Through revivals, camp meetings, and periodicals, they taught the doctrines of justification and entire sanctification as two gifts of the Holy Ghost.

In 1880 the forming of separate Holiness bodies began. Daniel S. Warner founded the Church of God with headquarters at Anderson, Indiana, in a split from a church of similar name organized fifty years before as part of the same restoration impulse that had produced the Disciples. The Salvation Army, which had been founded in England in 1878 by William Booth, a former Methodist, and which emphasized certain Holiness teachings, extended its work to North America in the following decade. In 1887 a nondenominational fellowship, the Christian and Missionary Alliance, was founded by A. B. Simpson, a former Presbyterian from Canada. Eventually it evolved into a new denomination. Independent congregations of various backgrounds multiplied until the denominations reacted with some alarm, especially the Methodists, who began to feel inroads on their congregations and conferences keenly. The history of the divisions, subdivisions, and unions of Holiness elements in new sects and denominations is complex. The most important single development grew from the First Church of the Nazarene, founded in Los Angeles in 1895, which soon spawned satellite churches and attracted others. By 1908 a series of unions formally brought the Church of the Nazarene into being as a swift-growing, revivalistic, perfectionist denomination, its Methodist background evident in its doctrine and polity. Within two years it was already reporting a membership of ten thousand; it increased more than fiftyfold within eight decades. A score of Holiness denominations of various sizes emerged from 1895 to 1905.[38] From the point of view of many in the major denominational families, such relatively small bodies were adding to the range of conservative "sects" on the fringes of Christendom and hindering efforts to bring a larger unity into the Protestant world.

Although the Holiness movement was at an early stage in its development into a new denominational family, it provided the seedbed for Pentecostalism, which continued many of its emphases while adding another that was distinctive. To the familiar Holiness concerns for conservative biblicism, premillennialism, strict moral codes, and faith healing, Pentecostals added the baptism of the Holy Spirit as evidenced by speaking in tongues. A line of demarcation between the two movements opened in the years before World War I: Holiness had paved the way for the Pentecostal movement and lost many members to it, but the two histories soon diverged.

Briefly, in the 1890s Benjamin H. Irwin, a Baptist minister and member of a Holiness association in Iowa, preached that beyond the experiences of justification and sanctification there was a third blessing—that of the baptism with the Holy Ghost and fire. At his services, emotional peaks reminiscent of the camp meetings of the Second Great Awakening occurred. Associations accepting this emphasis were gathered as the Fire Baptized Holiness Church in 1898. Associated with Irwin's revival meetings was a former Methodist, Charles F. Parham, who opened a small Bible school in Kansas where, at a watchnight service following a study of Acts 2, as 1901 dawned, a student and then others spoke in tongues— an experience interpreted as evidence of the baptism of the Holy Spirit. As news of the event spread, Parham traveled widely, conducting meetings. In 1905 he opened a Bible training school in Texas, where, despite the racial barriers, his students included a black former Baptist preacher

---

[38] The literature on the Holiness Movement is vast; its extent can be seen in Charles E. Jones, *Guide to the Study of the Holiness Movement* (Metuchen, N.J.: Scarecrow, 1974), and Donald W. Dayton, ed., *The Christian Higher Life: A Bibliographical Overview* (New York: Garland, 1984). A good basic work on the movement is Vinson Synan, *The Holiness-Pentecostal Movement in the United States* (Grand Rapids, Mich.: Eerdmans, 1971). For a useful treatment of the various Holiness churches, see Piepkorn, *Profiles in Belief*, vol. 3, *Holiness and Pentecostal* (1979); he discusses the background and situation in the 1970s of 61 Holiness and 130 Pentecostal denominations. See also Timothy L. Smith, *Called Unto Holiness: The Story of the Nazarenes: The Formative Years* (Kansas City, Mo.: Nazarene Publishing House, 1962).

of Holiness tendencies, William J. Seymour. Accepting the emphasis on the third blessing, Seymour moved to Los Angeles in 1906, where for three years he conducted the intense, sustained Azusa Street revival that soon attracted thousands, among them many future leaders, black and white, of various branches of Pentecostalism. Many were convinced that they had received the third blessing and spoke in tongues. They went out to spread the Pentecostal emphasis, not only in North America but also to other continents. Others who heard about the revival, some of whom came to see for themselves, concluded it was emotional nonsense, and all kinds of charges were hurled at the new movement, along with assertions that speaking in tongues could be wholly explained away by psychological analysis. Sharp criticism came from not only the older, established denominations but also Holiness and smaller conservative churches.[39]

At first the Pentecostal movement operated largely along nondenominational lines. But soon, often because of controversies, either new church bodies were formed, or some already founded turned to the new way. Important for the future of the movement was the work of Charles H. Mason, a former Baptist. After five weeks at Azusa Street, Mason returned to Memphis, Tennessee, to redirect his Church of God in Christ, which had been founded as a Holiness body in 1895, into what would later become the largest black Pentecostal church in the world. Mason's role was significant for the growth of the new denominational family, for his church held a legal charter, which meant that ministers ordained by him could legally perform marriages and secure clergy fare privileges on the railroads—a boon for revivalists and other leaders who were continually traveling. Some whites thus ordained stayed with the Church of God in Christ, which, along with other growing Pentecostal bodies, was at first interracial, though in a few years the racial line was drawn as the burgeoning denominations divided. Divisions also occurred for theological reasons, related primarily to the doctrine of sanctification. A number of such groups merged in Arkansas in 1914 to form the Assemblies of God, soon to become the largest of the Pentecostal denominations. Other controversies led to the formation of still other churches.

By 1920, therefore, two complex and rapidly growing denominational families had been added to the Protestant spectrum. Finding their original followings largely among poor and disinherited elements in American life, often in rural areas, many of these bodies followed familiar patterns of upward escalation economically and socially even as their appeal to

[39] In addition to the works by Synan and Piepkorn just mentioned, see Robert A. Anderson, *Visions of the Disinherited: The Making of American Pentecostalism* (New York: Oxford University Press, 1979), and Nils Bloch-Hoell, *A Study of the Origin, Development, and Distinctive Character of the Pentecostal Movement* (New York: Humanities Press, 1964).

those on the margins of society persisted. As still small, volatile movements in the early decades of the century, the country at large rarely took them seriously. Often the press treated them derisively by calling them such names as "holy rollers." But the foundations of what were to mature into a number of viable, vigorous churches were laid in the late nineteenth and early twentieth centuries, eventually at the cost of controversy and confusion in the older denominations. The new arrivals were not contained by the centripetal forces that were still holding the major Protestant churches together in a workable relationship. As the denominational spectrum significantly widened, linkages that had allowed Protestants to think of themselves as the predominant religious force in the nation in their version of a voluntary Christendom were being weakened. At the time leaders of the major denominational and interdenominational agencies did not know that these "curiosities" would later seriously rival or actually undermine the church-state pattern of the voluntary Christendom that had dominated so much of the religious life of the nineteenth and early twentieth centuries in America.

The Holiness and Pentecostal denominational families were counted as in the Protestant fold, but the continuing growth and increasing self-confidence of traditions outside the range of religious bodies classed as Protestant was of great significance in the first two decades of the twentieth century, though that became generally evident only later. Future changes in the relations between religion and government, however, can be better understood by attention to those years.

The Burgeoning of American Catholicism

In a passage on European immigration during the peak years from 1890 to 1920, Jay Dolan compactly described not only the arrival of more than eighteen million newcomers but also the significance of the complexity of this great influx:

> These immigrants came from quite different parts of Europe than their nineteenth-century predecessors. Large numbers of Italians immigrated during those years; scores of people fled from poverty and persecution in Eastern Europe and settled in the United States. Polish, Hungarian, Czech, Slovak, Ruthenians, Slovenians, and numbers of people from other exotic cultural backgrounds streamed into the United States. Americans had never seen such a mosaic of peoples from regions so culturally remote from the Anglo-Saxon heritage that for so long had comprised the bedrock of the American population.[40]

[40] "Immigration and American Christianity: A History of Their Histories," in *A Century of Church History*, ed. Bowden, 124.

The Roman Catholic church was greatly strengthened by this unprecedented migration. With an estimated twelve million members in 1900—
an inclusive reckoning of all persons baptized in the church—Catholics
gained some four million more by the time the country entered World
War I in 1917; membership was reported to exceed nineteen million by
1920. Obviously the church was gaining from the continued influx of
immigrants, which surprisingly surpassed an annual total of one million
no less than six times in the first fifteen years of the century. Nor were all
those arriving from Europe; there was also an influx of French-Canadi-
ans. The outbreak of the war in Europe soon checked the incoming tide,
but John Tracy Ellis concluded that almost 50 percent—three and a half
million—of those arriving between 1900 and 1920 were Catholics.[41]

Catholic resources were strained in the effort to provide sufficient
churches and schools to care for the newcomers. The distinctive Americanist movement had been brought to a halt, but the church worked hard
to help these Catholics from many backgrounds adjust to American life
and become patriotic citizens. In 1902 Pope Leo XIII congratulated the
Catholics in the United States on their remarkable growth; he declared
that its cause, "although first of all to be attributed to the providence of
God, must also be ascribed to your energy and activity." The pope commented on the promotion of every kind of Catholic organization "in harmony with the remarkable character of the people of your country." He
made the best of the separation of church and state. "True, you are shown
no special favor by the law of the land, but on the other hand your law-
givers are certainly entitled to praise for the fact that they do nothing to
restrain you in your just liberty."[42] There were indeed a multitude of
Catholic organizations, some of them expressly devoted to church extension. For example, the American Catholic Missionary Union had been
founded in the 1890s, and the Catholic Church Extension Society was
formed in 1905. At the local level, groups of immigrant Catholics regularly founded mutual aid societies in their efforts to find a place in their
new environment. Some groups predated the formation of a Catholic parish in their locales, but more often the initiative came from the clergy. By
1908 no less than thirty bands of diocesan priests were reaching out to
neglected parishes. Thirteen new dioceses, eight of them in the Midwest,
were established between 1903 and 1914 when Pius X was pope.

The growing influence and maturity of the American church was recognized by the papacy in 1908 when the apostolic constitution, *Sapiento
consilio*, removed it (along with other countries in the Western hemi-

---

[41] "The U.S.A.," in Roger Aubert et al., *The Church in a Secularized Society* (New York:
Paulist Press, 1978), 277.

[42] Ellis, ed., *Documents of American Catholic History* 2: 548.

sphere) from the missionary category and the jurisdiction of the Congregation for the Propagation of the Faith; this move formally gave the church equal status with that of European nations. American Catholics were now beginning to enter more aggressively into foreign missions. There had been little time or energy for such enterprises in the nineteenth century. The exceptions were few: short-lived efforts were made in Liberia in the 1840s, and a few missionary priests and members of orders served in such places as the Bahamas, China, Hawaii, and Central America. But in the year following *Sapiento consilio* the Saint Mary's Mission House near Chicago was opened as the first training center for missionaries going abroad. Two years later its importance was surpassed by the organization of the Catholic Foreign Mission Society, a community of secular priests better known as Maryknoll founded by James A. Walsh and Thomas Price. Its outreach was delayed by the war; its first band of priests left for China in 1918. Eventually it sent thousands of priests, brothers, seminarians, and sisters abroad.[43]

This rapidly expanding church, torn by inner tensions, was struggling to find a principle of unity. It had long been troubled by disagreements among the various ethnic traditions, now accentuated by the increasing numbers. Many of the more recent arrivals hoped to maintain their own traditions and languages, but they encountered a church struggling toward centralization at a time when the Irish clergy, who emphasized the priest's controlling role in parish affairs, made it difficult for lay people to assume decision-making roles. By 1900 two-thirds of the bishops were of Irish descent. In a number of midwestern dioceses, where the German element was in control, about one-seventh of the bishops were of that background. In either case many of the newer immigrants, especially from southern and eastern Europe, who found themselves uncomfortable but outnumbered, had difficulty securing priests who understood their old world traditions and languages.

This led to some bitter controversies as lay groups formed by new arrivals, were quickly learning the ways of democracy and struggled for traditions dear to them and priests familiar with their ways. This had happened before, even to the point of congregations withdrawing, but usually the bishops won in the end; time helped to heal the wounds. The continued growth of the parochial schools, of which there were more than five thousand by 1920, played an important role in reducing some ethnic tensions and encouraging a loyalty to the new country. But the schools also often reflected the demographic patterns of the host parish, and battles for their control among those of various nationalities erupted.

In the case of two sizable immigrant groups, however, the tensions

---

[43] Hennesey, *American Catholics*, 206, 218; Ellis, "The U.S.A.," 286.

were not sufficiently reduced to avoid schism. Catholic Ukrainians worshiped according to their distinctive Eastern rite in Europe, which had been accepted by Rome centuries before, along with the custom of a married clergy. But the American bishops, belonging to the Latin rite, were committed to clerical celibacy. The departure of Ukrainian congregations for the Russian Orthodox Church had begun in the 1890s; by 1916 more than 160 Eastern-rite Catholic parishes had transferred the allegiance of more than two hundred thousand people.

The other major schism was among groups of Polish Catholics. It also began in the 1890s with the separation of congregations over issues of the laity's role and ownership of property. In 1904 Francis Hodur, pastor of a Scranton congregation that had become independent over difficulties with their German pastor and Irish bishop, gathered various schismatic churches together to form the autonomous Polish National Catholic Church. Three years later Hodur was consecrated bishop by the Old Catholic archbishop of Utrecht. Although the majority of Poles remained with the Roman church, the new body grew to some quarter of a million members by midcentury.[44] The numbers who left the church in these splits were small compared to the vast size of the Roman Catholic church; in most cases the underlying tensions that the several schisms dramatized were kept in bounds. But the divisions illustrate the way immigration widened the religious pluriformity of twentieth-century America, though Protestant, Eastern Orthodox, and Jewish histories illustrate the fissiparous tendencies much more fully.

The dramatic growth of the Catholic church over a period of more than a hundred years had brought rich and varied Catholic traditions and a mixture of many nationalities together in the context of an often hostile, rapidly centralizing culture. Facing its great inner diversities made the church reach for larger patterns of unity so that it could rise to the challenges and opportunities of the twentieth century and fulfill a mission adequate to the faith it professed. As archbishop of Baltimore, Cardinal Gibbons was the titular head of the church, and it was a tribute to his own integrity and diplomatic skills that he remained a force for unity in a time of such tumultuous change. He was a highly respected figure within and beyond Catholicism; at an impressive celebration on the occasion of the fiftieth anniversary of his ordination, many celebrities were present, conspicuously President Taft and his predecessor, Theodore Roosevelt.

The archbishops exercised strong leadership in their own areas, and a

[44] Dolan, *American Catholic Experience*, 180–89; Piepkorn, *Profiles in Belief*, Vol. 1, *Roman Catholic, Old Catholic, Eastern Orthodox* (1977), summarized the history of the Ukrainian churches and the Polish National Catholic Church, 69–73, 280–83.

few played national roles. They met annually, but they lacked a permanent organizational structure and looked to Rome for authority. Growing in number and size, the various religious orders, not directly responsible to the diocesan structures of the church, were under their own leaders. Some lay organizations were thriving; for example, the Knights of Columbus, founded by New England Irish-Americans in 1882 as a fraternal benefit and insurance society, had spread to every state in the union (and beyond) within twenty-five years; eventually it became the largest body of Catholic laymen in the world.[45] Various efforts to provide a measure of cooperation and coordination among the growing network of lay movements had led to forming the American Federation of Catholic Societies in 1901. But some members of the hierarchy gave it only half-hearted support, and, because each organization in its membership retained its autonomy, it served primarily as an annual meeting for discussing and passing resolutions.[46] The federation was not able to provide the principle of unity the church needed in the face of twentieth-century realities. Not until the crisis of American entry into World War I did the church find and apply that principle.

In relation to the wider culture, the Catholic experience appeared ambivalent. On the one hand, Catholics were gaining in political power, especially in some cities where there had been concentrations of immigrants over several generations. James Hennesey has illustrated this development in Irish-Catholic Democratic strongholds of Boston, New York, Jersey City, Chicago, San Francisco, and Kansas City.[47] Another sign of growing Catholic visibility was the prominence of a number of well-known Catholics in national life. For example, Charles J. Bonaparte, related to the famous French family but American born, became secretary of the Navy in 1905 and then served as attorney general from 1906 to 1909. A devout Catholic, he was committed to keeping the spheres of religion and government clearly distinct. Edward Douglas White, appointed to the Supreme Court in 1894, became chief justice in 1910 and served until 1921, the last year of his life. Maurice F. Egan, former professor at Notre Dame and Catholic University, entered diplomatic service in 1907 as minister to Denmark, in which post he played a major part in the purchase of the Danish West Indies in 1916. The public role of such persons contributed to a better press for Catholics.

[45] The story has been well told by Christopher J. Kauffman, *Faith and Fraternalism: The History of the Knights of Columbus, 1882–1982* (New York: Harper, 1982).

[46] McAvoy, *History of the Catholic Church*, 345–46.

[47] *American Catholics*, 208. See also Hennesey, "Roman Catholics and American Politics, 1900–1960: Altered Circumstances, Continuing Patterns," in *Religion and American Politics From the Colonial Period to the 1980s*, ed. Mark A. Noll (New York: Oxford University Press, 1990), 302–21.

On the other hand, developments in Rome reinforced the persistent impression in general public opinion, especially as exploited by anti-Catholics, that the church was foreign. In the latter half of the nineteenth century, the classicist or neoscholastic position became dominant in Catholic theology, especially in Rome. From this perspective, the church was viewed primarily as a fixed, unchanging reality, a divine institution, a perfect society—immune to change and superior to other associations of humans. As the nineteenth century drew to a close, such convictions lay behind the cautious but effective silencing of the Americanist movement as such. But in Catholic seminaries and universities of both Europe and America, some priests and other scholars who encountered the rapidly developing fields of modern science, philosophy, history, and biblical studies were seeking to relate some new perspectives to traditional church teaching. In 1903 Pope Leo XIII was succeeded by Pius X, who became increasingly disturbed by the implications for the church's official teachings as interpreted from the neoscholastic position of what soon became labeled modernism. The center of the modernist movement was in France, but the church in America was affected by the determination of Rome to end what it perceived as a threat to the faith. This judgment, meted out with a heavy hand, did not discriminate between destructive criticism and the various patterns of creative scholarship that sought to renew the church's intellectual life by reference to modern thought.

In 1907 Pius X issued two encyclicals regarding modernism. *Lamentabili sane exitu* condemned sixty-five errors, drawn largely from modernist writings. *Pascendi dominici gregis* not only detailed modernist faults but also listed practical steps to end the movement. By interpreting the movement as a conspiracy based on agnosticism and immanentalist philosophies, the pope in his letter instructed bishops to tighten censorship and appoint vigilance committees in each diocese. Three years later an oath against modernism was required of all priests and candidates for that role. Thus neo-scholastic theology with its view of the church as static and unchanging through history was vigorously promoted and any evidence of liberal scholarship was quickly suppressed. Some notable European leaders of modernism were excommunicated, and some others in the Catholic world withdrew from the church.

On the American scene, continuing efforts to mediate between traditional orthodox interpretations of faith and church and modern thought were checked for a half-century. Movements toward intellectual renewal in several prominent American seminaries, notably St. Joseph's at Dunwoodie and St. John's in Brighton, related to the archdioceses of New York and Boston respectively, were halted.[48] With this triumph of con-

---

[48] See chaps. 9 and 10 in Christopher J. Kauffman, *Tradition and Transformation in*

servatism, the church in America moved into a period of consolidation and Romanization. Rome became both the spiritual and intellectual center of Catholicism in America. The emphasis was on the church as institution—orthodox, regularized, controlled from Rome through the hierarchy and the priesthood. The work of dioceses, parishes, and schools was supported by a network of ancillary Catholic organizations that in many areas tended to create enclaves of the faithful largely cut off from cultural contacts with others. "The combination of Americanist and Modernist crises, and particularly the powerful integrist reaction which set in after 1907," Hennesey concluded, "effectively put an end for the next fifty years to further development of Catholic thought in authentic American dress."[49]

All this, coming at a time when millions of immigrants were still pouring in, fed the familiar clichés that the Catholic church was foreign to American culture and a menace to the country's traditions. Resurgent anti-Catholic feeling reached its height in 1914, when about sixty anti-Catholic periodicals were being published. Most had little standing and small circulation, though the weekly *Menace* then had well over one million subscribers. The new surge, based largely in rural areas and small towns, never generated the force of the APA in the 1890s, and it soon passed. But it stirred considerable apprehension, for Catholics remembered the nativist furies of the past.

When war clouds began to gather, as Richard M. Linkh has explained, "Catholics were placed on the defensive and felt compelled to conduct themselves in a manner above suspicion proving their undivided loyalty at every turn."[50] Inasmuch as the church consistently taught and Catholics practiced love of country, clearly evidenced in times of war, to be regarded as unpatriotic hurt. Many Catholics believed in the melting pot theory of assimilation, in which the many streams of immigration would be fused into one American people, with each contributing its best to the whole. Cardinal Gibbons favored the concept and tirelessly emphasized the patriotic spirit of Catholics. So did the rapidly growing Knights of Columbus, recently characterized as "a classic instance of a minority's drive to assimilate into the larger society."[51] As early as 1893, a prominent leader of the Knights, Thomas H. Cummings, anticipated the "triple melting pot" variation of the theory, much later to be popularized by Will Herberg's book *Protestant—Catholic—Jew* (1955). Cummings wrote

---

Catholic Culture: The Priests of Saint Sulpice in the United States from 1791 to the Present (New York: Macmillan, 1988), 199–239.

[49] *American Catholics*, 217.

[50] *American Catholicism and European Immigrants (1900–1924)* (Staten Island, N.Y.: Center for Migration Studies, 1975), 135.

[51] Kauffman, *Faith and Fraternalism*, 71.

that "the best type of American is he who best exemplifies in his own life, that this is not a Protestant country, nor a Catholic country, nor a Hebrew country, any more than it is an Anglo-Saxon or a Latin country, but a country of all races and all creeds, with one, great broad unmolterable [*sic*] creed of fair play and equal rights for all."[52]

At a time when many Catholics were moving into increasingly prominent political and public roles in American life and knew themselves to be loyal Americans, it stung to be regarded as foreign and somehow alien, not only because of the Catholic melange of races and tongues but also because of the Romanization of their American church, which tended to cut them off from many aspects of cultural and intellectual life. The latter especially, Dolan concluded, "put Catholics in a strange stance; they were both 100 percent American, loyal patriots to the core, and 100 percent Roman, loyal Catholics to the core. It was a unique blend of religion and nationalism which most other Americans failed to understand."[53] Clear statements by American Catholic authorities who affirmed their acceptance of religious freedom and the separation of church and state were brushed aside not only by extremists among anti-Catholics but also by more moderate critics who feared the alleged political power of the pope in twentieth-century America. That the wave of intolerance of the second decade of the century soon quieted, however, was in part evidence of the mounting strength of Catholics in the United States and also of their ability, despite the difficulties, to claim a larger place in American public life.

The Maturation of Other Religious Traditions

Judaism

In the first fifteen years of the twentieth century, while immigration was having a significant impact on America's largest church, it was also swiftly turning Judaism into what would soon be recognized as one of the nation's major religious traditions. Estimates of the increase in the number of Jews in this period vary considerably, but general evidence points to a growth from a little more than one million to more than three million.[54] The discrimination and periodic persecution with which Christians had treated Jews for centuries was resurgent in Europe in the later nineteenth century, and millions turned their eyes toward America as a land of freedom and opportunity. The outbreak of pogroms in Russia in 1881

[52] Ibid., 167. For Herberg's interpretation of the triple melting pot, see his *Protestant—Catholic—Jew: An Essay in American Religious Sociology* (New York: Doubleday, 1955).

[53] *American Catholic Experience*, 320.

[54] Yahalom, "Church-State Separation and Education," 32.

had greatly increased the number of Jewish immigrants to the United States; a second wave of European anti-Semitism beginning in 1903 dramatically intensified the influx. It was evident to the newcomers that though the shape of Christianity in America differed in many ways from that of eastern Europe, nevertheless the environing culture and its dominant religious institutions still bore marks of an origin in Christendom. The point has been well made by Stuart E. Rosenberg. Very much aware that in federal law America was never a Christian nation, he observed that "in the light of social realities the atmosphere of American life, not only in the Puritan communities, on the frontier, and in rural areas, but also in the early twentieth-century cities was Christian in everything but law."[55] Primarily in those cities the new Jewish immigrants clustered, more often than not unable to speak the language of their new refuge and possessed of limited resources. Their presence in such growing numbers heightened the rising tide of social anti-Semitism, which was one reason the older, established American Jews, many from a German background, also resented them.

Most of those Jewish newcomers who wanted to practice their faith did not find themselves readily at home in the Conservative synagogues, even less so in those of Reform Judaism. The latter had formed their major national organizations in 1873 and 1889: the Union of American Hebrew Congregations and the Central Conference of American Rabbis. But those from the highly traditional Jewish enclaves of eastern and central Europe had an understandable mind-set against everything modern. Hence many new twentieth-century arrivals found a home in the growing number of Orthodox synagogues, often gathering new ones of their own, some small and poorly housed, but very important to them. Here they could celebrate holy days and festivals, speak Yiddish and the languages of the countries of their origin, and enjoy familiar social customs. By 1898, assisted by native Orthodox leaders, these synagogues were strong enough to form a national body, the Union of Orthodox Congregations, and four years later, a Union of Orthodox Rabbis of the United States and Canada. Numbers of the Orthodox synagogues remained independent, however, or were drawn to one of the separatist Hasidic groups. Although many immigrants of the period did not formally affiliate with any synagogue but considered themselves part of the Jewish people, in its institutional forms Judaism had become an increasingly important presence on the American scene, with its three main (and various minor) divisions. Gaining strength in part as a mediating force between the other two major strands, Conservative Jews then founded their major national

[55] *America Is Different: The Search for Jewish Identity* (New York: Burning Bush Press, 1964), 35.

organizations: the United Synagogue of America (1913) and the Rabbinical Assembly of America (1919).

Cautiously at first, Jews took an increasingly active part in making their views known in matters of religion and government. In the nineteenth century Jews had urged their rabbis to stay out of partisan politics lest any statement be read as the sentiment of their people. In many ways this hesitancy was by no means novel: as has been noted, many Protestant denominations had not wanted their ministers to be conspicuous in party politics, though a few were; again with some memorable exceptions such as Archbishop Ireland, Catholic clergy also were often cautious in letting their party preferences be known. Cardinal Gibbons, who accepted invitations at various times to offer prayers at both major party political conventions, in a sermon in 1912 declared that "it is not for me in this sacred pulpit or anywhere else publicly to dictate or even suggest to you the candidate of my choice."[56] Only slowly did the developing national institutions of Judaism find it appropriate to take clear stands on controverted issues. By the twentieth century they had gained a greater assurance in speaking out on certain public matters because of their growing numbers and the mounting prominence of some of their lay figures. For example, Oscar Strauss was the first Jew to become a member of the cabinet when appointed in 1906 as secretary of commerce and labor by Roosevelt; the support of Henry Morgenthau, Sr., ambassador to Turkey, for Wilson in 1912 gave the Jewish community unprecedented access to the White House, especially on matters of foreign policy; and Louis D. Brandeis was named as the first Jewish Supreme Court justice in 1916.

From a growing base and increased self-confidence, Jewish organizations now spoke more forcefully on issues that had long plagued them.[57] Leading Protestant denominational and interdenominational bodies continued to stand firm on their defense of the old blue laws; they not only argued the necessity of a weekly day of rest for reasons of health and as part of a network of social reforms but also affirmed that, as the majority of Americans were Christians, Sunday should continue to be the proper day. Those who wished to choose another day of rest were certainly free to do so, but for observant Jews and members of several small seventh-day Christian bodies that often meant economic hardship. It was especially difficult for recent immigrants, who did not know much about possible exemptions from Sunday laws or how to go about getting them. When strictly enforced, the consequence of such laws for observant Jewish businessmen and their employees meant they suffered the competitive

[56] As quoted by Ellis, *Life of Gibbons*, 2: 527.
[57] See Chap. 3,

disadvantage of working one day less per week. Such laws, therefore, encouraged the marginal to give up their Sabbath observance. "Others violated the blue laws," Yahalom has concluded, "and consequently thousands of these people were arrested each year, especially in the large cities."[58] She found the records fragmentary, for in many cases those violating the laws were brought before a police court for infractions and after minimal proceedings were fined or served time in jail. Often lacking resources and being unfamiliar with American legal procedures, the accused rarely appealed. Yahalom pointed to the result:

> They were not sufficiently immersed in American politics to discern the changing nuances in the attitude of the local administrations toward the blue laws. At times the administration took a tough stand toward violators of these laws, especially when the Protestant reform movements created waves, while the attitude grew more lenient at other times. For all of these reasons, the documentation of these cases is meager [29].

From the ranks of Orthodox Judaism what came to be known as the Jewish Sabbath Alliance of America was formed in 1905. For a quarter century it helped Sabbath-observant Jews by setting up agencies to help them find suitable employment, pursued legislative and legal activities, and cooperated with other branches of Jewry. In that same year the Central Conference of American Rabbis named a commission to work on the Sunday observance problem. In the following year this group merged with another to become the Committee on Church and State in order systematically to secure exemptions from the Sunday laws. Soon after its founding, Conservative Jewry's United Synagogue joined the movement through its Committee on Religious Observances.

In New York State, where there was the highest concentration of Jews in the country, Jewish organizations of various types worked together to broaden the exemptions offered under a Sunday law, without much success. The choice of strategies occasioned intense debates. Some preferred an emphasis on full exemption on First Amendment grounds for any who observed a day other than Sunday for religous reasons; others chose simply to request privileges for the disadvantaged. Many Reform Jews, who were particularly active in various campaigns for social legislation and aware that in some industries employees labored every day of the week, knew that realistically the only day of rest that could be won was Sunday. Hence, most Jewish energy went toward seeking exemption for those observing the seventh day as the Sabbath, rather than working for a change in the basic law. The issue remained tense into the later twentieth century,

---

[58] "Sunday Laws," 28.

but it was one matter important to American Jews on which they took a stand in the years before World War I.[59]

The number of Jews in America tripled in the early twentieth century; the growth changed many aspects of Jewish life, but their attitude toward the importance of the public school remained strongly positive. For most of these new immigrants, "the public school was an ideal means to an end; it was a melting pot which would bestow upon their children the knowledge of English and turn them into full fledged Americans."[60] But they did object to the use of Christian hymns, prayers, and observances in public education. Appealing to the principle of religious freedom, the Union of Orthodox Congregations protested to the New York City Board of Education, achieving some success by 1907.

Reform's Central Conference of American Rabbis took the lead in 1904 in sustained effort to free public schools of religious activity. Two years later its arm for this effort was renamed the Committee on the Relation of Church and State, signifying its concern with church-state separation as well as religious freedom. It circulated widely a bold, detailed document, "Why the Bible Should Not be Read in the Public Schools," that provided much information on specific cases and legal rulings in favor of upholding the rights of minorities in tax-supported institutions. The committee urged that action begin quietly at local levels and move to legislative and legal efforts only when necessary. Naomi Cohen has called attention to the significance of the new approach taken by the committee:

> Unlike the earlier arguments against Sunday laws, the Central Conference's statement went beyond a specific defense of equality for Jews. In fact, it singled out no particular religious group and could easily have been written by any defender of separationism. By building their case on general terms, the framers of the statement testified to their own integration within American society as well as to the changed climate of opinion. Americans in 1906 would be far more prone to heed arguments about Americanization and universal rights than the justice of one minority's grievances.[61]

In 1914 the Central Conference took a further step in passing a resolution opposing Christmas and Easter celebrations in public schools and institutions. In general, Jews clearly believed in and supported public schools, while working to eliminate persisting Christian practices and references within them.

The Jewish world was deeply troubled by the resurgence of anti-Semitism early in the twentieth century. In the United States, it was felt espe-

---

[59] Ibid., 29–43.
[60] Yahalom, "Church-State Separation and Education," 33.
[61] *Encounter with Emancipation*, 100.

cially as social discrimination and exclusion; in Russia it was brutally present in the pogroms of 1905. This led to fresh Jewish efforts to bring the various strands of their people into wider cooperation, as in the formation in 1906 of the American Jewish Committee, later the American Jewish Congress. Such organizations acted on behalf of civil rights for all. The committee, for example, mounted sufficient pressure to effect changes in American foreign policy with respect to Russia by 1911.[62]

In their work, such organizations reinforced what Jonathan D. Sarna has called "the standard Jewish line on church and state"; he explained that "the Central Conference of American Rabbis, the American Jewish Committee, and the American Jewish Congress expressed similar support for 'strict separationism' early in the twentieth century."[63] In their efforts to fight discrimination and seek equality, the various types of Jewish organizations broadened their own spheres of cooperation, and, on an ad hoc basis, worked also with some Catholic, Protestant, and nonreligious—even atheist—agencies for its specific ends. In pressing for full equal rights, Jewish concern promoted public institutions as nonreligious, not antireligious. On the basis of their historical experience, Sarna notes, Jews at that time favored "strict church-state separation as the only defense against a Christian-dominated state" (19). Only much later in the century did their "church-state dilemma" emerge, for their experience also taught them "to oppose secularization as a force leading to assimilation, social decay, and sometimes to persecution of all religions, Judaism included" (19). But early in the century, they faced a still self-assured voluntary Protestant establishment seeking to deal with the challenges and threats of a new century; the strategy Jews followed then seemed appropriate to the leaders of their diverse but rapidly growing and maturing population.

Eastern Orthodoxy

In the first two decades of the twentieth century immigration was also a major factor in more than doubling the size in America of a Christian tradition not classified as either Catholic or Protestant. The churches of Eastern Orthodoxy trace their continuities back to the early Christian movement in the East, long before the major division of the eastern and western churches in 1054. Estimates suggest that about one hundred thousand people belonged to these bodies in 1900, but claimed membership figures are believed too inclusive, derived often primarily from the

---

[62] Ibid., 234–38; see also Nichols, *Uneasy Alliance*, 36.
[63] "Christian America or Secular America?" 17, 19.

size of given ethnic groups associated with Orthodox churches, largely from Russia, Greece, and the Balkan countries. These churches have continued to grow through the twentieth century; some estimates indicate that they claim constituencies totaling some three million in 1990. As a number of these bodies with their distinctive ecclesiologies and liturgies eventually became prominent in ecumenical life and discussion, brief attention to a period in which their basic institutions were being developed provide significant illustrations of the way the religious spectrum was widening and changing early in the twentieth century.

The oldest of these churches to be gathered under episcopal leadership in the United States, the Russian Orthodox, came onto American soil when Alaska passed from Russian to American hands in 1867. Four years later, diocesan affairs for the United States were administered from San Francisco, but because increasing numbers of Russian immigrants were coming to the eastern coastal areas, the bishopric was moved to New York in 1898. St. Nicholas Church was built there; by 1905 it had become the cathedral of an archdiocese. As the Russian Orthodox church was the only canonical representative of Eastern Orthodoxy at the episcopal level in North America until 1917, for a while it helped to supervise some other Orthodox bodies of a variety of ethnic backgrounds: Greek, Serb, Albanian, Bulgarian, Romanian, Hungarian, and Ukrainian. The Russian Revolution caused serious difficulties for the church in America, and divisions resulted; by far the largest communion of Russian background is today known as the Orthodox Church in America.

The first Greek Orthodox congregation in the country to survive was formed in New Orleans in 1864, but growth was slow until extensive immigration from Greece occurred between 1890 and 1920. In 1918 the ecumenical patriarch of Constantinople (Istanbul) took steps toward the formation of the Greek Orthodox Archdiocese of North and South America, which was formally completed three years later. The Russian and Greek communions quickly became and have remained the largest among the Orthodox churches; others have developed their various hierarchies in the years since World War I and are often largely centered in particular geographical areas.[64] Most of these Eastern Orthodox churches are in communion with one another. Like other religious institutions in America, they have inevitably become involved with the network of governmental agencies, often at the local level. An important legal case involving

[64] Brief treatments of this family of churches as they developed in the twentieth century can be found in Piepkorn, *Profiles in Belief*, vol. 1. For a competent survey of general Eastern Orthodox history, theology, and spirituality, with brief attention to the American scene, see John Meyendorf, *The Orthodox Church: Its Past and Its Role in the World Today*, trans. John Chapin (Crestwood, N.Y.: St. Vladimir's Seminary Press, 1981).

the control of St. Nicholas Cathedral later wound its way through state and federal courts to the Supreme Court.[65]

This chapter opened with Santayana's comment in 1913 that the civilization characteristic of Christendom had not disappeared, yet another one had begun taking its place. "We still understand the value of religious faith; . . . . On the other hand, the shell of Christendom is broken."[66] The increase in the number and size of religious bodies in early twentieth-century America gave evidence of the continuing hold of religious faith among millions in a rapidly growing population. But the force of Christendom, even in the voluntary Protestant forms that contributed to a wide acceptance of certain common moral and cultural perspectives in the nineteenth century and provided many with a sense of national direction, was eroding. The continuing proliferation of denominations, the growing strength of Roman Catholicism, and the increasing presence of Jewish life meant that familiar ways of relating religious and governmental institutions were being undermined. In an increasingly mobile population, even traditions still based largely in particular geographical areas soon had outposts in other locations. The distinctive Church of Jesus Christ of Latter-day Saints, for example, after its "certain anguishing accommodations to American culture,"[67] adjusted to the new situation and continued to grow; by 1920, it had more than doubled its membership from the approximately two hundred thousand with which it began the century. The religious map of the country was steadily changing.

The signs that one order was passing while a new one had not yet taken shape were evident in the opposing ways a number of states in this period dealt with the question of religion in the public schools—a point where groups operating out of differing religious and educational viewpoints often collided with each other and public agencies. As noted, the broadly Protestant perspectives and practices in the tax-supported public schools had long been under attack for quite different reasons by Catholics, Jews, Mormons, and some others, increasingly joined by those whose views were informed by scientific, naturalistic, and humanistic currents of thought. This stimulated sharp reactions among many who had committed themselves to the public schools for a mixture of religious, educational, and patriotic reasons; for them education without some attention to religion was inadequate because it did not touch on things of greatest importance. Although the fight was an old one, it was renewed at the state

---

[65] See Noonan, *The Believer and the Powers That Are*, 314–21.

[66] Santayana, *Winds of Doctrine*, 1.

[67] Arrington and Bitton, *Mormon Experience*, 251.

level in many places during the twentieth century—some states going one way, some the other.

When the century opened, only one state—Massachusetts—had a law on the books making morning prayer or Bible reading in the schools obligatory. But within a few years after 1910 eleven states—among them Alabama, Delaware, Florida, Tennessee, and Pennsylvania—had followed suit, and one or both exercises were obligatory. Before 1900, however, only Wisconsin's court had upheld lower court rulings banning Bible reading in the schools. Five other states—Nebraska, Illinois, Louisiana, Washington, and finally South Dakota—then took that route, all but one before 1920.[68] Only a close study of each case could show the balances that led to such contradictory decisions, but clearly the struggle to redefine the role of religion in public education illustrates that a sweeping realignment of forces was proceeding. How many public figures dealt with the issue was revealed in a declaration of former president (and outspoken Protestant layman) Theodore Roosevelt, who said that in the interest of "absolutely nonsectarian public schools" it was "not our business to have the Protestant Bible or the Catholic Vulgate or the Talmud read in these schools."[69]

A study of church-state cases in state appellate courts by H. Frank Way has concluded that between 1870 and 1920 especially the state courts were moving away from a perception of America as a Christian nation toward a secular-based perspective. Although the volume of such recorded cases was not high, "the decisions indicate that courts began to assume a role in redefining church-state relations."[70] But the leading Protestant denominations, all continuing to grow in size and maintaining characteristic optimism, were confident that their evangelical and missionary crusades would win the day and that their dominant position would continue. The meaning of significant trends of their own times became clear only later.

With the advantage of hindsight, we can now see that seemingly unrelated and relatively minor changes by 1917, as far as church-state relations were concerned, were moving toward an emerging constellation of forces that were already reshaping the religious scene in America. Espe-

[68] Robert F. Drinan, *Religion, the Courts, and Public Policy* (New York: McGraw-Hill, 1963), 91–92; Jorgenson, *The State and the Non-Public School*, 135; Michaelsen, *Piety in the Public School*, 168–70. In his lengthy concurring Supreme Court decision in *Abingdon School District* v. *Schempp*, 374 U.S. 203 (1963) at 230–304, Justice William J. Brennan reviewed this history in considerable detail.

[69] As quoted by Brennan, *Abington* v. *Schempp* at 273. The footnote to the quotation reads: "Theodore Roosevelt to Michael A. Schaap, Feb. 22, 1915, 8 Letters of Theodore Roosevelt (Morison ed. 1954), 893."

[70] "The Death of the Christian Nation: The Judiciary and Church-State Relations," *Journal of Church and State* 29 (1987), 510.

cially at the state level, the courts were searching for fresh interpretations of church-state problems—interpretations quite different from the Supreme Court's 1892 decision in *Church of the Holy Trinity* v. *United States*.[71] The crucible of World War I had a significant impact on both religious and governmental agencies and on their interaction, as it had on so many aspects of American life.

[71] See Chap. 1.

7

Changing Patterns of Religion and Government: The Impact of World War I

THE OUTBREAK and rapid spread of war in Europe during the summer of 1914 caught most Americans by surprise. Few foresaw that it would last so long, escalate into a world struggle involving the United States, and eventually mark a major dividing line in Western history. "The Great War of 1914–18 lies like a band of scorched earth dividing that time from ours," wrote Barbara Tuchman in 1966, using terminology then made grimly familiar by the Vietnam War to dramatize the point. "In wiping out so many lives which would have been operative in the years that followed, in destroying beliefs, changing ideas, and leaving incurable wounds of disillusion, it created a physical as well as psychological gulf between two epochs."[1]

As the twentieth century has worn on, many interpreters have explored that gulf. For example, in his examination of modern literature since World War I, Paul Fussell has shown how that struggle has set its stamp on the ways we both use language and perceive reality. Long familiar and widely accepted patterns of understanding the world were not only challenged by the brutalities and dislocations of war but for many were also shattered beyond recognition. To those who lived through those days and its continuing aftermath, the previous epoch seemed characterized by naive innocence. Fussell called attention to Philip Larkin's poem "MCMXIV." Written about a half-century after that year and grounded in the knowledge of what had happened since that fateful summer, the poem concentrates its theme in its last line: "Never such innocence again."[2] Some had recognized that long before; in 1919 William Butler Yeats had penned his memorable lines, "The blood-dimmed tide is loosed, and everywhere / The Ceremony of innocence is drowned."[3] Henry F. May significantly located his brilliant study of *The End of American Innocence* between 1912 and 1917. In that half-decade few could grasp and fewer admit what the coming of the war in 1914 meant to them

[1] *The Proud Tower: A Portrait of the World before the War, 1890–1914* (New York: Macmillan, 1966), xiii.

[2] *The Great War and Modern Memory* (New York: Oxford University Press, 1975), 19.

[3] As quoted by Hans Kohn, in *World War I: A Turning Point in Modern History*, ed. Jack J. Roth (New York: Knopf, 1967), 37.

and their ideas, especially their progressive view of history. Not even after America entered the war in 1917 could people comprehend the impact. It took time for all but the most perceptive to realize that a world had been lost and that plagues of guilt, doubt, and complexity would henceforth continue to undermine the sense of confidence with which the century had begun.[4]

To be sure, in America tensions soon arose among those who took differing attitudes toward the war at its outset. Many of German (and some of Irish) background sympathized with the Central Powers, though the majority favored the Allies. Another gulf opened between those who argued for greater preparedness and those who feared militarism; prominent political and religious figures were arrayed on both sides.[5] The debates became very heated at times, especially when such events occurred as the sinking by torpedo of the British liner *Lusitania* on May 7, 1915. This tragedy cost nearly twelve hundred lives, one-tenth of them Americans. Stories of German atrocities were spread and often exaggerated. Yet the majority of Americans did not want to get actively involved in the war even as sentiment swung to the side of Britain and France.

In the election of 1916 Wilson ran on a platform that promised continued peace, prosperity, and progressive democracy. Greatest enthusiasm was aroused by the first plank, which led to the famous slogan that Wilson himself did not use, "he kept us out of war." The Democratic victory was narrow, for the Republican was the larger party, but the victors also retained control of both houses of Congress. In January 1917, Wilson set before the Senate a plan that called for a negotiated peace maintained by a league linking nations devoted to peace, but it was already too late, for Germany had decided to sink all ships, including neutrals, in a broadly defined zone around Allied nations. On one day in March, three unarmed American merchant ships were sunk without warning. Historians have long debated precisely what combination of various factors tipped the scales toward entry into the war, but in coming before Congress on April 2, 1917, Wilson stressed the German violations of American neutral rights and projected idealistic war aims. He used the phrase that was to be so often repeated—at first generally in deep seriousness, but in retrospect often in sceptical irony—"the world must be made safe for democracy." Four days later, on Good Friday, both houses of Congress concurred on a declaration of war, and the president signed the measure.

Immense changes in the fabric of American society were not long in coming. The patriotic spirit, high since the days of 1898 and expansion-

---

[4] *End of American Innocence*, 361–63, 387–94.

[5] David M. Kennedy, *Over Here: The First World War and American Society* (New York: Oxford University Press, 1980), 31–37.

ism, was now not only lifted higher but also became more pervasive in people's lives. It became important to say the right words and be ready to serve at home or abroad. Politics, business, and religion were expected to fall (or be pushed) into line. American entry into the conflict had come when progressive reform politics was at high tide, but now the agencies of regulation were put to new uses. "War necessitates organization, system, routine, and discipline," said a thoughtful interpreter of American life, magazine editor Frederick Lewis Allen. "The choice is between efficiency and defeat. . . . We shall be delivered into the hands of officers and executives who put victory first and justice second."[6] Not only manpower but also the economy was mobilized because the requirements of war compelled previously unprecedented cooperation between government and business. Through such agencies as the War Industries Board, the Railroad Administration, and the War Labor Board, the lengthening arm of the federal government organized and directed many aspects of the nation's economic and industrial life. Those who led such agencies deeply believed they were using their growing power for good; as Edward N. Hurley, head of the U.S. Shipping Board, exclaimed: "Great power may be used for goodwill or for evil. If possessed by the United States we may be sure it will be used for good."[7]

Protestant Cooperation in Wartime

Protestant churches in America had traditionally emphasized loyalty to legitimate political authority, and for the most part they willingly became purveyors of the patriotic spirit. Some prominent religious leaders joined the ranks of the militants in their enthusiasm and displayed growing intolerance of diversity. Evangelist Billy Sunday, for example, who called himself God's recruiting officer and declared that Christianity and patriotism were synonymous, prayed in the House of Representatives: "Thou knowest, O Lord, that no nation so infamous, vile, greedy, sensuous, blood-thirsty, ever disgraced the pages of history. Make bare thy mighty arm, O Lord, and smite the hungry, wolfish Hun, whose fangs drip with blood, and we will forever raise our voice to Thy praise."[8] George Mars-

[6] Ibid., 43, as quoted from *Nation*, April 26, 1917, 484–85.

[7] As quoted by Emily S. Rosenberg, *Spreading the American Dream: American Economic and Cultural Expansion, 1890–1945* (New York: Hill & Wang, 1982), 74.

[8] As quoted by Winfred E. Garrison, *The March of Faith: The Story of Religion in America Since 1865* (New York: Harper, 1933), 243; see also McLoughlin, *Modern Revivalism*, 444. During the period of extensive reaction against World War I, Ray Abrams collected many examples of the emotional mingling of religious and militaristic language in *Preachers Present Arms* (New York: Round Table Press, 1933).

den has shown how many others of conservative viewpoints "found the force of popular sentiment irresistible" and joined the chorus.[9] But numbers of the most widely heard religious voices speaking for an unqualified nationalism and ready to revile the enemy were on the liberal side of the theological spectrum. Like many others, Lyman Abbott invoked holy war imagery; on the title page of his *The Twentieth Century Crusade*, he said boldly that "a crusade to make this world a home in which God's children can live in peace and safety is more Christian than a crusade to recover from pagans the tomb in which the body of Christ was buried." He went on to interpret the war in highly idealistic terms when he asked a rhetorical question: "When did a nation ever show so much of this spirit of love, service and sacrifice as the American Nation does today?"[10]

With the fever of war gripping the nation, pacifists had a difficult time as public opinion ran against them. Looking back on the war period in 1922, William Adams Brown, a Presbyterian professor of theology at New York's Union Theological Seminary, characterized the pacifists as "radical Protestants" who "not only believe that Jesus' principles are applicable to state as well as to church, but that they are applicable now." Insisting that Jesus laid down a clear method for applying his principles, pacifists concluded that it forbade "the taking of human life for any purpose whatever," even for self-defense or in defense of others.[11]

A number of prominent Protestant leaders who had espoused some form of pacifism abandoned it; they found it ever harder to maintain genuine neutrality and discovered that they could identify with the war aims as eloquently enunciated by Wilson and others. Not all did; notable among the pacifists were Episcopalian Paul Jones who resigned from his diocese under pressure, Presbyterian Norman Thomas, and Unitarian John Haynes Holmes. The small historic peace churches, especially the Brethren, Mennonites, and Quakers, generally maintained a pacifist witness against war and saw many, but not all, of their young men of draft age become conscientious objectors. Convinced members of such small denominations that forbade its adherents to participate in war in their creeds or principles were permitted to enter alternative forms of noncombatant service. The claims of other individuals and groups that conscription violated their religious scruples or liberties were unanimously rejected by the Supreme Court.[12] Anyone who took a pacifist position could

---

[9] Marsden, *Fundamentalism and American Culture*, 149.

[10] Lyman Abbott, *The Twentieth Century Crusade* (New York: Macmillan, 1918), 56.

[11] *The Church in America*, 160. For the historical background, see Peter Brock, *Pacifism in the United States: From the Colonial Era to the First World War* (Princeton: Princeton University Press, 1968); see also his *Twentieth-Century Pacifism* (New York: Van Nostrand Reinhold, 1970).

[12] *Selective Draft Law Cases*, 245 U.S. 366 (1918); see Richard E. Morgan, *The Supreme*

be subjected to public criticism and hostility. Under the leadership of the influential Quaker philosopher Rufus Jones, with three Quaker bodies participating, the American Friends Service Committee was founded in 1917; it assisted conscientious objectors at home and sent relief workers abroad.

Although the militants among religious leaders were not all extremists, they were critical of the pacifists and often suspicious of those thought to harbor pacifist ideas. Yet between those two broadly defined groupings, one large and one small, there was an important third one. In his careful scholarly study of the role of the churches in World War I, John L. Piper, Jr., has documented "a middle ground position, which focused on ministry and sought to develop a wartime ministry without damning either war or the enemy."[13] Probably a large majority of American Christians, Catholic and Protestant, were in this category. Most abhorred war and had long hoped their country would not be drawn in, but once the decision to enter had been made they supported it loyally and patriotically and trusted that these sacrifices would lead to a warless world. Although their position, lacking the hard clarity of the extremes, has been easy to ignore, its recollection contributes to understanding the changing relations between religion and government in the war years, changes with lasting consequences.

As the signs of probable American entry into the war multiplied, the Federal Council of Churches, not yet ten years old, was in a position to provide leadership for Protestant churches in the coming crisis. Based in New York, it was officially supported by some thirty denominations, including many of the larger ones. More than a hundred thousand ministers and nearly eighteen million church members, over two-thirds of the Protestant totals, formally composed its constituency. The council was the creation of the denominations and could speak and act for them only by agreement, but it did not hesitate to use its resources and guide its members in dealing with problems all faced as war neared. In Piper's words, "the truly great opportunity of the Council and the years of real growth in cooperative Protestantism came during the war" (4). It soon became

Court and Religion (New York: Free Press, 1972), 56–57, and Norman Thomas, The Conscientious Objector in America (New York: B. W. Huebsch, 1923), esp. 88–91.

[13] The American Churches in World War I (Athens: Ohio University Press, 1985), 11. The book had its origins in his Ph.D. dissertation, "The Social Policy of the Federal Council of the Churches of Christ in America during World War I" (Duke University, 1964), which was then extensively revised and enriched by significant additions, especially on the role of Catholics in the war. I am much indebted to John Piper, not only for his writings but also for informative conversations concerning the topic. A general history of the army chaplaincy that includes this period was written by Earl S. Stover, Up from Handymen: The United States Army Chaplaincy, 1865–1920 (Washington, D.C.: Office of the Chief of Chaplains, Department of the Army, 1977), esp. chaps. 5 and 6.

clear that government officials, unprepared to deal with the separate denominations, preferred to work with agencies perceived to be representative. Some rather tentative cooperation also developed between Protestants and Catholics. Despite obvious differences, the wartime activities of Protestant and Catholic agencies showed some remarkable parallels.

The general secretary of the FCC, Charles S. Macfarland, had learned even before the war about certain difficulties faced by chaplains in the army and navy—low morale, compounded by the low ratios of chaplains to service personnel. In cooperation with another Protestant agency, the Home Missions Council, a Washington office was opened early in 1914 to take care of this and other problems common to the churches. An associate secretary, Henry K. Carroll, was appointed to guide its work. By talking with legislators, appearing at congressional committees, and writing numerous letters, Carroll became an important factor in getting through Congress an act that significantly improved the lot of naval chaplains. He also persuaded some denominations to create commissions on the chaplaincy and made the Washington office available as a clearinghouse for all Protestant candidates for the chaplaincy—of mutual advantage both to the churches that availed themselves of the service and to governmental authorities.

By early 1917 the Washington office had become the sole responsibility of the FCC and Carroll had resigned, so Macfarland himself spent much time at the nation's capital. He brought together a General Committee on Army and Navy Chaplains and, at the end of March, assigned Worth M. Tippy to head the office. The two officials worked out an agreement with the secretaries of war and the navy whereby the new committee would henceforth screen and nominate all Protestant candidates for chaplaincies (109–10, 115). The effort was timely, for now a channel was available to regularize the recruitment and selection of Protestant chaplains in cooperation with the government, not only for those churches associated with the FCC but also for other denominations that were willing to participate. The way was being prepared for the heavy responsibilities ahead.

Quite different forms of Protestant cooperation were those provided by the Young Men's and Young Women's Christian associations (YMCA, YWCA)—nondenominational lay organizations that enjoyed wide support among the churches. On the day war was declared John R. Mott, general secretary of the YMCA, sent a telegram to President Wilson offering "the full service of the Association Movement."[14] The next week the YMCA organized its National War Work Council to promote the physical, mental, social, and spiritual welfare of those serving in the army and navy, to strengthen the work of the chaplains, and to serve the

[14] As quoted by Hopkins, *John R. Mott*, 474.

churches. Before April was out, Mott had met twice with Wilson, who issued to the army an executive order, extending official recognition to the YMCA as a valuable adjunct and asset to the service and providing that it be rendered "the fullest practicable assistance and cooperation" at posts and stations, in camps and field (475). The details were turned over to Secretary of War Newton D. Baker, former reform mayor of Cleveland, and one of his staff, Raymond B. Fosdick, who had been active in police reform work in New York but now became head of the War Department's new Commission on Training Camp Activities. Both Protestants, these men thought of the YMCA as a nonsectarian agency and put it in charge of camp recreational activities. A large financial campaign was launched by the YMCA because a budget of three million dollars was deemed necessary for their work with the forces. Although it found wide support among church constituencies, the YMCA was not an agency of the churches and, because most association secretaries were not ordained, could not adequately provide for the ministry of word and sacrament to those in military service.

The primary agency of the churches to support such a ministry, carried on by chaplains, camp pastors, and prominent clergy on special assignments, was the FCC, and it gave much attention to that task when war came. Some visible militants as well as certain admitted pacifists (several of the historic peace churches belonged to the council), were related to member denominations, but the FCC played an important role in defining and affirming the middle ground between them. A special meeting of the council gathered in Washington on May 8–9, 1917; representatives of other cooperative mission and social agencies, including the YMCA and YWCA, were invited. Frank Mason North, president of the council at that time, set the tone by saying that the purpose of the meeting was neither to stimulate patriotism nor to assert loyalty, but to accept responsibility, define tasks, and determine a program. North had previously requested that William Adams Brown prepare a preliminary draft for a message to the churches, to be submitted to full discussion and revision. The draft was approved without substantial change.[15] The first part of the statement, "Our Spirit and Purpose," acknowledged that the government had been forced to recognize a state of war and that the president had "called upon all the people for their loyal support and their wholehearted allegiance" and affirmed that "as American citizens, members of Christian churches gathered in Federal Council, we are here to pledge both support and allegiance in unstinted measure." Moreover, the state-

[15] Published in full in Charles S. Macfarland, *The Churches of Christ in Time of War* (New York: Missionary Education Movement, 1917), 129–37. For commentary, see Piper, *American Churches in World War I*, 15–18, and Gorrell, *Age of Social Responsibility*, 282–84.

ment declared that a double responsibility rested on those who were both Christians and citizens: "We owe it to our country to maintain intact and to transmit unimpaired to our descendants our heritage of freedom and democracy. Above and beyond this, we must be loyal to our divine Lord, who gave His life that the world might be redeemed, and whose loving purpose embraces every man and every nation" (129). The nation's war aims were summarized and found to be those "for which every one of us may lay down our all, even life itself" (130). Acknowledging that some believed that Christians were forbidden to engage in war in any circumstances, the statement found that "most of us believe that the love of all men which Christ enjoins demands that we defend with all the power given us the sacred rights of humanity" (130). A number of "special duties" were listed: for example, being diligent in works of relief and mercy, keeping alive the spirit of prayer, caring for the welfare of those in service, maintaining vigilance against the spirit of vengeance, and protecting the rights of conscience. The second part of the document, "Our Practical Duties" (133–37), listed more immediate steps, reflected some points of the social creed of the churches, called for upholding moral, sexual, and spiritual standards, and commended the passage of wartime prohibition.

The message was widely circulated to its constituents. Some regularly scheduled denominational gatherings discussed it and responded in various ways; they made it clear that the churches wished to provide as normal a religious environment as possible for those in the armed forces. After much preliminary planning and work, the FCC, in its New York offices on September 20, 1917, created the General War-Time Commission of the Churches to coordinate the work of the denominations in the war effort. One hundred members served on it, many representing the various cooperating denominations; others named included outstanding ministers and laypersons, among them John Mott for the YMCA and Mabel Cratty, general secretary of the YWCA. The commission was chaired by Robert E. Speer, a well-known Presbyterian lay foreign missions executive; William Adams Brown was its very active secretary. The commission met four times between its founding and the completion of its work in April 1919. Its day-to-day work was supervised by the officers and a busy executive committee, which met twice a month. The commission sought to coordinate what was being done by the churches and to provide for or perform work not otherwise covered as needs arose—and the emphasis shifted toward the latter as time went on. It worked closely with the General Committee on Army and Navy Chaplains. It also spawned subcommittees: one worked with Catholic authorities on a Church Flag with the result that one offical flag was recognized; another arranged for Memorial Day, 1918, to be set aside for prayer. Realizing that sizable funds were needed for both the denominational and cooperative programs for the war period and postwar reconstruction, the commission launched an Interchurch Emergency Campaign, brought to a successful completion early in 1919, in time to help undergird the continuing ministries to those serving in occupation armies and moving through the sometimes tedious processes of demobilization.[16]

As has been noted, the progressive period was also the time when Jim Crow laws were in force, especially in the South.[17] The color line was evident to the Negroes, as African Americans were then called. They nevertheless largely closed ranks as patriotic Americans in support of the war, not confusing it with their own continuing struggle in opposition to the unjust discrimination they so often faced. Black troops, many assigned to stevedore duty, found themselves under white officers, commissioned and noncommissioned. Unfortunately, black chaplains were scarce, for the War Department had failed to include chaplains when it arranged for the commissioning of some Negro officers. Hearing reports of serious racial discrimination in the assignment and treatment of draftees, the General War-Time Commission of the Churches appointed a Committee on the Welfare of Negro Troops.[18] When Emmett J. Scott, who had been Booker T. Washington's private secretary for many years, was named as special assistant in charge of Negro affairs for the War Department, he was added to the committee.

The committee's field secretary, Charles Williams, conducted detailed surveys of moral and religious conditions in areas surrounding many major camps in the United States. He sent copies of his reports, which revealed the pervasiveness of racial prejudice, to the War Department; Williams thus kept Scott well informed and prepared the way for a better understanding of his work among his colleagues. Williams also pressed for more Negroes in the chaplaincy, officers' training schools, and ranks of noncommissioned officers. But when members of the FCC's committee, augmented by leaders of the council and the General War-Time Commission, confronted a group of War Department officials on September 25, 1918, results were minimal, though there was some reduction of segregation.

The FCC was painfully discovering the depth of racism through these experiences, which were writ large for the country in the terrible Chicago race riot in summer 1919. Two years later it created a permanent Commission on Church and Race, adding the racial problem to its list of social concerns. Piper has concluded that for many churches, an important outcome of their wartime efforts "was the Protestant discovery of racism as

---

[16] Piper, *American Churches in World War I*, 20, 35–48.

[17] See Chaps. 3 and 5.

[18] Cavert, *Church Cooperation and Unity*, 151–53; Piper, *American Churches in World War I*, 164–73.

a national issue in which they were implicated and their decision to add racial brotherhood to their social goals."[19] It was but the start of a long road for the cooperative movement.

Catholics Find Unity in Wartime

"When the United States was swept into that conflict [World War I] in 1917, American Catholic disunity was appalling," wrote John B. Sheerin in a biography of John J. Burke, a priest who contributed much to overcoming the disarray. "The American bishops had not met in formal assembly since 1884. There were 15,000 Catholic societies but almost no communication, coordination or cooperation among them."[20] Like many other Americans prior to entry into the war, most Catholics seemed to hope that American neutrality could continue and peace be negotiated. Some in the church, especially among Germans and Irish, tended to favor the Central Powers, but majority sentiment, as in the nation, was steadily moving toward the Allies. "The Church's persistent effort to unite her immigrant children helped to cement a polyglot nation pulled by conflicting loyalties," Edward Cuddy has concluded, "and her emphatic demands for loyalty to the United States and obedience to her leaders helped dispose millions of Americans for the painful enterprise of war when it finally came in April, 1917."[21]

At American entry, Cardinal Gibbons, emphasizing that "the members of both Houses of Congress are the instruments of God in guiding us in our civic duties," called for unreserved obedience to the country's call and legislators' decisions. [22] When the archbishops held their annual meeting on April 18, they dispatched a public letter of support to the president and pledged that the Catholic people "will rise as one man to serve the nation. Our priests and consecrated women will once again, as in every former trial of our country, win by their bravery, their heroism and their service new admiration and approval."[23] Catholic leaders had repeatedly stressed the importance of loyalty to country as a religious as well as a patriotic duty, and the war provided an opportunity to demonstrate it decisively. But church teaching did not identify loyalty and patriotism with nationalism; therefore, few Catholics were numbered among the vo-

---

[19] *American Churches in World War I*, 196.

[20] *Never Look Back: The Career and Concerns of John J. Burke* (New York: Paulist Press, 1975), 11.

[21] "Pro-Germanism and American Catholicism, 1914–1917," *Catholic Historical Review* 54 (1968), 454.

[22] As quoted by Ellis, *Life of Gibbons*, 2: 239.

[23] As quoted by Sheerin, *Never Look Back*, 36.

ciferous militants. There were also few pacifists, for this war could readily be defined as just in accordance with Catholic tradition.

The church had no central office or agency to carry on the work necessary to focus Catholic resources on the war. There was nothing comparable to the Protestant FCC; something similar had to be quickly developed under the pressures of war. The energetic John Burke, member of the Paulist fathers and editor of the order's journal *The Catholic World*, came to Gibbons with a plan that he had worked out with three friends. It was accepted with the concurrence and approval of cardinals John Farley of New York and William O'Connell of Boston. Burke had already taken the lead in organizing a Chaplains' Aid Association to provide the growing number of priests entering the chaplaincy with equipment for celebrating Mass, New Testaments, prayer books, and other literature. Now he became the energizing and directing force in arranging for a meeting at Catholic University on August 11–12 to which every diocese was invited to send a clerical and lay representative, along with those from the major national lay societies.

Given less than a month's notice, 115 delegates arrived; discussion seemed to falter until Burke as chairman outlined his plan. A mystic who lived an intensely religious as well as a busily activist life, Burke later explained that the plan "was given" to him out of his spiritual resources.[24] He envisioned a unifying agency overarching the boundaries of dioceses and societies, the National Catholic War Council (NCWC). The organization would "harmonize and nationalize the entire work of the Catholic body," based on representation from local councils in every diocese.[25] He saw the need for campaigns to raise necessary funds, which he estimated at five million dollars (it finally ran to ten times that). By passing four resolutions that became the charter of the new organization, the representatives unanimously approved and refined the plan, so that Catholics could "devote their united energies to promote the spiritual and material welfare of the United States troops during the war" (30).

In September Burke was named chairman of the NCWC's central committee. An office was soon opened in Washington, and an executive secretary secured. To enable the new council to play a larger role among the faithful, the hierarchy saw the need of bringing it more clearly under its own direction. The result was some reorganization in January 1918 that provided for a strong administrative committee of four bishops, chaired by the capable Peter J. Muldoon of Rockford, Illinois. The everyday work of the council, with Burke at its center, was carried on largely by an in-

[24] Ibid., 40; cf. 11–12, 38–46.
[25] Piper, *American Churches and World War I*, 28. For a summary of the work of the NCWC from 1917 to 1919, see 69–87.

formal fellowship of priests and laity, most of whom had been active in social thought, action, and ministry. From the outset, much like the Protestant General War-Time Commission, the NCWC proliferated committees. Piper dryly observed that "Burke had specifically denied any intention of creating a bureaucracy, but it came to look peculiarly like one" (73). Also like the commission, as the workload increased with the tempo of the war in 1918, the NCWC tended to get more deeply involved in operating programs through employed field secretaries.

Throughout its two-year life, the NCWC's concern for helping to bring the sacramental ministry to service personnel through chaplains remained central. Early in the century, the archbishops had created the Catholic Army and Navy Chaplains' Bureau; since 1913 Lewis O'Hern, like Burke a Paulist, had been its head. When America entered the war, there were only sixteen Catholic chaplains in the army and eight in the navy, with ten others attached to national guard units. When the NCWC was reorganized, the pope named Patrick Hayes as Chaplain Bishop, whose "diocese" included all priests named as chaplains. With the help of five vicars general and O'Hern as executive secretary, he brought strength and order to the chaplains' work. At that point Congress, responding to the growth of the armed forces, had authorized a much larger number of chaplains. The NCWC twice encouraged the bishops to help priests enter the chaplaincy, although they were much needed everywhere in a church whose recent expansion had been so rapid. Because the religious orders had responded well, it was suggested that the dioceses were now called to make some sacrifices, but it took the added appeal of the apostolic delegate from Rome to secure the numbers needed. By the end of the war, there were more than fifteen hundred Catholic chaplains in the services.[26] All this involved considerable cooperation between Catholic authorities and government officials.

The largest of the lay Catholic fraternal societies, the Knights of Columbus, played a significant and conspicuous role during the war, especially in its direct contact with military personnel. The Knights had already gained considerable experience before American entry when the order had worked among the nearly quarter-million National Guard troops stationed along the Mexican border. Paralleling extensive YMCA work, it had set up recreation centers open to all, without regard to creed or color. Of great benefit to Catholics in general, the openness of K of C centers also helped break down anti-Catholic prejudice. Its national board of directors, meeting on April 14, affirmed the patriotic devotion of its four hundred thousand members and its unconditional support of the president and Congress.

---

[26] Ibid., 108, 112–13; Sheerin, *Never Look Back*, 38.

A few weeks later, Supreme Knight James A. Flaherty reported to the president the order's desire to establish centers at military training camps, open to all, for the recreational and spiritual comfort of men in service. But the YMCA had already been put in charge of recreational activities by the War Department's Commission on Training Camp Activities, and the Knights had to convince Baker and Fosdick that from their point of view the YMCA was really not nonsectarian: there were no Catholic members on its National War Work Council. When consulted, YMCA representatives refused to add such members lest their bases of support be reduced. Not until late June did the government's commission finally invite the K of C to build its centers in the camps, and by December 1 seventy-three had been erected, while plans were being formulated for work overseas. All this cost money, and soon a K of C fund drive was undertaken with a goal of three million dollars. Later other well-established fraternal groups also gained access to the camps.[27]

The autonomous K of C was well into its program by the time the NCWC was formed. One resolution passed by the August 1917 founding meeting of the council heartily commended "the excellent work which the Knights of Columbus have undertaken in cooperating with the Government of the United States in meeting the moral problems which have arisen and will arise out of the war, and it is the opinion of this convention that the Knights of Columbus should be recognized as the representative Catholic body for the special work they have undertaken" (201). But some key leaders of the lay organization felt that the work in which they were so deeply involved was not being taken seriously enough by the new effort, and the K of C did not affiliate. Certain other lay leaders, prominent in the early months of the NCWC, were cool to the K of C and did not accept its claims that "it was the only viable social organization capable of attending to the social and religious needs of Catholic servicemen" (205). The K of C did create some ambiguities by appointing some priests as chaplains to its centers, appearing to take episcopal authority lightly, though the priests were paid by the dioceses from which they came. In preparation for the reorganization of the NCWC by the archbishops, Gibbons was able to persuade the K of C leaders to meet with his representatives; thus, the K of C war activities finally came under the NCWC umbrella. The K of C extended its activities abroad; at its peak it had a force of more than a thousand secretaries overseas with nearly one hundred fifty clubs and huts, and it raised millions of dollars for its extensive and highly praised services.

For an agency without precedent in American Catholic history, and one

---

[27] Kauffman has recounted in some detail the story of the K of C in the war; see *Faith and Fraternalism*, 190–221.

quickly put together, the NCWC achievement was impressive indeed. It did much to provide unifying bonds within the church, to improve Catholic morale at home and abroad, and to increase the respect of many others for a church that had long been seen as alien on American soil.

Judaism and the War

To bring a measure of coordination into Jewish support for the war, representatives of seven national bodies formed the Jewish Welfare Board (JWB) on April 9, 1917, only a week after American entry. It was headed by a member of the Conservative movement, Cyrus Adler, president of the Jewish Theological Seminary and of the United Synagogue of America. His deputy was David De Sola Pool, an Orthodox Jew who at the time was president of the New York Board of Jewish Rabbis, which had members from various streams of Judaism. In keeping with the critical nature of the situation, the JWB took on tasks unprecedented in American Judaism. It was not clear what the status of Jewish chaplains would be; in the Civil War four rabbis had been appointed as chaplains in hospitals, but their role in the military was not further defined at that time. Adler promptly met with Secretary Baker of the War Department to help draft the law to permit qualified candidates from all denominations to be chosen.

In keeping with Jewish concerns in matters of religious freedom and church-state separation, Adler thoughtfully addressed these issues in his presidential address at the annual meeting of the United Synagogue in 1917:

> No one believes more fully than I do in the complete separation of church and state. They are separated by the fundamental principles of the Constitution of the United States which provides that "Congress shall make no law respecting an establishment of religion, or prohibiting the free exercise thereof." This view has been repeatedly emphasized, and never more definitely than during the early years of the Republic, when in a treaty with Tripoli, negotiated under the presidency of Washington, and ratified by the Senate in the presidency of Adams, it was declared "the government of the United States is not in any sense founded on the Christian religion."
>
> Upon this ground virtually all Americans stand. Though occasionally this country is loosely spoken of as a Christian country, such a statement simply means that the majority of the inhabitants of the United States nominally profess some form of Christianity in a formal sense. The fact is not even established, as some have claimed, by the wording of an opinion handed down by the late Mr. Justice Brewer, the obiter dictum of an Associate Justice of the

Supreme Court of the United States not being competent to overthrow the Constitution.

But having said so much, it might be recognized on the other hand that the United States is not an irreligious or non-religious country. It has never been secularized, and in the greater part of the country the church is the most important center for the people, religious and social.[28]

Noting that provision had been made for the spiritual welfare of men in military and naval service with the permission of the government and in accordance with the law, Adler declared forcefully that "I would never consider it as waiving the fullest religious liberty that we should have Jewish chaplains for our Jewish boys in the Army and Navy" (21). He also welcomed the representation of the Young Men's Hebrew Association (YMHA) in the military services and called upon his organization to support it. In her study of American Judaism and the separation of church and state, Yahalom concluded that "his remarks typified the stands of all streams of Judaism which unreservedly supported a military chaplaincy."[29] In all, twenty-three rabbis served in the armed forces during the war. The JWB also gained access to training camps and constructed some buildings as centers for its work.[30]

The role of Jewish pacifists, who surfaced for the first time in American history, was not easy. In an "obligatory" war, as Orthodox Jewry defined World War I, exemption from military service was not sanctioned, even in matters of the observance of the Sabbath and the dietary laws. But Reform Judaism, with its strong concerns for international harmony and brotherly love, had supported peace movements and had to wrestle with the issue. The law establishing the military draft in 1917 permitted exemption on conscientious grounds only to members of recognized religious sects whose existing creeds or principles forbade participation in war. Strictly interpreted this would apply primarily to the historic peace churches, but government officials also considered pacifists of other traditions who could at least claim that the religious body of which they were members provided some backing for their position.

When several members of the Reform movement sought exemptions, therefore, they appealed to the Central Conference of American Rabbis for support. After long and intense debate in summer 1917, the conference passed this resolution: "While the mission of Israel is Peace and its constant endeavor and prayer are for Peace and Brotherhood among

---

[28] *Fourth Annual Report of the United Synagogue of America* (New York: Clarence S. Nathan, 1917), 20–21. For a somewhat different version, see Yahalom, "The Demands of War and the Principle of Freedom of Religion," 9–10

[29] "The Demands of War," 10.

[30] Piper, *American Churches in World War I*, 25, 138, 148–49.

men, yet when one's country is at war in behalf of righteousness and humanity, the individual Jew who claims this hope of Judaism as a ground of exemption from military service does so only as an individual, inasmuch as historic Judaism emphasizes patriotism as a duty, as well as to the ideal of Peace."[31] Ten rabbis voted against it, one of whom, Martin Zielonka, requested permission to have his statement printed in the record. He did not identify himself with the conscientious objectors and declared (in the mood of the time) that he was neither a pacifist nor a believer in encouraging "slackers"; instead, he found the war "one of the most righteous that any nation has ever entered into." Nevertheless, he also affirmed that "we as Jews should protect the honest and sincere conscientious objector who places his objection upon a religious ground. I believe that the eighth verse of the twentieth chapter of Deuteronomy can be and ought to be interpreted in this way" (176). But his was a lonely voice.

Yahalom interprets the failure of Reform to support its pacifist members as a response to the prevailing feeling in the wider society, especially in the large eastern coastal cities where so many recent immigrants were clustered, that Jews were ungrateful to their new homeland and were not sharing in the military burden. Because many prominent Jews of German background had been associated with peace movements before 1917, some distrust of Germany was also heaped on the Jews as a people, and any sign of pacifism was seen by some watchdogs as a German weapon. Anti-Semites, accustomed to embroidering whatever negative rumors they could find, did not hesitate to proclaim such charges. In fact, many recent immigrants were not called to serve in the military either because of poor health or because they were still in the naturalization process and not yet eligible.[32] Yet some Jewish leaders continued to affirm pacifist sympathies, notably the distinguished Reform rabbi, Judah Magnes.

One event that illustrates how religious and governmental affairs became interrelated in the war years and their aftermath was the approval Wilson gave to Britain's Balfour Declaration of 1917, which favored the establishment in Palestine of a national home for the Jewish people. Many Jews had become deeply involved in Democratic politics and had access to the White House, particularly through Ambassador Henry Morgenthau, Sr. and Justice Louis D. Brandeis. Such influences led Wilson to approve the Balfour Declaration before its actual publication on November 2, without consultation with the State Department. Because the United States was not at war with Turkey and Palestine was then under

---

[31] Isaac E. Marcuson, ed., *Central Conference of American Rabbis: Yearbook* 27 (1917), 175.

[32] Yahalom, "The Demands of War," 31–33.

Turkish jurisdiction, the State Department, knowing of divisions among Jews on the Zionist issue and the objections of certain Christians, did not favor the Balfour pronouncement.

Not until August 31, 1918, when it was clear that Turkey would soon be defeated by the British, did Wilson's public letter to Stephen S. Wise, a prominent Reform rabbi in New York who favored the Zionist position, make the president's endorsement officially and widely known. The letter won Wilson much Jewish acclaim but also evoked considerable anti-Zionist sentiment from some Jewish, Christian, and Arab sources. Wilson's action deeply involved the United States in a highly controversial matter, which was to grow increasingly complex throughout the course of twentieth-century history from the Paris peace conference onward.[33] Reminiscing toward the end of his life, Wilson soliloquized aloud to Wise, "To think that I, a son of the manse, should be able to help restore the Holy Land to its people."[34]

Interchurch and Interfaith Cooperation

In view of previous bitterness between Catholics and Protestants, the development of cooperation between them in 1917 and 1918 was unprecedented. Catholics were consulted when the General War-Time Commission decided to press for the appointment of one chaplain for every twelve hundred men after army reorganization in the summer of 1917 had set a much higher ratio. Hence when a petition to high government authorities was sent as representing "the Christian forces of America," it included the signatures of top leaders of a number of Protestant denominations, the Federal Council, and the Catholic hierarchy. In view of previous Protestant tendencies not to think of Catholics in referring to "Christian forces," this was a significant turn.[35] Representatives of the leadership group met with President Wilson, Secretary of War Baker, and other military and legislative officials in Washington on September 27, 1917. Piper explained that "throughout the hearing the churchmen shared their conviction that the separation of church and state did not prevent the coop-

[33] Selig Adler, "The Palestine Question in the Wilson Era," *Jewish Social Studies* 10 (1948): 303–34. On the possible influence on Wilson's views of William E. Blackstone, Methodist layman and author of the "Blackstone Memorial" of 1891 favoring the restoration of the Jews to Palestine, see the Ph.D. dissertation of Yaakov S. Ariel, "American Premillennialism and its Attitudes towards the Jewish People, Judaism and Zionism, 1875–1925" (University of Chicago, 1986), esp. 196–221.

[34] *Challenging Years: The Autobiography of Stephen Wise* (New York: Putnam, 1949), 186–87.

[35] Piper, *American Churches in World War I*, 119.

eration of religious and governmental agencies to facilitate an adequate ministry for the men in the armed forces" (120). Although it took months of heavy lobbying, including strong messages from John J. Pershing, commanding general of the American Expeditionary Force in France and his senior staff chaplain, Episcopal bishop Charles H. Brent, the desired bill was finally passed in May 1918 (121–22).

Another major development was interfaith cooperation. As the churches and synagogues carried out their wartime roles, they learned to work not only with various agencies of government but also with each other for stated purposes. In fall 1917, troubled by reports concerning the moral welfare of American troops in France, Burke as president of the NCWC wrote to Protestant and Jewish leaders asking for cooperation in requesting suitable government action and inviting them to a consultation on the matter in October. The group decided to write to Raymond Fosdick of the War Department's Commission on Training Camp Activities; they suggested that the policy the government followed at home on matters relating to reducing immorality among soldiers and suppressing "disorderly houses" (of prostitution) should also be applied in overseas countries where American troops were stationed. Fosdick agreed to an effort to implement the proposal and also suggested that the informal group might continue in a special advisory capacity for matters involving religion.

This led to the formation of the Committee of Six, chaired by Burke. The other members were Harry Cutler of the Jewish Welfare Board, and four from the General War-Time Commission of the Churches: Brown, Mott, Speer, and James DeWolf Perry, the Episcopal bishop of Rhode Island and senior Red Cross chaplain. Some Catholics criticized Burke for cooperating with Protestant leaders in the Committee of Six, but Gibbons urged him to continue.[36] The committee met more than a dozen times during the war; among other things the members seized the opportunity to stress the distinctively religious aspects of chaplains' responsibilities, for it was presently discovered (especially among Catholics) that "there were officials high in the government service, and officers high in military ranks, to whom the *Sacramental* meaning of the chaplaincy was a closed book."[37] Though set up at the suggestion of War Department leaders, the Committee of Six helped the churches and synagogues by representing their interests. Also, four religious organizations—YMCA, YWCA, K of C, JWB—became members of the War Department's Commission on

[36] Ibid., 111; Sheerin, *Never Look Back*, 42–43.

[37] Michael Williams, *American Catholics and the War: The National Catholic War Council, 1917–1921* (New York: Macmillan, 1921), 238.

Training Camp Activities, along with the War Camp Community Service, the American Library Association, and the Salvation Army.

The money needed by the churches and synagogues to carry out their religious, social, and recreational tasks with soldiers at home and abroad quickly exceeded original estimates. Many religious bodies and their agencies—the Protestant denominations and the FCC, the Catholic church and the NCWC, the branches of Judaism and the JWB—were involved in raising millions of dollars as the work swiftly expanded. Money was needed for the increasingly varied and extensive undertakings of these bodies; among them, for example, the network of visitors' and community houses operated by women's groups of the NCWC, the numerous hostess houses of the YWCA, and guest centers under the direction of the JWB—all of which provided women and families with places to stay near military centers. To oversee fund raising for this important work another interfaith committee was appointed, its members drawn from these three agencies.[38] That so many millions were raised by the various religious groups both separately and in cooperation testified to the qualities of patriotism and generosity aroused in the American people by the crisis of war.

As American involvement in the conflict was reaching its peak in summer 1918, new monies were needed. The government's Commission on Training Camp Activities proposed that the seven religious and welfare organizations related to it conduct a United War Work Campaign. When representatives of the agencies met in Washington in late June, however, Mott indicated that the YMCA was not ready to join such a campaign, as its own plans were well developed and it believed its constituency would shy away from a drive in which their contributions might flow to another program. To get around that difficulty the K of C representative proposed that donors might designate how their contributions would be used. But Fosdick as head of the commission was aware that the K of C was generally regarded as a fraternal group and that if it were part of the united drive, other such organizations would want equal status. On July 30, however, Fosdick proposed that the NCWC become the Catholic wartime organization officially recognized for war work, with the Knights of Columbus as its agent for recreational services. In response to a query about how he would deal with the charge that this meant that the government was recognizing the Catholic church, "Fosdick replied that he would say to any challenging Protestant denomination that if it could show that 35% of the men in the army belonged to its group, as the Catholics could do, he would recognize it."[39] The K of C reluctantly went

[38] Piper, *American Churches in World War I*, 146–51.
[39] Ibid., 78.

along when it was promised that its identity, achievements, and needs would be emphasized and not lost as part of the NCWC.

There was one more serious problem to be ironed out. In August, when the United War Work Campaign finally announced it would proceed, the secretary of war indicated it would be conducted in two parts: the largely Protestant groups (YMCA, YWCA, War Camp Community Service, and American Library Association) would lead off in November; and the others (NCWC, JWB, and Salvation Army) would go public in February. The Catholics protested sharply; they resented the discrimination of separate drives and feared that the second drive would be seriously disadvantaged. Supreme Knight James A. Flaherty sent a telegram to Baker: "I earnestly trust that the rumor you are to order two joint drives for recreation funds—one for the Catholics and Jews and the other for the Young Men's Christian Association and three other agencies—is not true. This would be drawing a religious line in time of war that cannot fail to cause criticism and disturbance throughout the country."[40]

As pressure mounted, a final conference was held in late August. There were some tense exchanges, for the famous K of C slogan, "Everyone Welcome, Everything Free," annoyed those agencies, especially the YMCA, that were not in a position to follow suit. By the end of the month a compromise had been hammered out: the slogan was retained, but the share of funds to go to the order reduced. Meanwhile, some nativist, anti-Catholic sentiments were surfacing, stirring up political difficulties. The matter was settled on September 3 by President Wilson, who in a public letter to Fosdick declared that it was his judgment "that we shall secure the best results in the matter of the support of these agencies, if these seven societies will unite their forthcoming appeals for funds, in order that the spirit of the country in this matter may be expressed without distinction of race or religious opinion in support of what is in reality a common service" (186). "The issues of church and state came very near the surface during this time," Piper candidly noted, "although they never really broke through into public debate."[41] In the interests of the common contributions to the nation and its military forces, religious institutions learned to work with both each other and governmental agencies, despite continuing tensions.

Meanwhile, the YMCA and YWCA had developed extensive plans for a campaign, but they threw their energies into the united effort when that decision was finally worked out. The other agencies, Protestant, Catholic, and Jewish, accommodated to what had been started. As general campaign director, the energetic Mott took the lead in getting the seven soci-

[40] Williams, *American Catholics and the War*, 184–85.
[41] *American Churches in World War I*, 83.

eties to work together harmoniously; for example, he made office space available to the NCWC at the YMCA headquarters in New York. A Committee of Eleven, made up of members of the participating organizations and chaired by Fosdick, was set up to coordinate policy. A goal of $170,500,000 was set. To devote his full time to the campaign, Mott turned over all his other responsibilities to his staff. He traveled in thirty-one states from mid-September to mid-November and focused especially on the big corporate and individual givers.

The intense public drive was scheduled for November 11–19, thus somewhat anticlimactically opening on the very day that the armistice was declared! But the excitement of victory did not hinder the effort. It was recognized that demobilization would take time, that occupation troops would be abroad for many months, and that reconstruction and rehabilitation efforts would be expensive. The goal was more than met; when all the returns were in, more than $188 million had been collected, which Mott called "the largest sum ever provided through voluntary offerings for an altruistic cause" in history.[42]

Aftermath

As the troops were brought home and demobilization proceeded, the need for cooperation among religious institutions lessened, and their relationship with governmental agencies soon became redundant. The major achievements had been primarily the varied far-flung ministries to soldiers in camps, at the front, and in hospitals at the hands of chaplains and secretaries of the K of C and the Ys, but the spectacular success of the United War Work Campaign was a high point for the institutions that backed those accomplishments. After the need had passed, the agencies and their network of committees slowly dissolved, though some were put to other uses. The General War-Time Commission of the Churches held its last meeting in April 1919. Some of the work it had undertaken was carried on by the FCC, and a number of the cooperative strategies and unified efforts that had proved effective were adapted to peacetime uses. The General Committee (later Commission) on Army and Navy Chaplains had proved its usefulness and continued as a permanent organization.

Cooperation with government agencies to provide relief and humanitarian aid to hungry and displaced persons outside the United States also continued. Herbert Hoover, an American mining engineer who had competently supervised the feeding of hungry Belgians after their country had

---

[42] Hopkins, *John R. Mott,* 535; see also 536–44.

been invaded early in the war, was chosen to head the Food Administration in 1917. There he stimulated agricultural production and increased the flow of food to Europe. He also played a conspicuous role in relief work in the postwar period. As Bruce Nichols has explained, as secretary of commerce in the Harding administration, Hoover worked with private voluntary agencies in the task of distributing supplies abroad; he required only that they affiliate with the government's American Relief Administration. Most, but not all, religiously motivated groups involved in relief work took that step; for example, the American Friends Service Committee, the Mennonite Central Committee, the American Jewish Joint Distribution Committee, the NCWC, the National Lutheran Council, the YMCA and YWCA, and the Southern Baptist Convention. "Besides ad hoc arrangements," Nichols reported, "religiously based agencies working with refugees routinely sought more frequent cooperative ventures than the missionary societies ever had."[43] In the face of desperate human needs caused by the war and its aftermath, the various agencies of a number of religious groups committed to the separation of church and state did not find these new relationships with governmental agencies objectionable.

The NCWC had proved so important for Catholic unity that it was transformed into another organization with the same initials—the National Catholic Welfare Council (the last word later changed to Conference). On February 20, 1919, at the somewhat delayed fiftieth anniversary celebration of the consecration of Gibbons as bishop, a message from Rome was received that indicated the pope wished for an organization to replace both the war council and the former annual meeting of the archbishops. In September, therefore, the bishops gathered for their first annual meeting as the new NCWC, elected their officers, including a number who had been prominent in its war activities, and chose Burke as general secretary (a position he held until his death in 1936). In a letter to the pope, Gibbons expressed his satisfaction with what had been done: "In this way the Hierarchy is now well organized to care regularly and efficiently and immediately for every important Catholic interest in the United States, and to this work of organization the bishops gave most of the time and wisdom of the meeting."[44] Catholics in the United States had clearly come to maturity during the years from 1880 to 1920, and their service to the country in the experiences of the war and in forming the continuing NCWC demonstrated it.

In the early postwar experiences of the Protestants, however, an effort to build on the cooperative achievements of the war years ran into disas-

[43] *Uneasy Alliance*, 40; see also 35–39.
[44] As quoted by Ellis, *Life of Gibbons*, 2: 305.

ter. The undertaking began on December 17, 1918, soon after the armistice, with a meeting of 135 prominent members of missionary and related agencies, among them many who had carried denominational and cooperative leadership roles during the war. They hoped to conduct a united Protestant fund drive in support of a significant advance in missionary and social work at home and abroad. Spirits were high from the excitement of victory in the war and the success of previous fund-raising campaigns by the denominations, singly and in cooperation with others. So the Interchurch World Movement (IWM) was born in an atmosphere of high confidence and expectation. Those who launched it, according to William Adams Brown, were caught up in a surge of confidence and hope: "The vision of a united church uniting a divided world, and under the spell of what they saw all things seemed possible. Difficulties were waved aside, doubters were silenced. In the face of an opportunity so unparalleled there seemed but one thing to do, and that was to go forward."[45]

The techniques of organization that had worked well in the war period were immediately put to work. In early February a general committee met, soon to swell to more than a hundred members. Mott was elected chairman of the executive committee, and S. Earl Taylor, a Methodist layman with wide experience in cooperative and fund-raising agencies, was selected as general secretary. They decided to mount an extensive program to survey needs and resources, to educate the constituencies, and to publicize the goals of the IWM widely in preparation for a massive financial campaign in spring 1920.

In his thorough study of the IWM, Eldon G. Ernst has described in considerable detail how the movement swiftly mushroomed during 1919 into "a highly complex, nation-wide Protestant machine of many departments and divisions," which chose as its objective and motto "the giving of the whole gospel to the whole world by the whole church."[46] About thirty denominations representing approximately 60 percent of Protestant church members participated in the movement's central budget by underwriting it pending the success of the campaign. Many well-known public figures publicly and actively promoted the IWM. Some felt that it was replacing the FCC; Charles S. Macfarland was told by many that the council should identify directly with the new movement. In his autobiography Macfarland remembered that he had been warned by one of its former presidents that "I was seriously endangering my own career and that of the Council" in resisting such a move.[47] But the general secretary

[45] *Church in America*, 119.

[46] *Moment of Truth for Protestant America: Interchurch Campaigns following World War I* (Missoula, Mont.: Scholar's Press, 1974), 53–54.

[47] *Across the Years* (New York: Macmillan, 1936), 190.

was convinced that the FCC should be sympathetic to the IWM but clearly detached from it.

By May 1920, the Interchurch World Movement had developed a massive bureaucracy organized on a business model with a staff of 2,612 employees; much of it was devoted to surveying the home and foreign mission fields of the world, to serving as the promotion agency of the churches as it refined old techniques and introduced new ones, and to producing vast numbers of bulletins, leaflets, pamphlets, periodicals, and books. By that time it had already spent well over seven million dollars of borrowed money underwritten by the denominations. But early in the year its leaders had been assured by John D. Rockefeller, Jr., speaking for a Board of Review, that the plans were "wisely and conservatively drawn."[48]

The financial campaign intended to reach almost every Protestant home in the country was set for the week of April 25–May 2, with a total goal of nearly $337 million (including the denominational allotments), $40 million of which was expected to be contributed by "friendly citizens" from the general public. In preparation, Rockefeller spoke before business groups in fourteen cities, and many wealthy Christians, some having little formal connection with a church, had been quietly approached. By May 2, however, a disappointing $124 million—more than $200 million short of the goal—had been subscribed. It was decided to push ahead. When the General Committee met on May 17–18, the denominational parts of the campaign had received close to $200 million in pledges, by all former standards a remarkable success. But the friendly citizen fund had chalked up only $3, not $40, million—and that was to be the source of support for the IWM apparatus with its huge staff. A second campaign for $10 million was launched so that the denominational underwritings would not have to be used, and the churches were asked to contribute directly to the movement's central budget.

Both efforts failed, however. In a month's time the second campaign had only $125,000 in pledges. Some denominations provisionally offered their continuing support, but a very cautious, limited action by Northern Presbyterians, followed by the withdrawal of the Northern Baptists, proved decisive. The latter, responsible for an underwriting debt of $2.5 million, voted after long debate to pay the obligation and pull out entirely. The executive committee of the IWM then saw little else to do but dismiss the staff of the movement and turn the matter over to the General Committee, which met on July 8. An effort was made to try to reconceive

<hr />

[48] Ernst, *Moment of Truth*, 109; on the role of Rockefeller, see also Charles E. Harvey, "John D. Rockefeller, Jr., and the Interchurch World Movement of 1919–1920: A Different Angle on the Ecumenical Movement," *Church History* 51 (1982): 198–209.

the movement on a much smaller scale, but it proved too late for that. Even its friends concluded it was over; some went so far as to describe its demise as "the greatest blow to Protestantism since the Reformation."[49] A committee appointed to see what could be done finally decided that, despite earlier claims, existing agencies could handle cooperative Protestant work. Such agencies as the FCC and the home and foreign missions councils were left intact and continued to develop their work. The valuable surveys that the IWM had undertaken were taken over by the Rockefeller-financed Institute of Social and Religious Research.

What had happened to cause the fall of the IWM? Begun in the flush of victory when the spirit of idealism was still running high and confidence abounded, and against the background of the sacrificial generosity of the war period, the IWM came to its big campaign a year and a half later when much had changed. Not many of the hopes that the war had aroused could be met in full, and some hardly at all. A sense of disillusionment had affected many persons, among them returned veterans who faced difficulties in relocation. A series of strikes, some marked by violence, disturbed the peace of the nation. The vast migrations of labor to industrial centers caused something of a reaction against strangers in settled areas, and the movements of blacks to the North precipitated major race riots in summer 1919. The violent course of the Russian Revolution triggered a "red scare." A serious blow to the internationalists, many of whom were ardent supporters of cooperative Protestantism with its commitment to missions, was the Senate's final defeat, on March 19, 1920, of American acceptance of the Treaty of Versailles with its provision for the League of Nations—not long before the IWM fund drive occurred. Hence the appeal came to a divided and troubled nation. Deep rifts were also appearing in Protestant ranks as the tensions between the complex liberal and conservative trends were beginning to harden into the bitter fundamentalist/modernist controversy of the 1920s—a factor that influenced the Presbyterian and Baptist actions.

The IWM had its flaws, too, in that it had not carefully enough defined its goals and purposes and had taken on more than it could handle. In the high enthusiasm following the victorious conclusion of the war, IWM leaders counted too much on one big financial campaign. They overestimated the unity among the denominations that had been evoked by the needs of war, and some thought that it promised a deep, continuing commitment to cooperation. From a later perspective the importance of the foundations that had been laid proved significant, but in the period of disillusionment following the war and the collapse of the IWM this was more difficult to see. Later analyses have also suggested that the IWM

---

[49] As quoted by Ernst, *Moment of Truth*, 151.

was a pragmatic movement little interested in deeper religious questions, including those directly related to the issues of denominational cooperation. There were indications that to a considerable extent it used prayer as a "promotive" instrument—as a way of generating power, practiced primarily for its results.[50]

How far the Interchurch World Movement's study of the extensive steel strike that began in September 1919 was responsible for the movement's failure has been much debated. The IWM's Department of Industrial Relations appointed a commission under Francis J. McConnell, a Methodist bishop and prominent social gospel leader, to investigate the strike thoroughly. On January 8, 1920, while its work was proceeding, the strike ended in decisive defeat, to the relief of many religious leaders along with much of the general public who were little aware of the strikers' side of the story. The commission's report, which pointed out that many steel workers labored twelve hours a day, seven days a week, some at less than minimum subsistence standards, was finally heard by the IWM executive committee on May 10—after the disappointing week of the main IWM financial campaign. Realizing the seriousness of the report's critique of the steel industry, the committee wanted to make sure its facts were right and had it further carefully scrutinized before unanimously voting on June 28 to have it published. Not until the end of July—when the life of the IWM was essentially over—did copies of the final report go to the White House and the press.

The report, soon published in book form, created a sensation, contributed to a change in the public attitude, and was credited in part for both the virtual end of the twelve-hour day and seven-day work week in the steel and some other industries and the improvement of the wage scale. Although the general social concerns expressed by some IWM departments may have been partly responsible for the fund drive's failure, the report itself came too late to be a significant factor. In retrospect, its achievement in contributing to shorter working days was seen as one of the high points of social gospel history.[51]

Ernst's estimates of the deeper significance of the IWM are striking. Quite early in his book he characterized it as "a dramatic cultural-religious event whose brief and stormy life would manifest the latter days of the century-old Protestant empire in America and forecast the emergence of a new age."[52] Near the end of his account, he wrote:

[50] Ibid., passim; most of Ernst's discussion about critiques of the movement is in his last chapter, 157–79, but see also 104 with reference to its instrumentalizing of prayer.

[51] Ibid., 115–36. The matter is discussed also in Gorrell, *The Age of Social Responsibility*, 315–19.

[52] *Moment of Truth*, 46.

In the last analysis, however, the single most important impact of the Interchurch World Movement on religion in America was its demonstration that crusading Protestantism—indeed Protestantism in general—was losing its traditional hold on the American people as a whole and on the social and cultural tone of the nation. Not only did the Interchurch World Movement mark a transition within American Protestantism in such areas as mood and spirit, developments toward cooperative unity, utilization of business methods and organization, and changing attitudes toward social involvement, but in its demise it also marked the changing status and role of American Protestantism itself as a religious force in America [170–71].

Even what most of the Protestant denominations had counted as a great triumph of the period—the passage of the Eighteenth Amendment—proved not to be very long lasting, and was to be repealed in the early 1930s.

The wartime cooperation between Catholics, Protestants, and Jews was a remarkable development in view of the deep-rooted animosities among these historic traditions, but it was based primarily on pragmatic needs and did not involve serious discussions of religious and theological matters. Though quieted for a time, the older tensions persisted and manifested themselves in continuing anti-Catholic and anti-Semitic currents in American life in the troubled years following the war. The issues of church and state continued to be a focal point for bitterness. The career of John A. Ryan illustrates the point.

On the one hand, Ryan was a notable progressive in his social thought, which he carefully based on Catholic teaching. In 1919 he drafted a program for social reform that so impressed the leaders of the NCWC that they adopted it and circulated it widely as "The Bishops' Program of Social Reconstruction."[53] It was known as one of the most significant of such statements issued by church bodies, becoming especially influential in the 1930s. But on the other hand, Ryan continued to articulate traditional Catholic positions on the role of the state. In a book written and edited in 1922 for the NCWC in which he commented on the 1885 papal encyclical on "The Christian Constitution of States," Ryan recapitulated the pope's argument: "If there is only one true religion, and if its possession is the most important good in life for States as well as individuals, then the public profession, protection, and promotion of this religion and the legal prohibiton of all direct assaults upon it, becomes one of the most obvious and fundamental duties of the state."[54] Obviously Ryan believed

[53] Reprinted in Ellis, ed., *Documents of American Catholic History*, 4: 589–607; see also Ryan's *Social Doctrine in Action: A Personal History* (New York: Harper, 1941), 144–51.

[54] Ryan and Moorhouse F. X. Millar, *The State and the Church* (New York: Macmillan, 1922), 37.

that there was only one true religion, but he hedged his views by insisting that the practical realization of Catholic hegemony in any country was so remote in time and probability that nobody should let it be disturbing. "It is true, indeed," he added, "that some zealots and bigots will continue to attack the Church because they fear that some five thousand years hence the United States may become overwhelmingly Catholic and may then restrict the freedom of non-Catholic denominations" (39). His hope that fellow citizens would be sufficiently realistic to see that the danger of Catholic religious intolerance would be so improbable and so far in the future that it should not occupy their time or attention was certainly not fulfilled, for his own statement was often quoted to keep the fires of controversy burning. Not until the Second Vatican Council was the issue authoritatively addressed by the Catholic hierarchy, leading to the promulgation of the "Declaration on Religious Freedom" by Pope Paul VI in 1965.

Summary: Four Decades of Change

The America of 1920 was a vastly different place from what it had been in 1880. It had doubled in size, and the population had become much more heterogeneous. Although outwardly there seemed to be little change in conventional ways of understanding the relations between church and state, there was not only a significant widening of the religious spectrum but also a decisive shift in the relative strength of the major traditions. Little seen at the time, the informal hegemony that the Protestant movement had long held over American religious and cultural life by its numerical pluralities and the power of its organizational networks was weakened. The voluntary establishment was being undermined. In retrospect, we can see that a considerable reconfiguration of the religious forces of the nation had already taken place. Externally familiar understandings of the separation of church and state seemed little changed, but the pressures of social religion and the progressive movement followed by the crisis of World War I had significantly increased relationships between religious institutions and governmental agencies. The postwar "return to normalcy," for which many had hoped, could neither reverse the deeper changes that had taken place nor erase the memory of the cooperation of religious bodies among themselves and with the government.

The Catholic church, brought into greater unity by the centralizing force of its annual meeting of bishops and the instrumentality of the National Catholic Welfare Conference, continued its remarkable growth, not free from but less troubled by the anti-Catholicism that it had faced before World War I. Having proved its patriotism in the stresses of war, the largest American church had come to a maturity of growing confidence in a nation in which it had often been viewed as an outsider.

Jews continued to be agitated by various Protestant missionary efforts to convert them; as Benny Kraut has summarized a complex situation, "to Jews the hostile atmosphere created was one more undesirable outcome of the Protestant triumphalism experienced in the 1920s."[55] But the organization of the three main strands of Judaism had been completed, and their wartime achievements and cooperation had increased Jewish self-confidence. Jewish leaders continued to press for the full equality and freedom they believed to be consistent with the Constitution.

Most Protestant bodies continued to grow in size for many years, and as the war had "produced a strong display of solidarity from all elements of Protestantism",[56] their sense of cultural and religious predominance remained largely unshaken until the 1930s.[57] Increasingly the fastest growing bodies tended to be among the newer movements outside the circle of the older denominations that had dominated the nineteenth century, but it did not appear then that some of them would eventually emerge as parts of major denominational families. It took time, combined with the reverses of the depression years, before many Protestants saw what had become apparent to the general secretary of the Federal Council of Churches by 1937: "We can no longer discuss the relation of Church and State, even in America, on the basis of the old assumptions which have held the field down to our own day."[58] The significance of earlier changes was beginning to sink in.

A number of prominent religious leaders who supported the progressive and social gospel movements had favored a more positive view of the state than had dominated most nineteenth-century reform thought and action. But as certain unanticipated consequences of a stronger role of government in social and economic life loomed, such as the licensing and zoning regulations of governmental bureacracies, some began to sense a drift away from a benevolent interpretation of the government's attitude toward the institutions of religion to one of stricter neutrality. The expansion of the agencies of both government and religion, dramatically highlighted during World War I, and coupled with the extensive widening of the religious spectrum, presaged the need for new ways to redefine for-

[55] "A Wary Collaboration: Jews, Catholics, and the Protestant Goodwill Movement," in *Between the Times*, ed. Hutchison, 208.

[56] Szasz, *Divided Mind*, 84.

[57] I have discussed this in *A Christian America*, chap. 7, "The Second Disestablishment (1920–1940)," 159–84.

[58] Samuel McCrea Cavert, "Points of Tension between Church and State Today," in Henry P. Van Dusen et al., *Church and State in the Modern World* (New York: Harper, 1937), 191.

mally what had long been conventionally referred to as the separation of church and state. The process of redefinition was accelerated in the 1940s by two landmark Supreme Court cases that incorporated the religious clauses of the First Amendment into the Fourteenth and made them applicable to the states (and by extension to all the arms of government).[59] The last half of the twentieth century has seen a continuing flood of cases dealing with religion and government, not only in the Supreme Court but also in state and local courts.

Of the many chapters of American religious, political, legal, and cultural history that lie behind the present church-state situation with all its complexities, those that occurred from 1880 to 1920 should not be neglected for a full understanding of the relationships between the institutions of religion and those of government in the twentieth century. Both governmental and religious institutions had changed significantly, and the difficult process of sorting out ways to relate them has been proceeding ever since.

[59] The free exercise clause was thus incorporated by *Cantwell* v. *Connecticut*, 310 U.S. 296 (1940), which affirmed the right of religious bodies to solicit publicly; and the establishment clause by *Everson* v. *Board of Education*, 330 U.S. 1, the New Jersey school bus case.

Selected Bibliography

Abrams, Richard M., ed. *The Issues of the Populist and Progressive Eras, 1892–1912.* New York: Harper & Row, 1969.

Adler, Selig. "The Palestine Question in the Wilson Era." *Jewish Social Studies* 10 (1948): 303–34.

Arrington, Leonard J., and Davis Bitton. *The Mormon Experience: A History of the Latter-day Saints.* New York: Knopf, 1979.

Bailey, Hugh C. *Liberalism in the New South: Southern Social Reformers and the Progressive Movement.* Coral Gables, Fla.: University of Miami Press, 1969.

Bailey, Kenneth K. *Southern White Protestantism in the Twentieth Century.* New York: Harper & Row, 1964.

Batten, Samuel Zane. *The Christian State: The State, Democracy and Christianity.* Philadelphia: Griffith & Rowland, 1909.

Beisner, Robert L. *From the Old Diplomacy to the New, 1865–1900.* 2d ed. New York: Thomas Y. Crowell, 1975.

———. *Twelve Against Empire: The Anti-Imperialists, 1898–1900.* New York: McGraw-Hill, 1968.

Bellah, Robert N., and Frederick E. Greenspahn, eds. *Uncivil Religion: Interreligious Hostility in America.* New York: Crossroad, 1987.

Bowden, Henry W., ed. *A Century of Church History: The Legacy of Philip Schaff.* Carbondale: Southern Illinois University Press, 1988.

Brauer, Jerald C. *Protestantism in America: A Narrative History.* Rev. ed. Philadelphia: Westminster Press, 1965.

Brewer, David J. *The United States a Christian Nation.* Philadelphia: John C. Winston, 1905.

Broderick, Francis L. *Right Reverend New Dealer: John A. Ryan.* New York: Macmillan, 1963.

Brown, William Adams. *Church and State in Contemporary America.* New York: Scribner, 1938.

———. *The Church in America: A Study of the Prresent Condition and Future Prospects of American Protestantism.* New York: Macmillan, 1922.

Bryce, James. *The American Commonwealth.* 3 vols. London: Macmillan, 1888.

Buenker, John D., John C. Burnham, and Robert M. Crunden. *Progressivism.* Cambridge, Mass.: Schenkman, 1977.

Carter, Paul A. *The Decline and Revival of the Social Gospel: Social and Political Liberalism in American Protestant Churches.* Rev. ed. Hamden, Conn.: Archon Books, 1971.

Cavert, Samuel McCrea. *The American Churches in the Ecumenical Movement: 1900–1968.* New York: Association Press, 1968.

———. *Church Cooperation and Unity in America, A Historical Review: 1900–1970.* New York: Association Press, 1970.

Christensen, Torben, and William R. Hutchison, eds. *Missionary Ideologies in the Imperialist Era: 1880–1920*. Aarhus: Aros, 1982.

Christiano, Kevin J. *Religious Diversity and Social Change: American Cities, 1890–1906*. Cambridge: Cambridge University Press, 1987.

Clymer, Kenton J. *Protestant Missionaries in the Philippines, 1898–1916: An Inquiry into the American Colonial Mentality*. Urbana: University of Illinois Press, 1986.

Cohen, Naomi W. *Encounter with Emancipation: The German Jews in the United States, 1830–1914*. Philadelphia: Jewish Publication Society of America, 1984.

Cornelison, Isaac A. *The Relation of Religion to Civil Government in the United States of America: A State without a Church but not without a Religion*. 1895. Reprint. New York: Da Capo Press, 1970.

Cross, Robert D. *The Emergence of Liberal Catholicism*. Cambridge: Harvard University Press, 1958.

Crunden, Robert M. *Ministers of Reform: The Progressives' Achievement in American Civilization, 1889–1920*. New York: Basic Books, 1982.

Cuddy, Edward. "Pro-Germanism and American Catholicism, 1914–1917." *Catholic Historical Review* 54 (1968): 427–54.

Danbom, David B. *"The World of Hope": Progressives and the Struggle for an Ethical Public Life*. Philadelphia: Temple University Press, 1987.

Davis, Moshe. *The Emergence of Conservative Judaism: The Historical School in 19th Century America*. Philadelphia: Jewish Publication Society of America, 1963.

Dolan, Jay P. *The American Catholic Experience: A History from Colonial Times to the Present*. Garden City, N.Y.: Doubleday, 1985.

Dorn, Jacob H. *Washington Gladden: Prophet of the Social Gospel*. Columbus: Ohio State University Press, 1967.

Driggs, Kenneth D. "The Mormon Church-State Confrontation in Nineteenth-Century America." *Journal of Church and State* 30 (1988): 273–89.

Drinan, Robert F. *Religion, the Courts, and Public Policy*. New York: McGraw-Hill, 1963.

Eighmy, John Lee. *Churches in Cultural Captivity: A History of the Social Attitudes of Southern Baptists*. Knoxville: University of Tennessee Press, 1972.

———. "Religious Liberalism in the South during the Progressive Era." *Church History* 38 (1969): 359–72.

Ellis, John Tracy, ed. *Documents of American Catholic History*. 4th ed. 4 vols. Wilmington, Del.: Michael Glazier, 1987.

———. *The Life of James Cardinal Gibbons: Archbishop of Baltimore, 1834–1921*. 2 vols. Milwaukee: Bruce Publishing, 1952.

Ely, Richard T. *The Social Law of Service*. New York: Eaton & Mains, 1896.

Ernst, Eldon G. *Moment of Truth for Protestant America: Interchurch Campaigns following World War I*. Missoula, Mont.: Scholars' Press, 1974.

Fairbank, John K., ed. *The Missionary Enterprise in China and America*. Cambridge: Harvard University Press, 1974.

Feldman, Egal. "American Ecumenism: Chicago's World's Parliament of Religions of 1893." *Journal of Church and State* 9 (1967): 180–99.

Firmage, Edwin B., and Richard C. Mangrum. *Zion in the Courts: A Legal History of the Church of Jesus Christ of Latter-day Saints.* Urbana: University of Illinois Press, 1988.

Fogarty, Gerald P. *The Vatican and the Americanist Crisis: Denis J. O'Connell, American Agent in Rome, 1885–1903.* Rome: Università Gregoriana Editrice, 1974.

Forsythe, Sidney A. *An American Missionary Community in China, 1895–1905.* Cambridge: Harvard University Press, 1971.

Freidel, Frank. *The Splendid Little War.* Boston: Little Brown, 1958.

Fussell, Paul. *The Great War and Modern Memory.* New York: Oxford University Press, 1975.

Gaustad, Edwin Scott. *Historical Atlas of Religion in America.* Rev. ed. New York: Harper & Row, 1976.

Gladden, Washington. *The New Idolatry and Other Discussions.* New York: McClure, Phillips, 1905.

Gorrell, Donald K. *The Age of Social Responsibility: The Social Gospel in the Progressive Era, 1900–1920.* Macon, Ga.: Mercer University Press, 1988.

———. "The Methodist Federation for Social Service and the Social Creed." *Methodist History* 13 (January 1975): 3–32.

Gowing, Peter G. "The Disentanglement of Church and State Early in the American Regime in the Philippines." In *Studies in Philippine Church History*, ed. Gerald H. Anderson, 203–22. Ithaca: Cornell University Press, 1969.

Grabill, Joseph L. *Protestant Diplomacy and the Near East: Missionary Influence on American Policy, 1810–1927.* Minneapolis: University of Minnesota Press, 1971.

Hammond, John L. *The Politics of Benevolence: Revival Religion and American Voting Behavior.* Norwood, N.J.: Ablex, 1979.

Handy, Robert T. *A Christian America: Protestant Hopes and Historical Realities.* 2d ed. New York: Oxford University Press, 1984.

———, ed. *The Social Gospel in America, 1870–1930: Gladden, Ely, Rauschenbusch.* New York: Oxford University Press, 1966.

Hennesey, James. *American Catholics: A History of the Roman Catholic Community in the United States.* New York: Oxford University Press, 1981.

Herron, George D. *The Christian State: A Political Vision of Christ.* New York: Thomas Y. Crowell, 1895.

Higham, John. *Strangers in the Land: Patterns of American Nativism, 1860–1925.* Rev. ed. New York: Atheneum, 1973.

———. *Send Them to Me: Jews and Other Immigrants in Urban America.* New York: Atheneum, 1975.

Hill, Patricia R. *The World Their Household: The American Christian Woman's Foreign Mission Movement and Cultural Transformation, 1870–1920.* Ann Arbor: University of Michigan Press, 1985.

Hofstadter, Richard. *The Age of Reform: From Bryan to F.D.R.* New York: Vintage Books, 1955.

Hopkins, C. Howard. *John R. Mott, 1865–1955: A Biography*. Grand Rapids, Mich.: Eerdmans, 1979.

———. *The Rise of the Social Gospel in American Protestantism, 1865–1915*. New Haven: Yale University Press, 1940.

Hudson, Winthrop S. *American Protestantism*. Chicago: University of Chicago Press, 1961.

———. "Protestant Clergy Debate the Nation's Vocation, 1898–1899," *Church History* 42 (1973): 110–18.

———, ed. *Walter Rauschenbusch: Selected Writings*. New York: Paulist Press, 1984.

Hunt, Thomas C. "The Bennett Law of 1890: Focus of Conflict Between Church and State in Education." *Journal of Church and State* 23 (1981): 69–93.

Huntington, William R. *The Church-Idea: An Essay Towards Unity*. 4th ed. New York: Scribner, 1899.

Hutchison, William R., ed. *Between the Times: The Travail of the Protestant Establishment in America, 1900–1960*. New York: Cambridge University Press, 1989.

———. *Errand to the World: American Protestant Thought and Foreign Missions*. Chicago: University of Chicago Press, 1987.

———. *The Modernist Impulse in American Protestantism*. Cambridge: Harvard University Press, 1976.

Jensen, Richard J. *The Winning of the Midwest: Social and Political Conflict, 1888–1896*. Chicago: University of Chicago Press, 1971.

Jordan, Philip D. *The Evangelical Alliance for the United States of America, 1847–1900: Ecumenism, Identity and the Religion of the Republic*. New York: E. Mellen, 1982.

Jorgenson, Lloyd P. *The State and the Non-Public School, 1825–1925*. Columbia: University of Missouri Press, 1987.

Kauffman, Christopher J. *Faith and Fraternalism: The History of the Knights of Columbus, 1882–1982*. New York: Harper & Row, 1982.

Keller, Robert H., Jr. *American Protestantism and United States Indian Policy, 1869–1882*. Lincoln: University of Nebraska Press, 1983.

Kennedy, David M. *Over Here: The First World War and American Society*. New York: Oxford University Press, 1980.

———; ed. *Progressivism: The Critical Issues*. Boston: Little Brown, 1971.

Kerr, K. Austin. *Organized for Prohibition: A New History of the Anti-Saloon League*. New Haven: Yale University Press, 1985.

Kinzer, Donald L. *An Episode in Anti-Catholicism: The American Protective Association*. Seattle: University of Washington Press, 1964.

Kleppner, Paul. *Continuity and Change in Electoral Politics, 1893–1928*. New York: Greenwood, 1987.

———. *Who Voted? The Dynamics of Electoral Turnout, 1870–1980*. New York: Praeger, 1982.

Kleppner, Paul, et al. *The Evolution of the American Electoral Systems*. Westport, Conn.: Greenwood, 1981.

Knudten, Richard D. *The Systematic Thought of Washington Gladden.* New York: Humanities Press, 1968.

Lacy, Creighton. *Frank Mason North: His Social and Ecumenical Mission.* Nashville: Abingdon, 1967.

Lee, Gordon C. *The Struggle for Federal Aid, First Phase: A History of the Attempts to Obtain Federal Aid for the Common Schools, 1870–1890.* New York: Teachers College, 1949.

Lindner, Eileen W. "The Redemptive Politic of Henry George: A Legacy to the Social Gospel." *Union Seminary Quarterly Review* 42, no. 3 (1988): 1–8.

Link, Arthur S., and Richard L. McCormick. *Progressivism.* Arlington Heights, Ill.: Harlan Davidson, 1982.

Linkh, Richard M. *American Catholicism and European Immigrants (1900–1924).* Staten Island, N.Y.: Center for Migration Studies, 1975.

Lowe, Eugene Y., Jr. "Richard T. Ely: Herald of a Positive State." *Union Seminary Quarterly Review* 42, no. 3 (1988): 21–29.

Lyman, Edward Leo. *Political Deliverance: The Mormon Quest for Statehood.* Urbana: University of Illinois Press, 1986.

Lynn, Robert W. *Protestant Strategies in Education.* New York: Association Press, 1964.

McAvoy, Thomas F. *A History of the Catholic Church in the United States.* Notre Dame: University of Notre Dame Press, 1969.

McDowell, John Patrick. *The Social Gospel in the South: The Woman's Home Mission Movement in the Methodist Episcopal Church, South, 1886–1939.* Baton Rouge: Louisiana State University Press, 1982.

Macfarland, Charles S. *The Churches of Christ in Time of War.* New York: Missionary Education Movement, 1917.

McLoughlin, William G. *Modern Revivalism: Charles Grandison Finney to Billy Graham.* New York: Ronald, 1959.

McSeveney, Samuel T. *The Politics of Depression: Political Behavior in the Northeast, 1893–1896.* New York: Oxford University Press, 1972.

Magnuson, Norris. *Salvation in the Slums: Evangelical Social Work, 1865–1920.* Metuchen, N.J.: Scarecrow Press, 1977.

Marsden, George M. *Fundamentalism and American Culture: The Shaping of Twentieth-Century Evangelicalism, 1870–1925.* New York: Oxford University Press, 1980.

Marty, Martin E. *Modern American Religion*, Vol. 1, *The Irony of It All, 1893–1919.* Chicago: University of Chicago Press, 1986.

May, Ernest R. *From Imperialism to Isolationism, 1898–1919.* New York: Macmillan, 1963.

May, Henry F. *The End of American Innocence: A Study of the First Years of Our Own Time, 1912–1917.* New York: Knopf, 1969.

———. *Protestant Churches and Industrial America.* New York: Harper & Bros., 1949.

Mead, Sidney E. *The Lively Experiment: The Shaping of Christianity in America.* New York: Harper & Row, 1963.

Meyer, Paul R. "The Fear of Cultural Decline: Josiah Strong's Thought about Reform and Expansion." *Church History* 42 (1973): 396–405.

Michaelsen, Robert. *Piety in the Public School: Trends and Issues in the Relationship between Religion and the Public School in the United States.* New York: Macmillan, 1970.

Minus, Paul M. *Walter Rauschenbusch: American Reformer.* New York: Macmillan, 1988.

Morgan, Richard E. *The Supreme Court and Religion.* New York: Free Press, 1972.

Nichols, J. Bruce. *The Uneasy Alliance: Religion, Refugee Work, and U.S. Foreign Policy.* New York: Oxford University Press, 1988.

Noll, Mark A., ed. *Religion and American Politics: From the Colonial Period to the 1980s.* New York: Oxford University Press, 1990.

Noonan, John T., Jr. *The Believer and the Powers that Are: Cases, History, and Other Data Bearing on the Relation of Religion and Government.* New York: Macmillan, 1987.

Palmer, Parker J., Barbara G. Wheeler, and James W. Fowler, eds. *Caring for the Commonweal: Education for Religious and Public Life.* Macon, Ga.: Mercer University Press, 1990.

Piepkorn, Carl. *Profiles in Belief: The Religious Bodies of the United States and Canada.* 4 vols. San Francisco: Harper & Row, 1977–1979.

Piper, John F. *The American Churches in World War I.* Athens: Ohio University Press, 1985.

Prucha, Francis Paul. *American Indian Policy in Crisis: Christian Reformers and the Indian, 1865–1900.* Norman: University of Oklahoma Press, 1976.

Quandt, Jean B. *From the Small Town to the Great Community: The Social Thought of the Progressive Intellectuals.* New Brunswick, N.J.: Rutgers University Press, 1970.

Rauschenbusch, Walter. *Christianity and the Social Crisis.* New York: Macmillan, 1907.

———. *Christianizing the Social Order.* New York: Macmillan, 1912.

———. *A Theology for the Social Gospel.* New York: Macmillan, 1917.

Reed, James Eldin. "American Foreign Policy, The Politics of Missions and Josiah Strong, 1890–1900." *Church History* 41 (1972): 230–45.

———. *The Missionary Mind and American East Asia Policy, 1911–1915.* Cambridge: Harvard University Press, 1983.

Reuter, Frank T. *Catholic Influence on American Colonial Policies, 1898–1904.* Austin: University of Texas Press, 1967.

———. "William Howard Taft and the Separation of Church and State in the Philippines." *Journal of Church and State* 24 (1982): 105–17.

Rosenberg, Emily S. *Spreading the American Dream: American Economic and Cultural Expansion, 1890–1945.* New York: Hill & Wang, 1982.

Roth, Jack J., ed. *World War I: A Turning Point in Modern History.* New York: Knopf, 1967.

Russell, C. Allyn. *Voices of American Fundamentalism.* Philadelphia: Westminster, 1976.

Ryan, John A. *A Living Wage: Its Ethical and Economic Aspects*. New York: Macmillan, 1906.

Ryan, John A., and Moorhouse F. X. Millar. *The State and the Church*. New York: Macmillan, 1922.

Santayana, George. *Winds of Doctrine: Studies in Contemporary Opinion*. New York: Scribner, 1913.

Sarna, Jonathan D. "Christian America or Secular America? The Church-State Dilemma of American Jews." In *Jews in Unsecular America*, ed. Richard J. Neuhaus, 8–19. Grand Rapids, Mich.: Eerdmans, 1982.

Schaff, David S. "The Movement and Mission of American Christianity." *American Journal of Theology* 16 (1912): 51–69.

Schaff, Philip. *Church and State in the United States: or The American Idea of Religious Liberty and Its Practical Effects*. New York: Putnam, 1888.

Sharpe, Dores R. *Walter Rauschenbusch*. New York: Macmillan, 1942.

Sheerin, John B. *Never Look Back: The Career and Concerns of John J. Burke*. New York: Paulist Press, 1975.

Shipps, Jan. *Mormonism: The Story of a New Religious Tradition*. Urbana: University of Illinois Press, 1985.

Shriver, George H. *Philip Schaff: Christian Scholar and Ecumenical Prophet*. Macon, Ga.: Mercer University Press, 1987.

Smith, Gary Scott. *The Seeds of Secularism: Calvinism, Culture, and Pluralism in America, 1870–1915*. Grand Rapids, Mich.: Christian University Press, 1985.

Smith, H. Shelton. *In His Image, But . . . : Racism in Southern Religion, 1780–1910*. Durham: Duke University Press, 1972.

Smylie, John E. "The Christian Church and the National Ethos." In *Biblical Realism Confronts the Nation*, ed. Paul Peachey, 33–44. Scottdale, Penn.: Herald Press, 1963.

Stokes, Anson Phelps. *Church and State in the United States*. 3 vols. New York: Harper & Bros., 1950.

Strong, Josiah. *Expansion: Under New World-Conditions*. New York: Baker & Taylor, 1900.

———. *Our Country: Its Possible Future and Its Present Crisis*. New York: Baker & Taylor, 1885.

Szasz, Ferenc M. *The Divided Mind of Protestant America, 1880–1930*. University: University of Alabama Press, 1982.

Thompson, Joseph P. *Church and State in the United States*. Boston: James R. Osgood, 1873.

Thompson, Robert E. *De Civitate Dei: The Divine Order of Human Society*. Philadelphia: John D. Wattles, 1891.

Turner, James. *Without God, Without Creed: The Origins of Unbelief in America*. Baltimore: Johns Hopkins University Press, 1985.

Varg, Paul A. *Missionaries, Chinese, and Diplomats: The American Protestant Missionary Movement in China, 1890–1952*. Princeton: Princeton University Press, 1958.

Way, H. Frank. "The Death of the Christian Nation: The Judiciary and Church-State Relations." *Journal of Church and State* 29 (1987): 509–29.

White, Ronald C., Jr. *"Liberty and Justice for All": Racial Reform and the Social Gospel (1877–1925)*. San Francisco: Harper & Row, 1990.

White, Ronald C., and C. Howard Hopkins. *The Social Gospel: Religion and Reform in Changing America*. Philadelphia: Temple University Press, 1976.

Williams, Michael. *American Catholics and the War: The National Catholic War Council, 1917–1921*. New York: Macmillan, 1921.

Wilson, John F., ed. *Church and State in America: A Bibliographical Guide*. 2 vols. New York: Greenwood, 1986- 1987.

Wilson, John F., and Donald L. Drakeman, eds. *Church and State in American History: The Burden of Religious Pluralism*. 2d ed. Boston: Beacon, 1987.

Wilson, R. Jackson. *In Quest of Community: Social Philosophy in the United States, 1860–1920*. New York: Oxford University Press, 1968.

Woodward, C. Vann. *The Strange Career of Jim Crow*. Rev. ed. New York: Oxford University Press, 1957.

Wuthnow, Robert. *The Restructuring of American Religion: Society and Faith Since World War II*. Princeton: Princeton University Press, 1988.

Yahalom, Shlomith. "American Judaism and the Question of Separation Between Church and State." Partial English translation of Ph.D. diss., Hebrew University of Jerusalem, 1981. (See Acknowledgments.)